Economic Development in Saudi Arabia

The changing political situation in the Middle East poses challenges for the economies of the region, and some see none more vulnerable to collapse than Saudi Arabia's. Yet as this study demonstrates, the fundamentals of the kingdom's economy are relatively robust, as over two thirds of GDP is accounted for by the non-oil sector, and impressive modern industries have been established, notably in petrochemicals. The financial system functions well, and despite substantial government debts, there is low inflation and currency stability. The private sector increasingly drives the economy, although job creation has been insufficient to prevent rising youth unemployment. The development challenges Saudi Arabia faces are similar to those of other middle-income countries, and three decades of diversification have made the economy less unique than it was in the oil boom years of the 1970s.

Rodney Wilson is Professor of Economics at the Institute for Middle Eastern and Islamic Studies, University of Durham. His main research interests are the trade and finance of the Middle East. His previous books for Routledge include *Economic Development in the Middle East*.

Durham Modern Middle East and Islamic World Series
Series Editor: Anoushiravan Ehteshami
University of Durham

1 Economic Development in Saudi Arabia
Rodney Wilson, with Abdullah Al-Salamah, Monica Malik and Ahmed Al-Rajhi

2 Islam Encountering Globalisation
Edited by Ali Mohammadi

3 China's Relations with Arabia and the Gulf, 1949–1999
Mohamed Bin Huwaidin

4 Good Governance in the Middle East Oil Monarchies
Edited by Tom Pierre Najem and Martin Hetherington

5 The Middle East's Relations with Asia and Russia
Edited by Hannah Carter and Anoushiravan Ehteshami

6 Israeli Politics and the Middle East Peace Process, 1988–2002
Hassan A. Barari

Economic Development in Saudi Arabia

Rodney Wilson
with Abdullah Al-Salamah, Monica Malik and Ahmed Al-Rajhi

LONDON AND NEW YORK

First published 2004 by RoutledgeCurzon

2 Park Square, Milton Park, Abingdon, Oxfordshire OX14 4RN
711 Third Avenue, New York, NY 10017

Routledge is an imprint of the Taylor & Francis Group, an informa business

First issued in paperback 2018

Copyright © 2004 Rodney Wilson

Typeset in Times by LaserScript Ltd, Mitcham, Surrey

All rights reserved. No part of this book may be reprinted or reproduced or utilised in any form or by any electronic, mechanical, or other means, now known or hereafter invented, including photocopying and recording, or in any information storage or retrieval system, without permission in writing from the publishers.

Notice:
Product or corporate names may be trademarks or registered trademarks, and are used only for identification and explanation without intent to infringe.

British Library Cataloguing in Publication Data
A catalogue record for this book is available from the British Library

Library of Congress Cataloging in Publication Data
A catalog record for this book has been requested

ISBN 978-0-7007-1729-3 (hbk)
ISBN 978-1-138-36211-6 (pbk)

 Printed in the United Kingdom by Henry Ling Limited

To all those Saudi Arabian doctoral students I have had the privilege of supervising

Contents

List of tables	x
List of figures	xii
Acknowledgements	xiii

1 Introduction 1

Development optimism 1
The challenges of globalisation 2
Explaining development 3

2 Which development paradigm? 6

Historical perspectives on market development 7
The goal of self-sustaining growth 8
The absence of feudalism 10
Emergent capitalism 12
Income distribution and development 15
The role of the state 17

3 Government economic policy 20

Economic planning 21
From planning office to ministry 24
Reorganisation of economic management 26
The Seventh Five-Year Plan 27
Lack of coordinated planning 28
Macroeconomic priorities 29
The burden of indebtedness 31
Fiscal choices 32
Government funding and foreign investment 33
Economic dualism 37

viii *Contents*

4 Oil, gas and petrochemicals 39

The development of the oil industry 40
Saudi Arabia's role in OPEC 41
Oil production 43
Oil pricing 45
Oil reserves, oil depletion and the future oil market 46
Contribution of oil to national economic development 48
Gas development 50
The petrochemical industry 53

5 The banking sector and financial markets 56

Early banking history 57
The development of commercial banking 59
Coexistence of conventional and Islamic finance 60
Competition for bank deposits and lending 62
Corporate finance and investment banking 65
The stock market 67
Managed funds 70
Finance and development 73

6 International trade and GCC economic relations 75

The economic rationale for Saudi Arabian trade 76
Regional implicational of international trade 78
Analysis of exports and import trends and assessment of
  stability 80
Trade surpluses and payments deficits 82
The trading partners of Saudi Arabia 85
The GCC and regional trade 87
The GCC single market 89
WTO accession 91

7 Employment issues 94

The demographic transition 95
Unemployment 97
Labour market trends 99
Structure of employment 101
The employment and replacement of expatriate labour 103
Education and training issues 106
Women in the workforce 108

Contents ix

8 Employment conditions in SABIC 111

ABDULLAH AL-SALAMAH

Industrialisation and job creation 111
The survey 113
Profile of the respondents 113
Training 115
Salaries 118
Promotion opportunities 119
Management decisions and labour relations 120
Working arrangements and time management 122
Conclusion 125

9 The role of the private sector 126

MONICA MALIK

The relationship between the private sector and the state 126
Ability of the private sector to initiate development 126
The efficiency of the private sector 128
Problems of management capability 129
Perceptions of the business environment and legal system 131
Views of the government's role in business 133
Shortcomings of the financial system 134
The inadequacy of the infrastructure 135
Excessive bureaucracy and regulation 135
Conclusion 137

10 The electricity industry 139

AHMED AL-RAJHI

Introduction 139
Restructuring of the electricity industry 140
Uncertainty in restructuring 140
Competition in production and monopoly in delivery 141
Functional transformation of the electricity industry 142
International experiences of reforming the electricity industry 146
The Saudi Arabian electricity industry: regulatory and
  organisational development 149
Salient features of the Saudi Arabian electricity industry 152
Policy issues and recommendations 161
Conclusion 163

Notes 165
Bibliography 178
Index 186

Tables

5.1	Saudi Arabia commercial bank size and profitability, 2001	64
5.2	Saudi Arabia listed commercial bank assets, $ billion, 2001	66
5.3	Arab stock market indicators, 2000	68
5.4	Share price indices by sector	68
5.5	Managed fund growth	70
6.1	Commodity composition of Saudi Arabian imports	81
6.2	Overseas payments and remittances from Saudi Arabia, SR billion	83
6.3	Balance of payment accounts of Saudi Arabia, SR billion	84
6.4	Saudi Arabia's non-oil trade with GCC countries, SR million, 2000	88
7.1	Population growth and composition	96
7.2	Labour-force projections for Seventh Development Plan	99
7.3	Participation rates for workforce	100
7.4	Structure of the labour force by economic activity, 1999	101
7.5	Factory employment	102
7.6	Manpower demand and supply projections, thousands	104
7.7	Structure of the Saudi Arabian labour force, 1999	105
7.8	Average monthly salaries, 2000	105
7.9	Planned student numbers during Seventh Development Plan	107
8.1	Educational level of SABIC employees surveyed	114
8.2	Occupation of SABIC employees surveyed	114
8.3	Families' acceptances of employees' job	115
8.4	Families' acceptances of time employees spend with them	115
8.5	Number of training courses attended	116
8.6	Importance of training to employees	116
8.7	Satisfaction with training policy	117
8.8	Satisfaction with skills acquired through training	117
8.9	Importance of salaries as a job attraction	118
8.10	Percentage pay increase	119
8.11	Satisfaction with salaries	119
8.12	Satisfaction with promotion opportunities	120
8.13	Satisfaction with management decision-making	121

Tables xi

8.14	Satisfaction with how managers/supervisors deal with employees	121
8.15	Satisfaction with procedures for job termination and transfer	122
8.16	Satisfaction with holidays and leave	122
8.17	Satisfaction with working hours	123
8.18	Satisfaction with scheduling of shifts	123
8.19	Satisfaction with working conditions	124
8.20	Satisfaction with safety and accident prevention	124
10.1	Government's share in electricity companies (in million SR)	151
10.2	The ratios of monthly peaks to year peaks for 1998	155
10.3	Electricity sold by type of consumption	156
10.4	Tariff structure for residential monthly consumption	158
10.5	Financial losses of SCECOs (in billion SR)	160
10.6	Revenue, cost and loss per kWh by SCECOs in 1998 (in halalahs)	160

Figures

4.1	Saudi Arabian oil production	44
4.2	Price of Saudi Arabian medium	46
4.3	Saudi Arabian oil exports	47
6.1	Balance of trade	80
6.2	Receipts from services and investment income	82
6.3	Destinations for Saudi Arabian exports, 2000	86
6.4	Sources of Saudi Arabian imports, 2000	86
10.1	Restructuring models for an electricity industry	144
10.2	Development of electricity generation and consumption	153
10.3	Investment requirements until 2020	154
10.4	Relative usage of fuel types by each region	157
10.5	Development of electricity prices (1971–2000)	159

Acknowledgements

In writing this book I owe a debt of gratitude to my colleagues in the Institute of Middle Eastern and Islamic Studies of the University of Durham. The Institute, with its excellent facilities, has provided a convivial atmosphere for the work involved, and I received useful feedback from staff and postgraduate seminars I was involved in relating to this work. I would also like to thank the library staff in Durham for their help, notably those servicing the Middle East Documentation Unit.

Some of the material contained in this book has been presented at conferences where the questions and comments of participants helped the author considerably. A paper on Saudi Arabia's trade relations with the European Union was presented at a seminar held at the Emirates Centre for Strategic Studies in Abu Dhabi in November 2001, and one on the kingdom's direction and composition of trade was presented at a conference at the Institute of Arab and Islamic Studies at the University of Exeter in September 2002. The material on investment was presented at a conference in Jubail in October 2000, and a paper on Saudi Arabia's role in the GCC was presented by the author at a conference at King Faisal University in Hofuf in February 2001. Some of the material on finance was presented at the Oxford Banking Forum held in Jeddah in September 2002. Material has also been drawn from a paper on 'Saudi Arabia in the Global Economy' presented at the American University of Sharjah in January 2003.

My greatest debt is to the postgraduate students from Saudi Arabia whose research I had the privilege of supervising. The research findings of Abdullah Al-Salamah and Ahmed Al-Rajhi are included in this volume, as is the work of Monica Malik, an expatriate with much knowledge of Saudi Arabia. These were presented at the conference of the British Society for Middle Eastern Studies held at the University of Cambridge in July 2000 at a session on the economy Saudi Arabia chaired by the author. I learnt much from the work on housing finance in Saudi Arabia of Hamad Saleh Al-Tasan, whose Ph.D. was successfully completed in 1998. Work on the thesis of Mohammed Bosbait on youth unemployment and of Abdullah Bohaimed on wage differentials in the kingdom was completed too late for inclusion in this volume, but the chapter on employment issues owes much to our discussions. The work of Salih Rashid xiv *Acknowledgements*

Al-Askar on the Al-Rajhi Banking and Investment Corporation is ongoing at the time of writing, as is the thesis of Sultan Al-Abdullatif on financial reporting in the kingdom and that of Salman Al-Dehailan on the role of women in the workforce. I have learnt a great deal from all these gifted young scholars, who typify the new generation of technically competent Saudis undoubtedly destined to contribute much to the kingdom's future development.

All too frequently foreigners' opinion on Saudi Arabia are shaped by discussions with other Western 'experts'. There is often too much discussion and too little listening to the views of Saudis themselves. The author hopes he has been a good listener to local nationals and that it is this which has shaped this study rather than any preconceived ideas on the subject.

1 Introduction

Much of the coverage of Saudi Arabia's economy in the Western media – and even more in scholarly studies – takes a very gloomy view. In terms of conventional measures such as per capita GDP, the country's economic development might appear to be going backwards. Per capita GDP amounted to 8,480 dollars in 2001 according to World Bank estimates, less than half the 1970s level. The kingdom's increasing population is portrayed as a troublesome burden and the economy viewed as on the brink of collapse, with future revenue from oil being problematic. Critics of government policy stress the continuing reliance on expatriate labour, as local manpower still seems unable to run the economy.

Development optimism

Yet the Saudi economy has not collapsed as the critics' dire warnings have been predicting for over two decades. Indeed, that economy seems remarkably resilient and government economic policy-making relatively robust.

In this study, a far more optimistic view is taken of Saudi Arabia's economic development while acknowledging its unevenness and paradoxes. Declining per capita income simply reflects generally lower oil prices and stagnant production allied to a rapidly rising population. The increasing indigenous population should be regarded as an asset not a liability, as ultimately the kingdom's future depends on its young people. A record proportion of the population, both male and female, are increasingly educated, with almost universal primary education and most proceeding to secondary education. Moreover, there are over 374,000 university students, the second largest number in the Arab world after Egypt, a much more populous country. Saudi Arabia has below-average illiteracy for the Arab world, with only 23 per cent of its population over fifteen unable to read and write, these being confined mostly to the older age groups. To its credit the government has given priority to education spending, even during the 1990s when substantial budget deficits emerged. It was defence spending that was cut, not education.

Although per capita GDP has declined, total GDP has continued to grow and by 2001 exceeded 186.5 billion dollars. Saudi Arabia's is by far the largest economy in the Middle East, being almost twice the size of that of Israel or

2 Rodney Wilson

Egypt, and in the Islamic world as a whole even the successful Malaysian economy is smaller. This economic size is not accounted for simply by oil; indeed, the share of oil in the GDP has declined considerably. Rather, manufacturing has expanded: from less than 5 per cent of GDP in 1981 to over 10.2 per cent by 2001, partly reflecting the world-class, export-focused, petrochemical industry that has been established as well as other energy-intensive activities such as steel making and fertilisers. The two largest companies in the Middle East are quoted on the Saudi Arabian stock market, namely Saudi Telecom and the Saudi Arabia Basic Industries Corporation (SABIC). In addition, a wide range of successful industries cater for the domestic and wider Gulf Cooperation Council (GCC) market, from food processing to pharmaceutical products and construction supplies. Despite the harsh desert climate, agriculture has also been a success, its share of GDP increasing from a mere 1.1 per cent in 1981 to 5.2 per cent by 2001. In the 1970s it was thought Sudan could become the breadbasket for Saudi Arabia; instead, it is the kingdom which exports grain to Sudan, not vice versa.

Services have grown the most rapidly, however: from only 18.4 per cent of GDP in 1981 to 43.1 per cent by 2001. This admittedly includes a vast array of activities, from taxi drivers and housemaids to sophisticated financial services and information technology. As is shown in Chapter 3, it is the service sector that provides most of the employment for Saudi Arabian citizens. This includes not only government services such as administration and teaching but also private services, such as banking, which largely employ local nationals. There are over three million Saudi Arabian citizens in the workforce of which over three quarters are working in the private sector, belying the view that only the government is willing to employ local nationals.

The challenges of globalisation

Saudi Arabia used to be regarded as an open economy though in many respects a closed society. The challenge for the House of Saud was to modernise the economy, while maintaining traditional values, and safeguarding the power structures of the state. To a considerable extent this balancing act between economic progress and social stability worked, despite the enormous changes oil wealth brought, with rapid urbanisation and the arrival in the kingdom of millions of migrant workers.

By the 1990s the twin-track policy of combining economic modernisation with the perseverance of the social status quo has begun to break down. This partly reflected domestic pressures, notably the rise in youth unemployment as the high birth rates combined with the rapidly declining infant mortality rates of the 1970s and 1980s resulted in a rapid population expansion and large numbers of Saudi Arabian citizens seeking to enter the workforce. It was also a result of high, but largely frustrated expectations, as Western materialism had an increasing impact on the wealthier families, leaving the poorer sections of society marginalised.

Introduction 3

Closer integration with the global economy is consequently a divisive issue in Saudi Arabian society, with most of the royal family and the merchant elite favouring economic liberalism but others – perhaps the majority – more doubtful about any possible benefits. These differences can be illustrated by the debate over foreign trade and investment, the former being analysed in Chapter 6 and the latter in Chapter 3, where government economic policy is discussed. Trade liberalisation was given a boost by the agreement to make the GCC a customs union in 2001 which involved the introduction of a common 5 per cent external tariff from January 1, 2003. This meant painful choices for Saudi Arabia, as hitherto some tariffs had been at a 20 per cent level in order to protect domestic producers from competition. It also threatened tax revenue losses, as tariffs were the major non-oil source of income. It was clear, however, that unless Saudi Arabia agreed to the tariff reductions at the Muscat summit in December 2001, the UAE, which had only a 4 per cent tariff, would not have been prepared to sign the customs union agreement.

As a consequence of past protectionist policies the kingdom has become less externally reliant, with exports – mainly oil – falling from 67.6 per cent of GDP in 1981 to 41.9 per cent by 2001. Imports peaked in the early 1980s but subsequently fell with the decline in oil income. During the 1990s imports were largely flat, and the balance of trade remained in surplus, even during 1998, which from the kingdom's point of view was the worst year for oil prices since the early 1970s.

Similar dilemmas to those over trade policy arise over foreign investment, which has been one of the major impediments to Saudi Arabia's joining the World Trade Organisation. The kingdom has sought to maintain local control of its oil resources, petrochemical industry and manufacturing and services catering for the domestic market. Although some sectors were opened up with the new investment laws of 2001 – notably downstream petrochemicals – many more remain restricted, especially the banking sector and the part-privatised telecommunications sector. Yet even the limited liberalisation encouraged an inward investment of 4.8 billion dollars in 2001, over half the total for the entire Middle East and North African region, demonstrating the large potential for gains. A great prize would be the 25 billion dollars which, it is estimated, will be needed to develop the kingdom's gas resources. Yet even here there is controversy, as discussed in Chapter 4 on the subject of oil and gas, with Saudi ARAMCO, the state oil company wanting to develop the gas itself with the reported approval support of the Oil Minister, while others – including Crown Prince Abdullah – favour ExxonMobil and certain Western companies as this could speed up the gas development process, assist economic diversification and cost less, at least in terms of upfront expenditures.

Explaining development

The study starts in Chapter 2 by attempting to discover which development paradigm best explains the country's economic history. Unlike in most

4   Rodney Wilson

developing countries, feudalistic structures were historically underdeveloped in the territories that now comprise Saudi Arabia, partly reflecting its lack of agriculture and limited Ottoman influence in comparison to the rest of the Middle East. A natural egalitarianism flourished throughout much of the traditional pastoral economy, with little accumulation of capital or wealth. Only in the trading centres of the Hejaz was there a degree of class formation, with merchants as the business elite, but even here, small family-owned establishments dominated. There was not even the class stratification found in the smaller Gulf countries, where dhow owners and pearling captains constituted the upper class while the pearl divers could be described as the working class.

The advent of oil and the accumulation of private fortunes by the more successful merchants and many members of the royal family resulted in the emergence of class divisions, which grew over time. It can be argued that this new upper and middle class owes its success to the state, for without state patronage it would not have achieved its success. Yet the position today is more complex, for although state connections may have helped to secure lucrative government contracts and agency monopolies in the past, there is now greater competition and a higher degree of transparency in Saudi Arabia than in most other Arab countries. Moreover, – and crucially – the great private fortunes accumulated by many Saudi Arabian nationals are often invested abroad and beyond state control. One study by the Saudi American Bank found that in 2001 85,000 Saudi families controlled overseas assets worth over 700 billion dollars. Their future prosperity depends more on the fortunes of the global economy and international financial markets than on local government patronage. The kingdom's growth may not yet be self-sustaining but that of many of its wealthiest citizens undoubtedly is.

Although oil has been crucial for the past development of the Saudi Arabian economy, it is no longer the main engine of growth. Rather, it is domestic market expansion that drives the economy, a consequence of population increase and a resultant growth in the number of consumers. As in advanced Western economies it is consumer expenditure that keeps the economy moving. It is changes in business and consumer confidence that affect the retail market, not simply oil prices.

Yet it may be premature to ascribe too much of the dynamism in the economy to the private sector, despite the increasing role that has been ascribed to business in recent development plans. This volume draws on survey work from three successful Ph.D. students at the University of Durham with whose studies the author had the privilege to be involved. Monica Malik's thesis demonstrates the frustration of business leaders in Saudi Arabia with government economic policy. Her interviews with thirty business leaders show that while a great deal has been achieved a considerable amount of work remains to be done, and that there is a lack of confidence that the government's ambitions for the private sector will be achieved. Indeed, it is alleged that government misunderstands the needs of the business community and must strengthen its capacity for economic management.

Introduction 5

Abdullah Al-Salamah, in his study, focuses on workers rather than management, his concern being the adequacy of working conditions in SABIC, the kingdom's largest manufacturing company with interests in petrochemicals and heavy industrial products. Although SABIC is regarded as one of the country's best employers, his survey of 312 Saudi Arabian nationals and expatriate employees shows their concern over the usefulness of the training they receive and their dissatisfaction over pay, promotion and the way grievances have been handled by management. In many respects their concerns reflect those of workers everywhere, demonstrating that the attitudes of the Saudi Arabian workforce are not so different to those of workers in the West and in other developing countries. They are willing to articulate their complaints, which helps to put pressure on employers for improvements in the terms and conditions of employment.

Ahmed Al-Rajhi, in his thesis focuses on the electricity industry, which has been extensively restructured with the separation of electricity generation and transmission. This has been carried out in preparation for the eventual privatisation of electricity generation, as in other Gulf countries, with new capacity to be constructed under build-own-operate schemes. The willingness of multinational companies to become involved naturally depends on electricity pricing but, as Ahmed Al-Rajhi shows, this is a complex issue giving rise to conflicts of interest between generators and private and business consumers. If states such as California have difficulty in getting the balance right – as threats of the collapse of its entire system in the late 1990s showed – how much more difficult is the problem in Saudi Arabia as an developing economy. There is also the issue of whether generation capacity should be located closer to the sources of energy (which means Eastern Province) or nearer to consumers in Riyadh or Jeddah. This has implications for regional economic policy.

Overall, an important objective of this book is to demonstrate that, although in the past Saudi Arabia was considered an exceptional economy because of its oil wealth yet limited non-oil economy, today it can be regarded as a more normal one. Its problems are typical of those facing developing countries, particularly deciding what the role of the state should be in economic management. The problems the state has to grapple with – notably budget deficits and rising unemployment – are similar to those found in many other countries. The mainstream development literature has, therefore, a good deal of relevance for the kingdom.

2 Which development paradigm?

The relevance of conventional models of economic development to Saudi Arabia can be debated. In the 1970s and 1980s there was an assumption that the economy was simply resource-based, and rentier in nature, with economic growth or contraction dependent on the price and output of oil.[1] The uniqueness of the economy was stressed, and it was viewed as atypical of developing countries; indeed, many questioned whether the country could even be classified as 'developing'. This issue still remains a matter of controversy, as in the kingdom's negotiations to join the World Trade Organisation some of the difficulties have centred on whether the country should be categorised as 'developing' or 'developed'.

A central premise of this study is that Saudi Arabia can be classified as a developing country and that conventional development theory is highly relevant. The economic structures, far from being simple, are complex. Hence the relationships between economic variables and the determinants of economic behaviour can best be understood by applying standard development models. These are required for any meaningful interpretation of economic trends.

Any successful development strategy has to be based on sound theoretical underpinnings. In so far as the kingdom's development plans encapsulate its development strategy, it is far from clear if this was, or even now, is the case. The first development plan covering the period from 1970 to 1974 was essentially a shopping list. The targets of the Seventh Plan, which covers the period 2000–2005, still remain in many respects an aspiration. They are a wish list rather than an attempt to address the serious underlying economic problems such as unemployment, the lack of competitiveness, the institutional rigidities and the difficulties in fostering an entrepreneurial rather than a dependency culture.

Economic diversification has been on the agenda for five decades, and much has been achieved in petrochemicals and energy-related industries, and to a lesser extent in developing industries to serve the local market.[2] The employment creation by these industries, most of which are capital-intensive, has been limited, with many of the jobs going to foreign nationals despite the policy of encouraging the employment of Saudis. There is also the issue of the long-term viability of the industries that has been debated ever since their

Which development paradigm? 7

inception,[3] and of whether they are capable of developing further or even maintaining their position in an increasingly competitive international environment where treaty obligations and membership of world organisations limits the scope for subsidies. Indeed, the whole issue of Saudi Arabia's position within the global economy – beyond its being a major supplier of crude oil – has yet to be addressed.

Historical perspectives on market development

Historical approaches that draw parallels with the development experiences of industrialised economies would appear to have some relevance to Saudi Arabia. Most of today's advanced industrial economies started with structures based on traditional agriculture, with change resulting from internal factors, such as improvements in communications, which enabled markets to operate on a larger scale. Change often came rapidly but was demand-generated by the spread of markets, was often accompanied by population growth which added to the demand for goods and services.

In the case of Saudi Arabia, most attention has focused on oil revenue and in particular on the development possibilities opened up as a result of the 1973–1974 and 1979 oil-price rises. Less attention has been paid to the emergence of a national market made possible by the creation of a modern infrastructure of roads, internal air transport, telecommunications and an electricity grid. Prior to the 1970s, although the kingdom was politically unified, economic transactions between the regions and cities were limited. Jeddah was the major port and commercial centre, but its economic links with Riyadh, the political capital, were restricted. Eastern Province, the centre for oil extraction, was a kind of enclave economy, dominated by Aramco, the Arabian American Oil Company, which employed mainly American expatriates and workers from outside the kingdom.

Arguably the major achievement of the oil era has been the creation of a national economy for goods, services and capital, and to a much lesser extent for labour. The distribution channels for imported goods, and in many cases the servicing arrangements, have become national rather than regional or local. Domestic industries have been established, with subsidised credit from the Saudi Industrial Development Fund,[4] to serve the national market, with protection through licensing and import tariffs.

The key medium-term issue now facing the non-oil economy is whether the widening of the market to a national scale has reached its natural limits, and whether future growth will simply be in line with gross domestic product growth, which may be modest. In the longer term there is the issue of whether domestic-market reliance can be maintained as the main driving force for the non-oil sector in an increasingly global economy where Saudi Arabia may be forced to curtail its subsidies and reduce protection. There are already regional pressures for reductions in protectionism from the GCC, and international pressures from the WTO and Saudi Arabia's Western trading partners.

8 *Rodney Wilson*

The goal of self-sustaining growth

Linear stages of economic growth theories – notably that espoused by Walt Rostow[5] – can help in put into context where economies such as that of Saudi Arabia have come from and where they are heading. The country has clearly emerged from the first traditional society stage, and some of the preconditions for take-off into self-sustaining growth associated with Rostow's second stage may have been met, notably in terms of the physical infrastructure. It seems unlikely that Saudi Arabia has entered the third take-off stage, and certainly it has not yet entered the fourth stage, the drive to maturity. However, for some Saudi citizens at least, the fifth has been attained: the age of high-mass consumption.

Although it is inappropriate to categorise Saudi Arabia in one of Rostow's stages, the approach is nevertheless helpful in identifying the obstacles to self-sustaining growth. The high mass consumption was facilitated by oil revenues, which are potentially sustainable on the basis of production and reserves for at least a period of eighty years. The crucial uncertainty lies in future prices and the level of world demand for oil. It is this uncertainty that prompted Saudi Arabia's efforts at diversification, which can best be viewed as a risk-reduction economic strategy. The problem is that economic diversification brings its own risks, not least the probability that some projects will fail to yield returns that could justify the investment. This may not matter if continuing subsidy remains possible until eventual viability is achieved; but already many subsidies have had to be either reduced or phased out completely, which underlines the need for project sustainability.

If the conditions for a take-off into self-sustaining growth do not yet exist in Saudi Arabia, what can be done to ensure that the kingdom will eventually overcome any deficiencies? Clearly the government has a potential role to play, but it can also be convincingly argued that its dominant role in the economy is actually part of the problem. State control over the disbursement of oil revenues has encouraged a rentier mentality and crowded out many potential private-sector initiatives. The private sector itself has an unhealthy dependence on government spending, which exacerbates the business cycles associated with oil-revenue fluctuations. Rather than private-sector activity varying in an anti-cyclical manner in relation to changing government expenditure, it tends to move in a pro-cyclical fashion.

Saudi Arabia has often been characterised as a classic example of a rentier economy, with the behaviour of both the government and the private sector driven by rent-seeking. The state seeks to maximise its revenue from oil to increase its power of patronage, and private-sector business seeks to obtain monopoly privileges for services provided to government in addition to exclusive franchises to distribute imports and licences to manufacture that enable the businesses to earn monopoly rents. This alliance between the state and politically favoured business serves the interests of both parties well but ultimately creates resentments and tensions from the excluded majority, who are unable to obtain similar favours.

Which development paradigm? 9

Rather than pressing for greater transparency in government contracts, an opening-up of distribution channels and a relaxation of the industrial permit system those excluded lobby – largely unsuccessfully – to be among the included. The authorities react with minor concessions, which are sufficient to keep alive the hopes of those outsiders most likely to qualify as insiders. New industrial licences are granted every year, but not in numbers significant enough to 'spoil the market' for established producers. New local firms are occasionally awarded government contracts, though most go to previous contractors. There are always new products to be imported and distributed, yet again established trading companies gain most, though not all, of this business. This is sufficient to preclude demands for more fundamental change.

It seems highly improbable that a rentier economy should take off into self-sustaining growth. Some in Western Asian economies such as Saudi Arabia see the so-called 'crony capitalism' of East Asian economies as similar to their own. Such a parallel is, however, mistaken as although a close relationship exists between governments and leading businesses in most East Asian states, many of these enterprises are focused on exports rather than the domestic market. Their governments can to some extent protect the businesses in the internal market, but they cannot shelter them from international competition. Even disguised subsidies are providing increasingly problematic in a world trading system increasingly subject to WTO rules and procedures. Governments of newly industrialising nations cannot in any case afford to finance such subsidies, especially if they are in debt to the International Monetary Fund, which disapproves of interventionist policies.

In the case of Saudi Arabia it is only the largely state-owned enterprises such as SABIC, the Saudi Arabian Basic Industries Corporation, which are subject to international competition. The private sector is almost wholly dependent on the domestic market. In such circumstances the relationship with the state is far more crucial; hence it is not surprising that much entrepreneurial effort goes into cultivating ministries and ministers rather than into product development or marketing.

In development literature the concept of absorptive capacity refers to the ability of countries to make productive use of foreign investment flows or aid, which is linked to their existing resource endowment and development potential.[6] In the case of the oil-exporting economies of the 1970s, it was asserted that they were acquiring more foreign exchange receipts than could usefully be deployed domestically, the policy implication being either the imperative of investing surplus funds externally in international financial markets or of increasing the absorptive capacity by improving the physical and human capital base. A failure to achieve self-sustaining growth may reflect limited absorptive capacity, and an increase in the latter may be one precondition for such growth.

Ragaei El Mallakh identified, back in the 1970s and early 1980s, the factors limiting absorptive capacity in Saudi Arabia as inadequate administrative capacity, manpower shortages and the inability of the physical infrastructure to

10   *Rodney Wilson*

absorb increased expenditure.[7] These factors undoubtedly inhibited the implementation of the second development plan during the period 1975–1980, when supply bottlenecks resulted in inflationary pressures and the government having to curtail its own expenditure despite substantial surpluses in revenue. Now, some twenty years later, the administrative capacity has improved considerably, both within the Ministry of Planning and the spending ministries, and the kingdom has a physical infrastructure that compares favourably with those of most developed countries in terms of highways, ports and telecommunications, although the user costs with respect to voice and data transmission are relatively high, reflecting the lack of competition. The question of manpower remains more problematic, as though immigrants filled the gap relatively high turnover among these groups plus work-permit controls and fees lead to increases in employment costs. Furthermore, despite the substantial growth in the Saudi Arabian population and labour force, suitably trained local nationals are often unavailable for key jobs such as electricians, plumbers and maintenance engineers, the preference for white collar jobs in government administration remaining in spite of the reduced number of these now available.

The absence of feudalism

Marxist theory sees economies developing from simple hunter-gatherer modes of production which represent a type of primitive communism to a form of feudalism based on settled agriculture with landlords controlling the means of production and tenants undertaking much of the labour. Eventually from this capitalism may emerge, together with industrialisation and urbanisation, which in turn give rise to the kind of class tensions that create revolutionary conditions leading ultimately to the triumph of socialism. Though such a sequencing may now appear far-fetched – especially since the collapse of the centrally planned economies – a Marxist historical analysis based on economic determinism can help in understanding the development processes at work in any economy, even such an unlikely candidate for Marxism as Saudi Arabia.

Though classifying Saudi Arabia's stage of economic development with the use of Marxist analysis may be problematic the kingdom does appear to exhibit some of the features of pre-capitalism and capitalism but arguably few of the characteristics of feudalism. In Saudi Arabia, settled agriculture is possible on less than two per cent of the country's total land area amounting to 45,000 square kilometres, and of this only around 6,000 square kilometres is actually cultivated. Livestock-rearing on scrubland was historically the main form of agriculture, but pastoral life tends to be associated with primitive communism rather than feudalism, as lands are grazed in common and there are tribal rather than individual rights. The tribes, of course, have their leaders, but there is little income differentiation as possessions have to be constantly transported, which precludes the accumulation of material wealth. There is also a form of economic democracy, as consultation takes place over the use of grazing land and such matters as where and when sheep and goats – and hence the tribe – should move.

Which development paradigm? 11

With virtually the whole country receiving less than a hundred millimetres per year of rainfall, which is often unpredictable, most agriculture has to be based on irrigation, even in Asir Province in the south-west, where in the higher regions there are forests and some rain-fed agriculture. In Asir most farms are small owner occupied units, usually of less than one hectare, as opposed to the large estates generally found under feudalistic conditions. This is largely a consequence of the hilly terrain and the fragmented nature of the holdings which usually consist of small, terraced fields. Land-tenure reform involving redistribution has thus never been an issue as in other Arab states such as Egypt, Syria or Iraq, where large estates were broken up by reforming governments seeking to eliminate the old feudal order.

Government policy in Asir has been largely supportive of existing smallholders, with subsidised loans provided through the Agricultural Bank and a number of water and dam projects. Although the area is poor, conditions compare favourably with the Yemeni side of the border which has received virtually no state support. Major government programmes for agriculture have been implemented in the Hofuf and Qatif areas of Eastern Province, where the whole Al-Hasa oasis was remodelled, with new irrigation and drainage systems serving 52,000 farms.[8] Despite the introduction of changes, land holdings in this region remain small, though larger than those in Asir.

None of these government policies towards agriculture could be regarded as supportive of feudalism or an attempt to create capitalist or even pre-capitalist conditions in rural areas, as family farming modes of production remain largely undisturbed. This is also the case with the nomadic way of life of Bedouin tribal groups dependent on sheep, goats and camels, even though they represent a diminishing part of the population as urbanisation proceeds. The help given to agriculture in the 1970s was partly a response to the decline in the previous decade, when the drift to the urban areas of young men in search of government employment resulted in a partial breakdown of farm activity.[9] Efforts to boost wheat, sorghum and barley production in that decade can also be viewed as an attempt to ensure that local producers benefited from the rapid expansion in the market for foodstuffs with the oil boom and the arrival of large numbers of migrant workers requiring to be fed. Domestic food self-sufficiency was not spelt out as a policy objective in development plans or other official documents, but by the 1980s because of grain subsidies, the kingdom became a net exporter of wheat, with meat being the main food import.

The main agribusiness developments in rural areas have been the egg and poultry schemes which, since 1980, have satisfied most local demand. These are private business ventures, often undertaken by grain merchants, and are in some respects capitalistic in nature. However, although there are location advantages in being a local producer of fresh produce, these enterprises would not be self-sustaining without the help of government grain subsidies. Even with such subsidies, profits from agribusiness developments are generally low because of high overheads, not least the cost of keeping the processing plants cool during

12   Rodney Wilson

the summer months to meet hygiene standards. The larger firms, which have a stock market quotation, have been the worst-performing companies locally.

Emergent capitalism

The absence of feudalistic economic relations arguably facilitates the transition to capitalism, yet it would be misleading to classify Saudi Arabia as an emergent capitalist society. Capitalism implies an internal dynamic for profit generation resulting from the profitability of the business enterprise. Marxist and neo-Marxist models of capitalist development stress the existence of class formation in society, the determinants of class being position within an economic hierarchy based on property rights or a lack of such rights. In such a system with industrialisation there is a transition from feudal landlords to industrial capitalists that clearly has little relevance to the situation in Saudi Arabia. To a considerable extent the state has usurped the functions of capitalists, but it does not employ exploitative modes of production with respect to its own citizens, any exploitation in the system being largely confined to the migrant workers. Indeed, local citizens often enjoy subsidised employment in government, although it is increasingly difficult to provide such work for more than a limited minority.

Profitability of capitalist enterprises can arise from a competitive advantage reflecting low costs, or the ability to exploit some unique characteristic of the product being sold, which gives a natural monopolistic advantage. In the case of Saudi Arabia, competitive advantage is problematic as labour costs are higher than in most developing countries. Admittedly transportation costs are low, reflecting the sound infrastructure and lack of congestion, but this assists imports as well as locally produced goods destined for the domestic market. Distribution margins are relatively high given exclusive dealer arrangements. These tend to encourage importing rather than local manufacturing, despite the low-cost finance available for the latter from the Saudi Industrial Development Fund.

Apart from certain processed date products that appeal primarily to local tastes, little is manufactured locally which can be regarded as having unique characteristics. The local supplies of basic and intermediate petrochemical products, polymers and fertilisers provide opportunities for related downstream industries, and great efforts are being made to attract investment in these sectors, but many other countries have similar products available. Proximity to markets is arguably more important than proximity to input supplies. In practice this means domestic-market reliance for Saudi Arabian industry as the regional market is limited and the UAE and Qatar produce similar goods.

At present basic and intermediate petrochemical products are mostly exported, which is likely to remain the case for the foreseeable future. Michael Porter's diamond model arguably has more relevance to SABIC's future success than to traditional models of capitalist development, the four conditions being factor of production availability, demand conditions, firm strategy, structure and rivalry and related and supporting industries.[10] In the case of SABIC, capital availability is less of a constraint than for competing petrochemical schemes in

Which development paradigm? 13

Iran. Labour is an issue, the constraint being the policy of increasing the share in the workforce of local nationals, which adds to costs. Demand conditions are externally determined by global economic developments, but strategy, structure and rivalry are accommodated through the joint venture arrangements with leading multinational oil and chemical companies. Related and supporting industries refer to upstream links to ARAMCO and downstream links to existing and planned businesses making use of the petrochemical products.

The transition to capitalism in Saudi Arabia can be viewed in terms of a conflict between traditional social forces and modernism. The attempt to safeguard traditional values is seen as in potential conflict with the demands of a modern, industrialising economy. For instance, business constraints on time management might appear to be at odds with the need to pray five times a day. The sexual segregation of the workplace or denying women the right to drive could be regarded as adding to costs and impeding efficiency. In practice, however, most Saudis manage to reconcile social and religious obligations – which are willingly and often enthusiastically accepted – with employment demands. The pattern of the working day is very different to that in the most developed countries, but that is not to deny the fact that most work gets done.

Tim Niblock rejects the notion of explaining development or lack of development in Saudi Arabia in terms of a conflict between traditionalism and modernisation.[11] Rather, he believes that greater insights into the forces for change can be obtained by delineating social groupings. The processes of development can then be examined in terms of social and political interaction rather than simply in narrow economic terms that often have little real bearing on underlying social conditions. He identifies urban merchants as a key social group, given that much of the development planning and the substantial investment in infrastructure and industry of the 1970s and 1980s was strongly supported by this group, who hoped to have their income augmented as a result – a hope that was largely fulfilled. The merchants had, and continue to have, a strong interest in the political stability of the kingdom, and are, therefore, largely supportive of the royal family, the military and the National Guard.

Field studies of Saudi Arabian managers, many of whom come from merchant families, reveal the extent to which they differ from their Western counterparts in terms of attitudes. Ibrahim Al-Awaji found basic loyalties were to family and kinship groups, with much evidence of collective rather than individualistic behaviour.[12] Fahad Al-Shalan found that the attitudes of public sector managers were influenced by religious and social norms, and that they largely adopted a consultative decision-making process.[13] Al-Malik, however, who compared private with state-sector executives, found the former had more individual authority and power, higher salaries and greater job satisfaction.[14]

Islamic beliefs are acknowledged by most Saudi Arabians as of relevance to their entire lives, including their business and financial affairs, even though, as elsewhere many – perhaps even the majority – do not live up to the demands of

14   *Rodney Wilson*

the divine guidance contained in the Koran or adhere fully to Islamic shariah law. As capitalism, like socialism, is essentially materialistic, and as interest-based transactions, though condemned in the Koran,[15] form an important part of the system, it is always likely to meet with a certain amount of opposition from within the country. Some of the kingdom's leading companies, such as the Dallah Al-Baraka Group, openly promote transactions that comply with strict Islamic law as opposed to secular commercial codes, and the financial institution with the largest number of branches, Al-Rajhi, is a self-designated Islamic bank. The essence of an Islamic economic system is the market, but a just one, employing fair transactions. This is of course the ideal rather than the norm, but still a very different kind of economic model from that prevailing within many forms of capitalism, including those inspired by Calvinism.

Wahhabism, like Protestantism, has proved remarkably adaptable to change despite its fundamentalist underpinnings. The stress on adherence to the shariah law has proved no impediment to accepting – and, indeed, welcoming – modernisation and change. Considerable emphasis has been laid on *ijtihad*, the right to interpret and reinterpret shariah law when economic circumstances have altered, and an attempt to reconcile modern financial and commercial practice with the demands of Koranic teaching, including the prohibition of *riba* or interest. While Islamic law is strictly enforced, in areas where Koranic revelation is silent, civil or complaints courts have been established to deal with business disputes.[16] Saudi Arabia subscribes to the Hanbali School of Islamic jurisprudence, often regarded as liberal on economic and business issues while – like other schools – being strict in the dieds of personal morality and criminal law.

There are advantages in being a latecomer rather than a development pioneer as this means that lessons can be learnt from the errors of others. In Saudi Arabia's case there was a desire not to repeat the mistakes made with industrialisation in Egypt, where state-run industries geared to the domestic market proved notoriously inefficient. In Saudi Arabia, the private sector was encouraged to play a significant role in industrialisation, with low cost loans made available from the Saudi Industrial Development Fund from the 1970s to finance up to half the costs of new projects, but without state ownership. Joint ventures with foreign multinationals were also encouraged, notably in the case of Saudi Arabia Basic Industries Corporation (SABIC) projects.

There were also lessons to be learnt from the excesses of Iran before and after the Islamic Revolution of 1979. Western capitalism was never given free rein in the kingdom as it was in the former country under the Shah, where this created tensions within a deeply religious society. Yet no special laws were passed to Islamise the banking system of Saudi Arabia comparable to the Iranian legislation of 1983. The Saudi religious establishment has made no attempt to formulate policies in the field of economics or development that conflict with those of the government, nor has it emerged as an independent source of power as with the Iranian Council of Guardians.

Income distribution and development

Simon Kuznets postulated that in the initial stages of economic development inequality of income would increase but that eventually, with the building of social institutions, policies of redistribution would be introduced restoring a greater degree of equality.[17] Numerous empirical studies have been conducted to test Kuznets' hypothesis, with rather mixed findings, but in the case of Saudi Arabia there is insufficient data to facilitate empirical testing. Nevertheless there is considerable evidence of substantial inequality in income and wealth which has increased markedly since the oil boom of the 1970s. During the Ottoman period and the reign of King Abdul Aziz there was only a modest degree of wealth and income inequality, with even the royal family living fairly frugal lives. The richest strata of society were the merchants of the Hejaz, although those involved in supplying goods and services to Aramco in the 1940s and 1950s earned reasonable incomes. However, position rather than wealth determined status and there was little stress on material goods in Wahhabi Muslim society. Indeed, for the Wahhabis the emphasis was on a simple lifestyle with spiritual values been seen as much more important than material possessions.

While a great deal of attention is paid to the legitimacy of how money is made, through *halal* or *haram* transactions – the former being permitted, the latter forbidden – there is much less emphasis on distributive justice. Fatwa have been issued to legitimise stock market transactions by individuals of high net worth, which is no longer seen as a form of *gharar* or deception, but less attention has been paid by the ulema to the needs of the poor and unemployed. Fourteen per cent of those living in Saudi Arabia still have no access to sanitation and over a quarter of the population remain illiterate.[18] The Bedouin are largely neglected by the state, though admittedly government schemes set up to encourage more permanent settlement so as to facilitate the schooling of their children have mostly failed simply because the Bedouin themselves are reluctant to abandon their traditional nomadic lifestyle.

There is no personal income or property tax in Saudi Arabia, most state revenue apart from that accruing from oil coming from import duties. The tax system is not designed to be progressive but rather simply to raise revenue for the purpose of covering government expenditure. Corporate taxes are more significant than personal ones, with those imposed on business income varying from 25 per cent for small enterprises with an annual turnover of less than 100,000 Saudi riyals to 45 per cent for those with one of over 1 million riyals. Income accruing to non-residents from investments in Saudi Arabian business or professional activities is subject to income tax, with the rate ranging from 5 per cent for taxable income of up to 16,000 riyals to 30 per cent for that exceeding 66,000 riyals.[19] The principle of tax bands – a key feature of any progressive tax system – is, therefore, accepted practice in Saudi Arabia.

The chief tax involving redistribution is *Zakat*, an Islamic wealth tax, the payment of which is regarded as one of the five pillars of Islam along with the

16 *Rodney Wilson*

profession of faith, prayer, fasting during Ramadan and pilgrimage during the haj. *Zakat* can be regarded as a form of almsgiving, but in Saudi Arabia the government is made responsible for its collection through the Department of *Zakat* and Income Tax. It is levied at one-fortieth of the value of liquid wealth or two-and-a-half per cent per annum, a category that includes bank balances and personal holdings of precious metals such as gold and silver but not property or items of equipment or furniture. In Saudi Arabia, *Zakat* is paid by local and GCC nationals and Saudi and GCC owned entities, partnership and limited-liability companies. The Koran stipulates that the the proceeds from it should be used to support the poor, orphans, widows, freed slaves and debtors,[20] an injunction that guides the policy of the above-mentioned Department.

Islamic inheritance laws also provide an important mechanism for the redistribution of wealth, as all sons are entitled to an equal share of an inheritance, this being twice that of the daughters. If a male head of household dies, one-eighth of the wealth goes to the widow, but the remainder is passed to the children immediately rather than upon their mother's death as in most Western countries.[21] There is no inheritance tax, but where there are no children the widow receives one-quarter of the wealth, the remainder accruing to the state after the payment of debts and legacies.[22]

Although the application of Islamic law has helped to reduce inequality of income and wealth, in other respects government policy has worsened inequality. Oil-rich countries can be regarded as distributive states in the sense that an important function of the state is to redistribute oil revenue, which gives the government the power of patronage. This, however, means winning the support of influential groups rather than adopting more inclusive policies that might help the poorer sections of society. Policies aimed at redistributing income might have the effect of undermining political support in societies where only a limited amount of solidarity exists between different income groups, especially in cases where the higher-income group includes many actually belonging to the royal family.

Disparities of income and wealth may matter less where there is a high degree of opportunity for social mobility. Historically there was relatively little social differentiation in the Arabian peninsula, the main distinction being that observed between pastoral nomads and urban merchants and craftsmen. The advent of oil created a new privileged class of Saudi Arabian civil servants and military personnel, but these groups have not succeeded in securing access for their offspring to jobs similar to their own as government ministries cannot afford to increase payroll numbers and the military spends increasingly on equipment rather than manpower.

In Saudi Arabia social differentiation is not based on clothing as there remains an external visual egalitarianism, although women from the higher-income groups, especially those who travel, increasingly emulate their Western counterparts when dressing for within the home or abroad. Housing reflects status, notably in the size and opulence of dwellings for a minority, with others being forced by economic circumstances to live in cramped apartment buildings

Which development paradigm? 17

originally intended for immigrant workers. Interest-free finance from the Saudi Real Estate Development Fund has largely helped higher-income families as those on low incomes cannot afford to take out loans, even if these are highly subsidised.

Mohammed Riad El-Ghonemy notes that despite the affluence found in Saudi Arabia, the widespread poor nutritional status and high illiteracy rate mean that the kingdom has more in common with less developed countries than with those enjoying higher incomes. He cites high rates of anaemia and malnourishment amongst poor children from large families, as well as parasitic infections.[23] Yet among higher-income groups obesity and diabetes seem to be common; indeed, there is a positive correlation between level of income level these health problems according to a survey undertaken in Eastern Province.[24] On a more positive note, infant mortality rates in the country have declined significantly and by 1998 averaged 20 per 1,000 live births, well below the rates in Egypt or even Jordan.[25] Life expectancy has increased to seventy-two years, only slightly below that of developed countries. It is also worth noting that considerable advances have been made in female education which results in Saudi Arabia having a far more favourable gender development index than those of most other Arab countries, including Algeria, Egypt, Jordan and Iraq.[26]

The role of the state

Much has been written on the changing role of the state in the Middle East, especially since economic reform and structural adjustment measures were introduced during the 1980s and privatisation during the 1990s.[27] The collapse of Communism, the retreat of Arab socialism and increasing tendencies towards globalisation have also resulted in a great deal of reflection on where states are heading. Charles Tripp sees this literature as of limited applicability in the context of the Middle East, the real issue being how the state itself is defined, which involves more than simply government.[28] He discusses the state as community, as hierarchy and as coercive apparatus. Although Tripp's analysis was largely designed to be applied to the northern Arab states rather than the Gulf oil-producing countries, the focus on definitions and categorisations is useful as it helps to clarify the position of the state in Saudi Arabia, which is not simply a transitory matter.

Islam is not confined by state boundaries, and Saudi Arabia has attempted to project its influence through pan-Islamic institutions, notably the Organisation for the Islamic Conference, which it plays a major role in funding. Nevertheless the territorial integrity of the Saudi state has created a closer sense of community and identity in the wider Islamic world, not least because of the inheritance passed down from Wahhabism and King Abdul Aziz, who brought the Hejaz and most of the Arabian peninsula under his control. Wahhabism had its origins in the Arabian heartlands of the central Najd. Ibn Abd al-Wahhab, the eighteenth-century founder of the movement, aimed to recreate in Arabia a state similar to that of the earliest days of Islam.[29] From Ibn Taimiyah it took the notion that the

18 Rodney Wilson

state and religion must be linked; indeed, that the institution of government way indispensable for regulating the affairs of men.[30] Power – or, in other words, Tripp's coercive apparatus – is necessary for the duty of commanding good and forbidding evil.

The trade-off between the desire to give allegiance to the state and the need for coercion has changed much since the Hejaz came under the control of King Abdul Aziz in 1925. In the early twentieth century significant religious differences existed between the more tolerant Hejazis and the more puritanical Wahhabis, notably over the pilgrimages to saints tombs, the issues of intercession and the dubious religious practices of certain pilgrims, including the playing of music, at the Kaaba in Mecca.[31] The Hejazis were inclined to be tolerant towards the pilgrims – upon whom their livelihood depended – whereas the Wahhabis were opposed to all intercession, believing in pure, direct communication through prayer between believers and God.

Ultimately, despite the more extreme Wahhabis being held in check by King Abdul Aziz, Wahhabi influence over the Hejaz became stronger. The economic dependence of the region on the Najd with the development of oil replaced the earlier dependence on the pilgrimage trade. The increasing economic links between the two areas and the creation of a unified market reduced the need for state coercion. It would be misleading to project the history of the early twentieth century into the twenty-first and exaggerate the regional differences that exists within Saudi Arabia.

A more important issue is that concerning the relations between the Jeddah's Fiqh Academy, the most respected source of religious guidance, and Riyadh's Ministry of Islamic Affairs, which has little connection with Hejaz-Najd differences. One obvious question is whether the Academy controls the Ministry or the other way round. The answer is probably neither; rather that each one influences the other, although in modern terminology the Academy can be regarded as the 'content provider' and the Ministry as the means of dissemination, both domestically through the *Da'awa* and guidance centres established in every Saudi Arabian city, and internationally through intergovernmental institutions such the Organisation of the Islamic Conference and charitable agencies including the World Assembly for Muslim Youth.

In practice economic management has not been a contentious issue in Saudi Arabia, the main differences arising over the speed of change rather than over policy issues. Economic debates within the kingdom usually involve business leaders, representatives from chambers of commerce and the commercial banks, academics and ministers. Such discussions tend to be about specific initiatives, such as the recent foreign investment laws of 2000, rather than about whether the economy should be advancing in a capitalistic, socialist or Islamic direction. The emphasis is on pragmatism rather than ideology, with often little interest being expressed in possible competing economic systems, including the tenets of Islamic economics.

The greatest challenge for the state within the sphere of economics is arguably the institutional capacity to deliver. A survey undertaken by

Which development paradigm? 19

Abdelrahman Al-Hegelan of the Saudi Arabian Ministry of Finance and Monte Palmer to evaluate the developmental capacity of the bureaucracy revealed serious shortcomings in most areas.[32] The areas where deficiencies were found included psychological drive, flexibility, communications, client relations and impartiality. Although the survey, carried out in the early 1980, covered 123 senior civil servants, there is little evidence that much has changed in the intervening years.

Power has undoubtedly shifted between and from ministries, however, with the role of the Ministry of Planning being downgraded since the 1970s and early 1980s, in many respects the heyday of economic planning. Then, as the state had substantial oil revenues, the first three plans that indicated government spending priorities were crucial both in determining what infrastructure got built and the overall direction of the economy. The targets in more recent plans have been more aspirations as they rely on private-sector initiatives that may not prove sustainable after the initial burst of energy has subsided. There has also been an emphasis on consolidation, which implies fewer new initiatives on the part of the government.

In 1999 the Supreme Economic Council was established to give a higher priority to the economy, coordinate ministerial actions and provide leadership and direction in economic decision-making rather than simply responding to events. The chairman of the Council is Prince Abdullah, deputy premier and commander of the National Guard. This demonstrates its significance. Economic power is seen as essential for political power, and the fall in Saudi Arabia's share in global output and per capita income during the 1980s and 1990s was viewed with concern. However, there was no basic policy change, the Supreme Council reaffirming that it would adhere to the principles of a free economy, free markets for capital, goods and services. In practice this meant the internal market, as restrictions on inward investment, import duties and banking controls remained. Unsurprisingly, there was no mention of a free market for labour.[33]

Given that three of the ten objectives of the Supreme Economic Council refer to the control of public debt, increasing the income of the state in line with the growth of the national economy and the diversification of revenue sources, this implies an enhanced role for the Ministry of Finance. Reference is also made to the need to increase savings and domestic investment, improve social welfare and ensure a fair distribution of income, create employment and enhance the private sector and the ability of the national economy to cope with global change. It is by no means clear that all these objectives are compatible, notably the aims of increasing social welfare and ensuring a fair distribution of income that may conflict with an enhanced role for the private sector, or the aim of increasing government revenue that may conflict with and crowd out private investment. It is still unclear to what extent the Supreme Economic Council will be an institution for consultation and debate or an executive authority with the ability to direct ministers.

3   Government economic policy

The long-term official objectives of Saudi Arabian government policy since the 1970s have been to diversify the economy, reduce the kingdom's dependence on oil revenue, build up its infrastructure, maintain stable prices and promote sufficient economic growth to ensure the provision of satisfactory employment opportunities for at least all male citizens. Now, a quarter of a century after the oil boom, would seem an appropriate time to evaluate how far these objectives have been achieved. Not surprisingly, the picture is a mixed one.

Since the 1970s there have been major changes in the economy, including some degree of diversification. The infrastructure is impressive by regional standards, with good highways, ports and airports, and considerable investment in basic utilities – notably water supplies – though perhaps less adequate investment in telecommunications, the electricity industry or urban services. Also commendable is the low rate of inflation, averaging only 0.9 per cent during the period 1991–2000, and the exchange-rate stability, with a peg of SR 3.7450 riyals to the US dollar being maintained.

The performance of the real economy has been less successful, with economic contraction rather than growth, inadequate job creation for local citizens and an ever-increasing number of unemployed young university graduates and school leavers. Gross national product remains highly sensitive to oil price and production levels even though the share of oil in GDP fell from over two-thirds in the early 1980s to nearer one-third by the late 1990s.[1] This was not less a result of successful economic diversification than of a decline in oil prices. In fact, GNP in 1998 – admittedly a depressed year for oil prices – was almost 10 per cent below its 1981 peak, and it was only improved oil prices in 2000 that resulted in GDP rising to its highest ever level.

Even more depressing is the trend in per capita GNP, which since 1980 has been falling steadily, largely a function of population increase and directionless GNP. In 1980, GNP per capita was almost 14,000 dollars, one of the highest levels in the world. By 2000, with population growth from 9.7 million to over 22 million, the GNP per capita figure was only 7,863 dollars, though at least thanks to oil price increases this was an improvement on the 1998 figure of below 7,000 dollars.[2] The kingdom has evolved from being a high-income

Government economic policy 21

nation to at best a middle-income economy, even though it would be simplistic to equate this alone with development failure.

The main weakness of government policy has been its inability to secure any degree of independence for its own finances from oil income. No alternative sources of taxes have been identified, which has led to substantial budgetary deficits and borrowings every year since the early 1980s, the only exception being 2000 when the oil price was temporarily high. Oil revenue has accounted for around three-quarters of total government revenue since 1982, despite temporary declines in 1988 and 1998 with very low oil prices, no real attempt has been made to extend the tax base. This is a symptom of political weakness, a lack of confidence on the part of the government in its ability to persuade citizens of the merits of paying more in taxation for improved public services or increased security.

The government itself – and, indeed, Saudi Arabian citizens – have paid a heavy price for this lack of government leadership, procrastination and indecisiveness. Spending and investment plans have repeatedly been scaled down and projects postponed or abandoned. Current expenditure has of necessity been given priority over investment merely to enable the government to continue paying its own employees. The cost of debt servicing has increased and the government has pushed itself into an economic corner with little scope for new initiatives. Faced with an inability to back any plans they may have with finance, all ministers can do is exhort others, notably the private sector, to take action; yet not surprisingly local businessmen have, over more than two decades, become increasingly sceptical about the government's capacity to act or to effect any meaningful change.

It is arguably the content – or, indeed, lack of content – of government economic policy which is to blame for the kingdom's unsatisfactory performance rather than the policy instruments themselves. Nevertheless it is instructive to examine in detail how the economic policy instruments have been applied and used – notably the Five-Year Plans, annual budgets and investment laws. A great deal can be learnt from this experience, and even where it is negative, which is all too often the case, the issues remain of whether it is worth continuing with Five-Year Plans, how tax and budgetary reform can be introduced and whether the investment laws need further revision if they are to be attractive to foreign companies and local citizens.

Economic planning

Development planning is often associated with socialist or Communist states where the government has control over resources and seeks to use its administrative powers to determine how funding is allocated rather than relying on markets and the private sector. It is associated with market failure and a belief that only governments can manage externalities and undertake resource mobilisation on a large scale.[3] Such planning assumes highly centralised decision-making, with the ministry responsible for planning having a

22   Rodney Wilson

considerable degree of power, including the ability to veto spending initiatives by other ministries. The Soviet Union adopted economic planning from the 1920s onwards;[4] while Turkey was the only Middle Eastern country to attempt such centralised planning, under Atatürk's policy of étatism in that decade and the one succeeding it.[5] In the Arab world, centralised planning was adopted from the late 1950s by the Arab Socialist Union in Egypt, a country considered by a leading advocate of planning, Oskar Lange, to possess a great advantage in that area because of its cotton exports and Suez Canal earnings,[6] although such ideas prove disastrous in the 1960s. Planning was also adopted in Ba'athist Syria and Iraq, as well as in South Yemen under the Marxist regime that took over from the British.

Ideologically, Saudi Arabia was far removed from such policies, as it had no foreign exchange controls and few trade barriers. The government aimed to encourage business, not hinder it; indeed, the merchants and traders were an important constituency. Hence the notion suggested by Samir Amin, that relations between the plan and the market were 'a cover for the tripartite socialism-capitalism-statism conflict',[7] did not apply in Saudi Arabia. Planning can, however, be interpreted and implemented in four basic ways,[8] at least two of which have arguably been adopted in the kingdom since the time when a planning strategy was first devised in the 1960s.

First, planning can refer simply to designing a public expenditure programme in the light of anticipated resources, a methodology that has been applied in the kingdom. Second, it can refer to targets for input resources of capital and labour and output calculations, an exercise that has been only partially undertaken there in the sense that employment and investment goals have been set but no detailed output projections. Third, planning can involve setting targets for the economy as a whole and giving an indication of how much will be invested in each sector, a model that has been employed from Riyadh. Finally, planning may refer to the means of enforcement used to ensure that the private sector meets its targets, mechanisms that have seldom been spelt out in the kingdom and which even in recent times have been vague due to the government's reluctance to become too deeply involved with influential local businessmen and merchants.

In other words, in Saudi Arabia planning has been more a macroeconomic exercise than a form of detailed microeconomic management, with the political and social environment ensuring that plan implementation does not intrude too much into indigenous business and commercial life. In particular, it was the need to ensure budget discipline that first brought the idea of planning to the fore, as although the kingdom possessed increasing oil wealth from the 1950s onwards, a serious economic crisis occurred between 1955 and 1957 largely as a result of unplanned, and somewhat haphazard and uncoordinated, spending by government ministries.[9]

Anwar Ali, first head of the Saudi Arabian Monetary Agency, favoured economic planning, and in 1959 an economic development committee was set up comprising the Ministers of Agriculture, Education, Health, Oil and

Communications, although this did not function very effectively. In 1960 a World Bank mission to Saudi Arabia recommended the establishment of a Planning Board which was duly set up in 1961, but although it was given responsibility for drawing up an economic development policy, the ministries refused to take its advice seriously or adapt their spending plans in the light of the priorities which the Board agreed.[10] The reality was that the ministries were more politically powerful than the Board and were not prepared to cede any powers.

The failure of the new system to prove effective was blamed on the Board rather than ministers, and in 1965 it was abolished. Following reports by the Ford Foundation and the United Nations Team for Social and Economic Planning, a new Central Planning Organisation (CPO) was established. In some respects this organisation was even weaker than its predecessor its role being simply to advice ministries and estimate the costs of implementing policies agreed by the Council of Ministers. Nevertheless the CPO was responsible for drafting the kingdom's First Development Plan covering the period 1970–1975, with the actual document appearing in 1969.

The aim of the First Plan was for 'Saudi Arabia to maintain its religious and moral values, and to raise the living standard and welfare of its people, while providing for material security and maintaining economic and social stability'.[11] In other words, there was to be development but not Westernisation, the aim being to preserve the traditional fabric of society while increasing prosperity – an elusive goal for any nation. Despite the lip-service paid to religious and moral values in the introduction to the First and subsequent Plans no explanation was given as to how the social status quo was to be maintained during the kind of economic transformation envisaged. Rather the stress was on the purely economic objectives of higher growth, diversification to reduce oil dependence and the development of human resources through an increased provision of education.[12]

The major achievement of the Plan was arguably in the discussion it generated about spending priorities. These were determined politically by ministers rather than by the planners, but ministers were at least aware of what the Plan said, even if they conveniently ignored targets that did not suit their own agendas. In practice many of the targets were met or exceeded, notably in the fields of education and transport, but this was largely due to rising oil revenues and the establishment of the Public Investment Fund rather than as a result of the planners themselves having much control over resources; although the President of the CPO sat on the board of directors with the governor of SAMA, the Finance Minister and two other ministers. Housing and telecommunications failed to meet their targets, but the planners had no direct input in these fields. Fouad Al-Farsi suggests that the most significant outcome of the First Five-Year Plan was the experience gained by the planners themselves.[13] The CPO monitored what happened so that there was at least an historical record of economic developments which could be referred to in the subsequent plan.

24　*Rodney Wilson*

The Second Plan, covering the period 1975–1980, was designed and implemented in much more favourable circumstances than its predecessor as a result of the quadrupling of oil revenues between 1973–1974. The issue was less one of resource constraint than of the country's ability to absorb this new revenue in productive investment. The emphasis on education and training continued, but ambitions could be scaled up, although it was recognised that a doubling of the foreign workforce, including teachers, would be required. The cornerstone of the plan, however, was the creation of two new industrial cities at Jubail and Yanbu, where major, world-class petrochemical, steel and aluminium, refining and desalinisation plants were to be located.[14]

From planning office to ministry

A justifiable question is: would these developments have occurred without the CPO? The answer is undoubtedly yes, as although these developments were included in the Plan it was the Ministry of Commerce and Industry which was charged with their design and implementation, decentralised royal commissions being responsible for the development of each city. Although the planners' powers were increased in October 1975 when the CPO became the Ministry of Planning, those of the individuals within the Ministry of Commerce and Industry with responsibility for industrial development were increased even further as a new Ministry of Industry and Electricity was established, while the remit of the former ministry was restricted to commerce. In 1975, as the number of ministries increased from fourteen to twenty, the fact of planning becoming one was in any case less significant than it might have been five or even ten years earlier.[15]

The CPO and its successor, the Ministry of Planning, might have had more influence had it been perceived that Saudi Arabian citizens were more closely involved in the instigation and drafting of ideas in the early plans. The Stanford Research Group, which worked within the CPO from 1967, was largely responsible for the work on the first two Plans, but consisted largely of Western professionals who were allowed a good deal of autonomy and discretion.[16] The extent to which the CPO president and latter the Planning Minister merely rubber-stamped their work as opposed to directing it is arguable.

In some respects the Second Plan represented the high point of this type of exercise in the kingdom, as though five more plans have since been issued it is debatable whether this is due to a continued commitment to planning or – more plausibly – institutional inertia. There is a sense in which planning has become a routine, almost mechanical exercise, and in so far as there have been any new economic initiatives or ideas in the country in the last two decades it is clear that the input from the Ministry of Planning has been minimal. As each new plan is unveiled it is written about in the press and receives critical appraisal by economic commentators, after which much of the content is ignored for four or five years, when the next plan appears. There is then an evaluation of the extent to which targets have been either met or missed, but any success or failure is not

Government economic policy   25

the responsibility of the planners themselves, who lack the power to ensure targets are met. With no penalties for failure or rewards for success either in the Ministry of Planning or anywhere else, planning has become a somewhat erudite exercise to some extent removed from the economic realities facing most Saudi Arabians.

SAMA, in its 1978 review of the Second Plan, for example, stated that there had been vigorous implementation, but then went on to discuss how the need to adopt an anti-inflationary stance in fiscal policy was an important priority, and how the planners could not be held responsible for the oil sector's failure to achieve its targets as this depended on international forces.[17] Given this lack of control, it might have been better if the Planning Ministry had adopted scenario planning, with multiple targets allowing for different oil-price projections and an attempt to consider what the economic consequences of each oil-price assumption might be.

By the time of the Third and Fourth Development Plans in the 1980s the oil-revenue position was much less satisfactory and funds to finance investment had to be cut and ambitions scaled down. Hence there was more emphasis on consolidation and on completing existing projects rather than on new ventures.[18] The themes of economic diversification and human resource development continued, but stress was laid on increased economic and administrative efficiency and the developing of other minerals besides oil, although little progress was made on the latter. These goals were easy to agree, but as the civil service and the state sector became ever more obliged to absorb Saudi Arabian graduates to create employment, this conflicted with the goal of administrative efficiency. Substantial investment in education continued, but issues such as the quality of provision were not addressed.

As the government had relatively fewer resources at its disposal from the mid-1980s onwards, planning became ever more ineffective, with the private sector expected to play an increasing role in the economy and in particular to meet the targets for the employment of local citizens; yet few incentives were offered to business in order to achieve these goals. The completion of many of the key infrastructure projects by the early part of that decade meant that resources could be freed for investment in human rather than physical capital, but this did not translate in the short or even the medium term into a successful policy of replacing non-Saudis with local citizens in the private sector, except perhaps in the fields of banking and financial services.[19]

In the Fifth and the Sixth Plans the emphasis was on continuation, but again the planners reiterated the familiar calls for greater economic diversity, an enhanced role for the private sector, investment in education and the creation of more employment for Saudis. This represented a 'wish' list, as the planners were unable to control a volatile economy dependent on international oil-price developments, while domestically the Minister of Planning carried little political clout. Investment in education could have been increased if, say, defence spending had been reduced, but the latter was outside the remit of the plans even though it accounted for over one-third of government spending.

Reorganisation of economic management

By the late 1990s it was apparent that the Ministry of Planning was becoming increasingly ineffective and that reform of economic management was needed to ensure at least a degree of coordination between spending ministries, if not their political control. Although it would have been mistaken to characterise the kingdom as experiencing an economic crisis, unemployment was rising, especially among the youth, an increasing amount of government revenue was simply being used to service debt and the economy did not seem to be heading in any clear direction. The flight of capital continued, there was little foreign investment, and the various joint-venture arrangements dating from the 1970s involving overseas involvement in the banking sector and SABIC seemed to be fossilised.

A political solution was clearly needed, as the basic problem for the Ministry of Planning was that it had responsibility without power. Economic and developmental issues were arguably too low down on the government's agenda in so far as it had any longer-term objectives than simply day-to-day management. There had been some economic vision back in the 1970s, with the planning of the new industrial cities in Jubail and Yanbu and the implementation of major infrastructure schemes, as well as the spread of schools and hospitals throughout the kingdom but by the late 1990s the government seemed to have stalled and there was drift in economic management.

It was against this background that the Supreme Economic Council was set up, largely because the oil-price falls of 1998 and their economic impact brought developmental issues higher up the political agenda. A more senior government member than the Minister of Planning was needed to take the lead; hence it was the Crown Prince and First Deputy Premier Abdullah, the effective leader of the country given King Fahd's poor health, who took the chair. The Second Deputy Premier Prince Sultan, who hitherto had been little involved in economic affairs, served as vice-chairman. With Crown Prince Abdullah also serving as commander of the National Guard and Prince Sultan as Minister of Defence, these two men jointly had an overview of the financial implications of security needs and were able to see what resources were available, and trade-off between economic and defence concerns.

Other members of the Supreme Economic Council included the Minister of Finance and National Economy and the Ministers of Planning, Commerce, Labour, Petroleum and Industry together with the Governor of SAMA.[20] Meetings of the Supreme Economic Council have taken place weekly since its formation in August 1999, though not all members attend every meeting and Crown Prince Abdullah and Prince Sultan are often absent; however, ultimately what matters is that they are in control and that all papers and documents relating to the meetings are received by their offices and reviewed by their advisors.

The remit of the Supreme Economic Council includes responsibility not only for development planning but also for fiscal and trade policy. This enables it to survey both short-term economic management and long-run strategy and also to

Government economic policy 27

focus on imbalances in both internal budgetary and external payments. The aim is also to also to design new policies, of which the most notable during its first two years of operation were the new law on foreign investment and the establishment of both the General Investment Authority and the Human Resources Development Fund.[21] The Supreme Economic Council also had some input into the final drafting of the Seventh Five-Year Plan that covers the period 2000–2005, although a great deal of the content had been written beforehand.

The Seventh Five-Year Plan

Targets in the original draft of the Seventh Plan were revised upwards as the planners became more confident, with oil revenues exceeding 62 billion dollars in 2000; almost double the 32 billion dollars originally forecast, and with the surplus on the current account of the balance of payments rising to 21 billion dollars. The Seventh Plan provides a detailed list of macroeconomic objectives and much information on goals set for each sector of the economy. However, there is little discussion of policy choices or of the rationalisation behind the target setting. Many of the targets could have been met if oil prices had remained above 25 dollars per barrel, but the subsequent price falls meant this was problematic. Even had the most favourable oil-pricing and production scenario occurred it was still unlikely that the kingdom would have become significantly more diversified by 2005, or that economic growth would have been self-sustaining without significant further injections of oil revenues.

The Seventh Five-Year Plan was approved by the Council of Ministers in September 2000. It was hoped that 817,000 additional jobs could be provided by 2005 – an ambitious target.[22] Initially, with the budget in surplus thanks to higher oil prices, the Plan looked to have much more chance of success than either the Fifth or Sixth. The targets in the Seventh Plan looked ambitious given the performance of the Saudi Arabian economy in the 1990s, but by 2000 they seemed quite modest and conservative. The planned target was for real GDP growth to average 3.16 per cent over the period 2000–2005; but the growth in 2000 exceeded 15 per cent. With the higher oil prices of that year the ambitious investment target also seemed more attainable, as the Plan envisaged an average investment growth of 6.85 per cent annually and the share of investment in GDP rose from 22.7 to 25.4 per cent.[23] The planners anticipated that most of the investment would come from the private sector given the squeeze on government resources with the 1997–1998 fall in oil prices. With the much higher oil prices of 1999–2000 the government was itself in a position to boost investment in the eventuality of a private-sector shortfall as occurred in 2000, when the budget surplus amounted to almost 7 billion dollars despite government spending rising to almost 84 billion dollars.[24] Unfortunately, as the oil-revenue situation deteriorated in 2001 and 2002, prospects for the planned targets being met seemed much less likely, demonstrating once again how short-term optimism and even euphoria can soon be dissipated when government income is so dependent on oil-price developments in international markets.

28 *Rodney Wilson*

Yet it is not so much the level of investment that matters, but the returns on that investment. The latest petroleum revenue windfall of 1999–2000 proved a mixed blessing as it reduced the pressures on the government for economic reform. Although there was much discussion of the new investment laws introduced in the spring of 2000 permitting the foreign ownership of new industrial ventures in many fields, reforms aimed at attracting external involvement can be no substitute for domestic reforms. The Seventh Plan discussed privatisation policy but in very general terms rather than providing a list of activities to be privatised.[25] There was no discussion of how privatisation was to be achieved or of the advantages and disadvantages of the different possible methods.

Lack of coordinated planning

It is clear that there has been little engagement between the development planners and those involved in utilities scheduled for eventual privatisation. The Saudi Telecommunications Company (STC) was created in 1998 out of the Ministry of Posts, Telephones and Telegraphs in order to facilitate the privatisation of this industry, but initially progress was limited.[26] The company remained in the state sector, with most staff unchanged from when it was part of the Ministry. JP Morgan, Booz Allen Hamilton, Clifford Chance and PricewaterhouseCoopers were brought in as advisors on procurement and marketing, but their remit did not extend to drawing up specific proposals for an initial public offering. There were some discussions about allowing a foreign partner – most likely the American telecommunications company Lucent Technology – to take a minority stake of less than one-third, but this was rejected on the grounds of security.[27] Lucent Technology and Ericsson of Sweden were awarded a 60-million-dollar contract to expand and enhance the mobile phone system, but this is merely work being commissioned by the STC and involves no equity financing.[28]

The plan would have been an opportunity to discuss how sectors such as telecommunications could be restructured. As it seems that foreign ownership of STC is unlikely to be permitted, the intention appeared to be to allow a gradual privatisation involving an initial public offering through the local stock exchange. The initial tranche at one–third of the company was finally sold in December 2002.[29] Replacing a public monopoly with a private fixed-line monopoly will not bring competition and it is not clear how the plan's objective of twenty-five telephone lines per hundred of the population is to be achieved. The cost of telephone calls, especially international ones, is very high by international standards, and the connection fee for mobile access of 450 dollars was one of the highest in the world.[30] The potential for telecommunications in Saudi Arabia is enormous, with a possible two and a half million Internet subscribers by 2005, a higher number than anywhere else in the Middle East. Yet there is a reluctance to tackle the vested interests that may still frustrate these developments, with too much weight given to suppliers rather than to consumers.

Government economic policy   29

There is also opposition to restructuring and privatisation in the electricity industry, as although the plan target is for 793,000 new subscribers to be connected to the network, it is unclear how this will be handled. The Saudi Electricity Company (SEC) has designed an ambitious project to treble electricity generation capacity by 2025, but its plans for the immediate future are limited to regional interconnection in order to establish a national grid.[31] At present the regional companies are still being integrated into SEC, which is creating a giant state owned monopoly. There has been discussion of separating generation from transmission, and allowing private companies to become involved in generation, but these ideas have still not been agreed and are not referred to in the Seventh Plan.

The targets for employment creation for Saudi Arabian citizens were not achieved during the Sixth Plan covering the period 1994–1999 largely because of the private sector's failure to expand recruitment sufficiently. The public sector actually exceeded its target, as the Plan had forecast an additional 95,000 jobs, but 139,000 new jobs were provided by the government itself and state-sector industries over the period 1994–1999.[32] Only 21.8 per cent of employees in the public sector are non-Saudi out of the one million employed, whereas in the private sector 61.3 per cent of the 6.1 million employees are non-Saudi. This illustrates the dilemma for policy-makers, as there seems to be a conflict between privatisation and economic reform and Saudi-isation, which needs direct state support.

To resolve this conflict the Seventh Plan aimed to improve the skills of Saudi Arabian school and college leavers so as to make them more attractive to private sector employers. Places in technical education were to be increased to 55,000 by 2005, with the building of ten new technical colleges and seventeen multi-purpose secondary technical institutes.[33] Vocational training centres were to be expanded, and it was hoped that 46,000 trainees would graduate during the planning period. Whether this will prove effective remains to be seen.[34] Private-sector employers are required to pay Saudis more than migrant workers, and it is virtually impossible to sack local citizens. On the other hand, compulsory medical insurance is being introduced for all non-citizens. This will increase the relative attractiveness of employing Saudis, whose insurance costs are covered by the government. Even more significantly the Seventh Plan envisages almost half a million of the new jobs planned for Saudis as being created through further restrictions on the work permits issued to foreigners, especially in retailing.

Macroeconomic priorities

The Saudi Arabian government has been successful in maintaining the stable macroeconomic conditions that are regarded by many as crucial for any take-off into self-sustaining development. Back in the 1970s the oil-revenue boom resulted in inflationary pressures, but since then price stability has been a prime objective of government economic policy. The average rate of inflation over the period 1990–1996 was only 2.1 per cent annually, and since then there has been

30 Rodney Wilson

price stability with falls of 0.6 per cent in 1998 and 1.3 per cent in 1999[35] and a rise of 1.2 per cent in 2000,[36] this modestly higher figure reflecting the oil-price rises of 1999 as there is a lagged effect between oil-revenue increases and rises in aggregate demand in the Saudi Arabian economy. As the oil price has subsequently fallen, the outlook is for virtually no inflation. The rise in the value of the dollar in 2000 and 2001 – to which the Saudi Arabian riyal is pegged – constrained import prices, as many goods come from the Euro zone and Asian countries and the riyal has appreciated against these currencies.

The peg with the dollar is regarded as the cornerstone of currency management in Saudi Arabia, not least because the prices of oil and petrochemicals are dollar-denominated. Although most oil goes to the Far East, the contracts and payments are in dollars. The dollar is also important for imports. The United States is the kingdom's most important importer supplier, accounting for almost 19 per cent of the total. Most imports from Japan, the second largest supplier, are also dollar- rather than yen-denominated. It is only imports from Europe that are denominated in other currencies, either in euros or – in the case of the United Kingdom – in sterling. There has been some debate from time from time to time about pegging the currency against a trade-weighted basket, and even on the merits of having oil prices denominated in some international unit of account. The IMF's special drawing right would be one possibility, to which the Islamic dinar – the currency unit of the Jeddah-based Islamic Development Bank – is pegged. However, as most of Saudi Arabia's official and private asset holdings are also in dollars this reinforces the case for using the United States currency as the peg.

It is the objective of exchange-rate stability that determines macroeconomic policy rather than explicit targets for prices or money-supply growth. Money supply growth is monitored, and though in theory interest-rate variations are precluded as an instrument of monetary policy by the Islamic prohibition of *riba,* in practice SAMA's policy is similar to that of other central banks. The ban on *riba* is interpreted as applying to interest transactions with bank clients, where administrative charges and fees are applied to conventional loans. For dealings between SAMA and the commercial banks repurchase agreements (repos) are used involving treasury bills, government bonds and foreign-exchange swaps. These transactions averaged 350 dollars million a day in 2000, indicating the extent of money-market development in the kingdom, with repurchase rates changing frequently in line with changes in dollar rates.[37] The rates set by SAMA on riyal repurchases are at a premium to dollar rates reflecting local currency risk factors, but there is no attempt to increase rates in order to reduce bank lending capacity, using repos as an instrument of monetary policy. There is also no direct control of bank lending – another possible instrument of monetary policy – as it is felt this could damage the bank's relationships with their major clients, who include members of the royal family and leading merchants.

Fiscal policy instruments are the chief means of controlling macroeconomic activity, but in practice this means government spending as opposed to taxes.

Government economic policy 31

Oil revenues – the main source of government income – are externally rather than domestically determined. There is no income taxation in Saudi Arabia, but import duties do rise and fall in a pro-cyclical manner and serve to some extent as automatic stabilisers. Income growth results in a rise in imports and a rise in duties and vice versa. Government spending is the main instrument through which the Ministry of Finance exercises control over the economy, as the Minister constrains the plans of the spending ministries during periods when oil revenue falls but permits some latitude in spending when oil revenue rises. These policies of allowing expenditure increases during the upswing and curtailing expenditure during the downswing are nevertheless the exact opposite of what Keynesian economists might recommend.

The burden of indebtedness

There has only been one year since 1983 when the government has actually run a budget surplus, that being in 2000.[38] Even then the projected surplus of twelve billion dollars translated into an actual surplus of six billion due to lower oil prices and higher-than-expected government expenditures. The reduction in oil prices after 2000 resulted once again in a serious fall in Saudi Arabia's government revenue and a consequent fiscal deficit with the Ministry of Finance in Riyadh predicting a doubling of the budget deficit to twelve billion dollars for 2002.[39] To control public expenditure the cabinet meeting under King Fahd decided to freeze the pay of all government employees and halt the creation of any new permanent jobs in government ministries. The public spending target has been set at 54 billion dollars to avoid further borrowing from foreign banks.[40] As almost three-quarters of Saudi Arabia's government revenue still derives from oil, state finances are extremely vulnerable to oil-price and production fluctuations. It is by no means certain that fiscal restraint will work in 2002 given previous experience of spending overruns.

The budget deficit is predicted to be around 8 per cent of GDP for 2002, a figure that would not be worrying if the expectation was for a fall in the medium or even the longer term. Given the uncertain outlook for oil prices, and the long-run downward trend in constant dollar prices that has been apparent for almost twenty years, there is clearly a need for fiscal reform in Saudi Arabia. Without such changes foreign indebtedness is certain to increase. The kingdom's external debts already amount to 25 billion dollars, higher than that for any Arab country apart from Egypt.[41] As Saudi Arabia is in debt to international banks, it is in many respects in a worse position than Egypt, whose indebtedness is largely to international agencies and the United States. Saudi Arabia's debts are, therefore, more expensive to service and cannot be written off in return for political favours as happened with Egypt after the Gulf War.

In addition to its external debt the Saudi Arabian government has borrowed heavily from its own commercial banks. According to the official figures issued by the Saudi Arabian Monetary Agency, local commercial bank claims on the government amounted to over 33 billion dollars by 2001, and the figure is rising

32 Rodney Wilson

by almost 500 million dollars each month.[42] One Saudi Arabian economist, Ihsan Bin Hlaika, estimated government domestic debts at 173 billion dollars[43] (possibly an exaggeration), but the debts of public sector enterprises are at least double the SAMA figure, which shows that internal debt has more than doubled since 1996. In addition to the cost of servicing this debt by government, there are also costs for the rest of the economy. Commercial bank funds lent out to government reduce the amount of finance that can be provided for the private sector, a process known as 'crowding out'. In Saudi Arabia's case, lending to government already amounts to over two-thirds of the sum lent to the private sector, and within three or four years, without fiscal reform, lending to government will exceed private lending. Saudi Arabia could learn from Turkey's disastrous experience in this respect, where the banking system suffered a crisis as the government itself proved unable to service its internal debt.

Fiscal choices

Most of the government's non-oil revenue comes from customs duties, which until 2001 were applied at a standard rate of 12 per cent, with a lower 4 per cent rate for food, medicine, books, precious metals, military equipment and machinery for local industries. A 20 per cent rate was applied to cement, iron and steel products, furniture and detergents in order to protect local industries.[44] These rates were reduced to 10 per cent in 2001 to comply with the transition to a customs union agreed by the Gulf Cooperation Council. The tariff reductions were also seen as helpful to Saudi Arabia's membership application to join the World Trade Organisation. With the timetable for the customs union brought forward to January 2003 at the Muscat summit of December 2001,[45] and with a new low common tariff of 5 per cent agreed, it is clear that the government will lose much of its non-oil income unless alternative sources of revenue are found.[46]

The religious tax, *Zakat,* is applied at a rate of 2.5 per cent per annum to the profits of Saudi Arabian companies and to the liquid wealth of individuals, but this revenue is earmarked for social welfare purposes and, therefore, makes no direct contribution to the financing of general government expenditure.[47] As the rate is specified in shariah religious law, it cannot be increased. Under the foreign investment law introduced in 2000 corporate taxes on non-Saudi businesses were reduced, rates of 20 to 30 per cent now being applied to the profits from non-Saudi businesses depending on the level of income. Similar rates apply to capital gains taxation.[48]

The introduction of personal income tax in Saudi Arabia would prove unpopular with local citizens and undoubtedly lead to greater calls for the government to be financially accountable to taxpayers as well as pressures for wider political reforms. High-net-worth individuals, including members of the royal family, are opposed to taxes likely to result in the redistribution of income or wealth. It is argued that the Islamic inheritance system redistributes wealth within extended families, and there is provision for charitable donation; hence

Government economic policy   33

government should not introduce estate duties. Yet given the magnitude of Saudi Arabia's private wealth – with 85,000 high net-worth individuals owning foreign assets valued at over 700 billion dollars according to Saudi American Bank estimates[49] – the temptation by a reforming government to introduce personal taxation would be great.

Given the resistance to income taxation, the most likely development in the medium term may be the introduction of sales taxes to replace import duties, or perhaps even a value-added tax system of the type being introduced in Morocco and Tunisia, and being considered by Egypt. This type of indirect tax could result in short-term price rises, but with little inflation in Saudi Arabia this is unlikely to prove a problem.

An alternative to raising taxation would be to cut budget allocations, defence expenditure – which accounts for almost 37 per cent of all spending – being a possible area, especially given the improved relations with Iran and the settlement of the borders with Yemen.[50] Education spending, which accounts for one quarter of the total, is more difficult to cut: Saudi Arabia has a young population, with 6.4 million of school age out of a total of 16.2 million local nationals, plus a further 1.5 million in the 20–24 university-student age group. Some cuts have been made to health and transport spending as well as subsidies, all of which are politically sensitive. Allocations to specialised development funds have also been reduced, but this may have an adverse effect on future economic growth.

Privatisation of utilities could also bring in useful receipts for government, yet as already indicated progress so far has been slow. The greatest potential sources of revenue from sell-offs are: the telecommunications company; Saudia, the national airline (whose privatisation was first proposed back in 1994); the postal service; the electricity sector; and the railways. However, apart from telecommunications, there is no timetable for the privatisation of any of these. The decision on February 4, 2002 to transfer the responsibility for privatisation to the Supreme Economic Council may help to overcome opposition as this signals a more determined stance from Crown Prince Abdullah, but whether this actually speeds up the programme for these industries remains to be seen.[51]

Overall the Saudi Arabian budgetary position is unsustainable, and merely hoping for a repeat of the oil-price rises of 2000 will not provide a lasting solution. No single measure can remedy the situation, but a combination of cuts in defence spending, privatisation of utilities and the introduction of a sales or value-added tax could help significantly. The time for rhetoric about economic reform is past in Saudi Arabia, and government action is needed if real GDP growth is to become less oil-dependent and advance by more than the 0.8 per cent predicted for 2002.

Government funding and foreign investment

The state itself has undertaken most investment, given that from the 1970s it had more than adequate resources to finance basic infrastructure, major industrial developments and even smaller projects that could have been financed entirely

34 *Rodney Wilson*

commercially. Saudi Arabia's substantial foreign exchange earnings, as the world's largest oil-exporting country have enabled the government to avoid having to rely on inward investment flows to contribute to the balance of payments. The government historically has sought to insulate the non-oil economy and the majority of the population from foreign influences. There has been a desire to maintain national control over all economic activities and to protect the interests of local businessmen from foreign competition. Since the early 1970s the oil industry has been under majority Saudi Arabian ownership, allowing production levels to be determined by the Ministry of Petroleum and Mineral Resources rather than by multinational oil companies.

Foreign investment has, however, been needed to establish petrochemical, fertiliser and other oil-related industries in order to take advantage of the technical skills and market access of the multinational oil and chemical companies.[52] This has been harnessed through joint ventures under majority Saudi Arabian ownership so as to ensure foreign interference is limited. The investment law introduced in May 2000 reversed this policy by permitting one-hundred-per cent foreign ownership in most sectors.[53] The law provided for a new Saudi Arabian General Investment Authority (SAGIA) to encourage foreign companies to become involved in the kingdom. SAGIA has taken over the functions of research and information-gathering and dissemination of the Saudi Consulting House as well as investment licensing powers from the Ministry of Industry and Electricity.

Why was this new policy introduced in 2000? There would seem to be three major factors responsible for the new investment laws. First and foremost was the kingdom's bid for membership of the World Trade Organisation, which has been actively pursued by the Minister of Commerce, Osama Faqih. It was made clear to the kingdom's negotiators during meetings in Geneva in April 2000 that liberalisation of the foreign investment laws was a prerequisite for membership. The monopoly control of major export industries by SABIC, the Saudi Arabian Basic Industries Corporation, was not seen as in the interests of fair and transparent international competition. There have been disputes with the European Union over feedstock pricing for petrochemical exports, the position on which could be clarified through benchmarking if alternative foreign-owned industries existed in the kingdom.

A second factor favouring foreign investment was the government's inability to fund the capital expenditure needed for a major expansion of manufacturing and basic utilities without adding even further to the debt burden. An alternative would be to raise capital for new ventures on the local stock market, but investors would have been reluctant to risk their capital without the reassurance of there being a foreign partner involved who was experienced in the field. Foreign investment is wanted not just for the finance it provides but also because of production or product knowledge, access to foreign markets and perceived brand strengths. There are no internationally known Saudi Arabian brands, SABIC being the only company that has launched foreign media campaigns to increase potential client awareness.

Government economic policy 35

The third factor has been the liberalisation experience of the other Gulf Cooperation Council (GCC) states. Businessmen in Saudi Arabia see the benefits Bahrain and Dubai have obtained from inward investment and would like to see more business generated for the kingdom. Although Jeddah remains the commercial capital of Saudi Arabia, its international role is very limited and its chamber of commerce sees its potential as a trading centre serving both sides of the Red Sea and beyond. It may be premature to envisage a duty-free zone being created comparable to Jebel Ali near Dubai, but there is little doubt that foreign investors would be extremely interested in such a venture if it could get off the ground.

The level of foreign investment in Saudi Arabia has been very disappointing in recent years, with accumulated capital inflows amounting to a mere 4 billion dollars over the 1984–1997 period, compared with almost 40 billion dollars for Malaysia and 50 billion dollars for Singapore.[54] Only 20 per cent of recent inflows have gone to the private sector, and investment outflows have greatly exceeded inflows. It is by no means certain, however, that the new investment laws will succeed in the short term in halting Saudi Arabia's decline in relation to other GCC countries. The Supreme Council for Petroleum and Mineral Affairs, which was established in February 2001, has confirmed that it is not seeking foreign investment in upstream oil-related activities, which will remain the responsibility of ARAMCO, the Arabian American Oil Company. Rather it is in downstream activities that foreign investment is welcomed, as an alternative to yet more SABIC joint ventures.

Under the new foreign investment law, one hundred per cent foreign ownership of plant is permitted, and though initially the position regarding land and real estate was less certain, SAGIA was able to announce that foreign companies could also own land in industrial areas. Under the land ownership regulations of July 2000 non-Saudi Arabian investors were allowed to own or even rent out business premises providing the value of the investment exceeded eight million dollars from the date when the land was acquired.[55] This effectively precluded foreign residents from acquiring land or housing for their own residential use unless they possessed considerable wealth, and even then clearance was required from the Ministry of the Interior. Any land ownership by foreigners in the holy cities of Mecca and Medina was prohibited.

The foreign investment law only covers investments in new projects, not takeovers of existing ventures. There was a reluctance to allow foreigners to own direct shareholdings in established Saudi Arabian companies. Since 1997 foreigners have been permitted to invest in a mutual fund run by the Saudi American Bank that invests in Saudi Arabian equities, and this has recently been extended to other mutual funds, but the domestic capital market has yet to be opened up to foreign investors. SABIC itself is the second largest company in the Middle East, with a market capitalisation of almost 10 billion dollars, but any takeover by a multinational oil or chemical company is unlikely to be permitted for the foreseeable future.

36 *Rodney Wilson*

This also applies in the field of banking, where the Saudi Arabian institutions are too small to be global players but there is a reluctance to open up the sector. All banks in the kingdom have to be at least 60 per cent Saudi Arabian-owned, and there is very little real competition in the provision of banking services. Consequently, much business is lost to Bahrain and even London when it could be generating revenue and well-paid jobs in Riyadh and Jeddah. The same applies to the local provision of fixed-line and mobile telephone services: Saudi Arabian consumers would benefit from much cheaper call charges if foreign entrants were allowed into the market.

The main attraction of the new investment laws to foreign companies was the provision to cut the corporate tax on foreign companies and joint ventures from 45 per cent to 30 per cent, the same level enjoyed by Saudi Arabian companies.[56] However, even this was introduced in a rather cumbersome way, with the government paying 15 per cent tax on behalf of the foreign company rather than abolishing the 45 per cent rate. Such half-hearted gestures did not inspire lasting confidence as there was concern that once an investment was undertaken, future budgetary pressures might result in the government deciding to cancel the rebate. Also welcome to foreign investors was the right to apply for subsidised loans from the Saudi Industrial Development Fund, but this was also dependent on the government being able to inject fresh capital into the Fund, an issue over which there remains considerable uncertainty.

The negative list proved disappointing for many potential foreign investors, as some of the items where investment appeared to be welcome in the earlier guidance produced by the Ministry of Industry and Electricity – notably power generation and telecommunications[57] – were subsequently excluded.[58] In many respects the negative list includes those areas of greatest interest to foreign investors, notably oil exploration, drilling and production. The manufacture of military equipment and clothing is also excluded, as is even military catering, but given the high level of defence spending a policy that favoured domestic production would seem appropriate, especially as the offset programmes associated with some defence acquisitions – such as the supply of Tornado aircraft from the United Kingdom – have proved less than effective. Other activities on the extensive negative list include air and land transportation, printing and publishing, radio and television, security services and distribution and retailing, although there is much brand franchising in the kingdom with local businessmen acting as franchisees.

Although the chairman of SAGIA, Prince Abdullah bin Faisal bin Turki, has tried to depict the new investment laws as a major policy change, it is clear that their success will be limited unless there is a reduction in the number of activities on the negative list. There have been some moves in the electricity industry, with the Council of Ministers approving in November 2001 a decree for the establishment of a power regulator.[59] This paves the way for the establishment of independent power generators, who could be foreign companies. There have also been hints by Crown Prince Abdullah that the number of items on the negative list might be reduced or even the entire list

Government economic policy 37

abolished. At the same time one of the Crown Prince's main concerns is to attract foreign investment in agriculture, which is not seen by most multinational companies as a priority area given global oversupply.[60]

Economic dualism

Even if the new investment law succeeds in increasing foreign investment in Saudi Arabia, it will not solve more fundamental economic problems. Over two million additional jobs will be needed during the period 2000–2005, yet heavy industry can only create a limited number of them. The new ethylene cracker announced for Yanbu and the planned expansion of Hadeed, the Saudi Iron and Steel Company, is resulting in fewer than 5,000 jobs. Many more jobs could be created in distribution and services such as banking, but as already indicated these are on the negative list as far as foreign investment is concerned. Saudi Arabia already exhibits many of the features of a dual economy, with well-paid jobs for a minority of its citizens and others now prepared to accept work paying as little as 160 dollars a month. The domestic terrorist incidents of the late 1990s and 2000, and arguably the participation of Saudi Arabian nationals in the events of September 11, 2001, may be as indicative of domestic social tensions as they are of frustration over the status of Jerusalem, the failed Middle Eastern peace process and opposition to Israeli and American interference in the Arab and Muslim worlds.

Transforming a dual structure into a more highly integrated economy is a difficult task. Expenditure multipliers can help, in so far as those engaged in the new industries spend their wages on locally produced goods and services rather than imports. In an open economy such as that of Saudi Arabia, where imports account for around one-third of GDP, leakages abroad are clearly considerable, though not as great as in the 1970s and 1980s when imports accounted for over 40 per cent of GDP. Leakages of expenditure abroad should reduce over time as the economy grows, but this process has to be measured in decades rather than years, and globalisation may slow down or even reverse this trend, as Saudi Arabian consumers increasingly demand the same goods as their Western counterparts, goods that cannot be supplied locally.

Supply linkages can also facilitate domestic economic integration and reduce dualism. The crude-oil sector is no longer as isolated, as there are supply linkages into refining, petrochemicals and energy-intensive industries that utilise gas, which was formerly flared off. Local service industries have developed to serve the needs of ARAMCO, the Arabian American Oil Company. Yet linkages between the export-orientated sector and import substitute industries appear to be weak, as are those with the commercial sector and agriculture. It is not clear how the links can be enhanced, as the modern export sector has specialist and highly sophisticated requirements which imply global rather than local sourcing. Items such as oil and gas pipelines can be supplied locally, but Saudi Arabia has merely a construction supply industry rather than a capability to produce and deliver industrial inputs.

38 *Rodney Wilson*

Despite the planners' efforts Saudi Arabia's economic growth has inevitably been unbalanced rather than balanced, with oil and oil-related activities as the leading sector while commerce and agriculture lag behind. Industry accounts for around half of GDP, with much of this referring to the oil industry, as manufacturing still accounts for less than 10 per cent of GDP. Agriculture contributes around 7 per cent of GDP, and services the remainder. Pursuing any alternative to an unbalanced strategy would not have proved effective, however, as no sector other than oil could have served as an engine of growth given the kingdom's poor non-oil resources. Both services and manufacturing can be regarded as dependent sectors rather than as having the potential to take off into self-sustaining growth. Even much of the modern development in agriculture would not have occurred without subsidy from oil revenues and demand which was ultimately generated through multiplier effects from government spending, itself dependent on oil revenues.

It would be simplistic to conclude that government policy had failed because Saudi Arabia's economy has not diversified sufficiently away from oil dependence or achieved self-sustaining growth. Much has been achieved over the period of the seven Five-Year Plans since 1970, most notably in the provision of infrastructure and urban growth. Macroeconomic stability has largely been achieved with low inflation, a comfortable external balance despite sharply fluctuating oil prices and the maintenance of a pegged exchange rate eliminating most currency uncertainty. Government finances have been less satisfactory, and the workings of the real economy have proved disappointing, with unimpressive private-sector performance and rising unemployment as ever-increasing numbers emerge from colleges and universities. Nevertheless the kingdom's economy has been modernised and the quality of some services, such as banking and finance, is as good as in many Western countries. Education provision could be much improved, but is still reasonably good by regional standards. Despite these achievements it appears that there has been a degree of government failure which has contributed to a failure of labour markets to achieve equilibrium. Government policy has also failed to ensure that the supply side of the domestic economy responds adequately to the demands of an ever-increasing population. The demographic pressures in the kingdom can turned to advantage if domestic-market expansion becomes the major engine of growth as opposed to simply oil.

4 Oil, gas and petrochemicals

There is an extensive literature on dependence on natural resources and economic development, much of it focusing on the negative consequences of declining long-term export prices and export earnings instability. In the 1970s much of this literature appeared to have little relevance to Saudi Arabia as the world's leading oil exporter, given the buoyant price of oil. Critics of oil dependence tend to use arguments based on the experience with natural gas in Holland, sometimes described as Dutch disease. Buoyant natural resource revenues from oil or gas push up the exchange rate and make other sectors of the domestic economy uncompetitive, not only in export markets but also in the home market as imports flood in.

In the 1980s the World Bank commissioned a study of the effects of revenues on economic development entitled *Oil Windfalls: Blessing or Curse?*[1] The focus was largely on the negative impact of oil, although admittedly the remit did not cover Saudi Arabia. Here the stress is on the benefits that oil has brought rather than on the negative. Although oil dependence has created problems for Saudi Arabia, there can be no doubt that the kingdom would not have become, without oil, the largest economy in the Arab world and the second largest in the Middle East after Turkey. Oil revenues have been used to finance a modern, generally efficient infrastructure, and an education system that has brought literacy and numeracy to virtually everyone in the kingdom even if it still has shortcomings.

Nevertheless, despite these positive benefits the question must still be raised of how well has the oil industry been managed. What has been the kingdom's role in OPEC, the Organisation of Petroleum Exporting States, and how far has this served the national interest? As the so-called 'swing producer' Saudi Arabia has often been the member forced to make the greatest production cutbacks during periods of oil glut and weak prices. Have the short-term revenue sacrifices been worthwhile in terms of longer-term benefits?

Saudi Arabia also has significant natural gas, although proven reserves are much lower than those of neighbouring Qatar or Iran and substantial investments are required to harness the supplies. Diversification into gas production can however reduce export earnings vulnerability to oil-pricing developments, and gas can be used as a major energy source for local industry. Nevertheless, how

40 *Rodney Wilson*

best to manage the gas development strategy has vexed Saudi Arabia's policymakers since the late 1990s, for reasons that this chapter tries to explain.

Rather than simply export crude oil and gas, the major export diversification since the 1980s has been into petrochemicals, with the kingdom becoming one of the leading international producers of methanol, ethylene, styrene, vinyl chloride monomer, butane, caustic soda, sulphuric acid and MTBE, the octane enhancer that replaces lead in petrol. Saudi Arabia, and in particular, SABIC, the Saudi Arabian Basic Industries Corporation, has learnt much from hosting these industries, but their contribution to local employment has been limited and in many respects Jubail and Yanbu, where most of the these industries are located, have become enclave economies with only limited links to the national economy.

The development of the oil industry

Oil was first discovered in Bahrain, but given Saudi Arabia's geographical proximity it seemed sensible to undertake some preliminary exploration work. In 1930 John Philby, an advisor, suggested to King Abdul Aziz that mining engineers should be called in to survey the natural resources of what was to become Eastern Province. By 1932 a mining engineer, Karl Twitchell, was optimistic about the presence of oil, and the King was advised to find a company interested in securing a concession. Not trusting the British, the King agreed that an American company, Standard Oil of California (SOCAL), should be given a sixty-year exclusive concession, that was signed on July 14, 1933.[2] The only oil not covered by this agreement were small concessions in the neutral zones bordering Iraq and Kuwait where two other smaller US oil companies, Getty Oil and Arabian Oil, were given exploration and production rights.

Although there were negative results from the first six experimental wells drilled from 1935 onwards, the seventh well drilled in Damman in 1938 revealed substantial reserves of oil. In fact, what had been discovered 1,440 metres down was the world's largest oilfield. By this time Texaco had been brought in by SOCAL as a partner, and the merged operations became the Arabian American Oil Company (ARAMCO). Later in 1944 Esso (which became Exxon) and Mobil were brought in, with the revised ownership distribution being 30 per cent each for Standard Oil of California, Texaco and Exxon and 10 per cent for Mobil.[3] SOCAL invited in these partners, as it was primarily a production company that lacked the market access of established refiners and retailers such as Exxon and Mobil.

This foreign corporate ownership structure was to remain in force until the time of the Arab–Israeli conflict of 1973, unlike Iraq and Iran whose oil industries had been nationalised, in Iran's case as early as 1951 by the then prime minister, Muhammad Mossadegh.[4] Arguably this had the advantage of giving the Iranian government control of production levels, but in practice as the major oil companies boycotted Iranian oil in retaliation there was no market for the oil, the Iranian economy deteriorated and Mossadegh was overthrown two years latter, supposedly with the assistance of the CIA. Saudi Arabia profited from these

Oil, gas and petrochemicals 41

developments in Iran as, with the chief Middle Eastern producer at that time virtually eliminated from the market, ARAMCO's Western partners took the initiative in increasing investment in Saudi oil, given the lower levels of perceived country risk.

Although the Saudi Arabian authorities did not control the level of oil production, they had secured a profit-sharing agreement with ARAMCO which entitled them to half of all revenues from oil sales. The original fifty-fifty profit sharing agreement had been with Venezuela in 1943 to secure additional US oil supplies during the Second World War, but the formula was also adopted for Saudi Arabia from the late 1940s when oil began being exported in significant volumes. As the oil companies were able to offset these royalty payments against corporate taxation in the United States, this encouraged investment in Saudi Arabian oil despite the profit-sharing overhead. However, the royalties could not be offset against retail-sales taxes on oil, which were to become more significant in the longer term.

Many of the arguments between the oil-producing countries and the multinational oil companies were subsequently over how the profits were determined, as clearly these were dependent on pricing. It was tempting for the companies to use low transfer prices for oil exports to maximise profits in the consuming countries where corporate taxes were lower rather than record high profits in the producing countries and pay half over to the governments. Venezuela was initially more concerned with this issue than countries such as Saudi Arabia, but there was a desire to see pricing transparency. Consequently, a system of posted prices was adopted from 1950, initially by Shell, but the partners in ARAMCO felt they had to adopt the same practice rather than risk criticism.[5]

Saudi Arabia's role in OPEC

Saudi Arabia was one of the five founder members of OPEC together with Iran, Iraq, Kuwait and Venezuela. Agreement was reached on the organisation's establishment at a meeting held in Baghdad on September 14, 1960. This was partly in response to controls on oil imports by the United States, which had been made mandatory the previous year, and a unilateral reduction in posted prices by the major Western oil companies. The idea of forming some kind of alliance of the Arab oil-exporting countries had been under discussion since the setting up of the Arab League in 1945, but Saudi Arabia was less enthusiastic about this initiative – especially once Egypt and Iraq – had become republics – and remained wary of the motives of Nasser in particular. Despite being a member of the Cairo-based Arab League, Saudi Arabia was more concerned with revenues than with following an Arab political agenda, and it recognised that in economic terms OPEC could be more effective as a countervailing force to the Western oil companies if non-Arab producers were involved.

OPEC was ineffective in the 1960s largely because the Western oil companies retained control of supplies and individual OPEC members had an interest in expanding production. Saudi Arabia's role was largely reactive as opposed to

42 Rodney Wilson

proactive, but it was willing to see the organisation expand with the entry of Qatar in 1961, Libya and Indonesia in 1962, Abu Dhabi in 1967 and Algeria in 1969. Later, in 1971, Nigeria was admitted, followed by Ecuador in 1973 and Gabon in 1975. It was of course notable that Egypt, despite having some oil, was not admitted, and that to some extent Iraq's role was weakened by the expansion of the membership, especially with the inclusion of so many non-Arab members.

As a consequence of the 1967 Arab–Israeli war and the failure of the Arab boycott on oil supplies to the United States and the United Kingdom, OAPEC, the Organisation of Arab Petroleum Exporting Countries, was established in 1968. Saudi Arabia felt obliged to participate, but it was still mindful of its special relationship with the United States concerning oil and other matters, and generally acted as a voice of moderation in both OPEC and OAPEC. By 1973, however, with the eruption of a new Arab–Israeli war, the kingdom had become disillusioned with American policy on Palestine and was a willing participant in the subsequent oil embargo organised by OAPEC which resulted in the substantial price increases.

This was undoubtedly a watershed both for the relations between oil producing and consuming nations and for Saudi Arabia's role within OPEC and OAPEC as the world's leading oil-exporting country. The balance of power had started to change between OPEC and the oil-consuming countries by the late 1960s, notably with the revolution in Libya and the emergence of the United States as the main oil importer given its own diminishing reserves and production. European state-owned oil companies, including Elf and Total of France and Agip of Italy, were prepared to get involved in countries such as Libya, and the major multinational companies – the so-called 'seven sisters', BP, Exxon, Gulf, Mobil, Shell, SOCAL and Texaco – had lost some of their monopoly buying power.[6]

Within ARAMCO the American sisters continued their traditional ownership and management role, and there was little pressure for change before 1973, even though the oil companies elsewhere were ceding control to government owned oil companies. Indeed, Saudi Arabia arguably benefited from these external development, as the ARAMCO shareholders, notably Exxon and Mobil, were prepared to invest more in Saudi Arabian production to maintain their access to supplies and share of world oil production.

This position became politically unsustainable after the October War of 1973, as although Saudi Arabia was not directly involved apart from its participation in the embargo, it could not be seen to have its production controlled exclusively by US companies, either internally or externally, despite the sixty-year concession agreed between the kingdom and SOCAL beginning in 1933. In 1974 negotiations started between the government and the American owners of ARAMCO about the state taking a majority ownership stake, with the companies to be bought out using future petroleum revenue. Initially the aim was for the government to take a sixty per cent stake, but this was unsatisfactory from the perspective of the oil companies, as without any measure of control in the subsequent joint venture there was a reluctance to continue equity participation

Oil, gas and petrochemicals   43

that implied risk. Almost as soon as the sixty per cent stake was agreed and implemented retroactively to January 1, 1974, negotiations started over full nationalisation. These lengthy negotiations were concluded in June 1977, when Saudi ARAMCO was created: a one hundred per cent government-owned company but with the former American oil partners providing some specialised management and technical services on a fee basis. The former ARAMCO partners incorporated locally to provide these services, notably Chevron, the successor to SOCAL, whose expertise had always been in oil and gas-field reservoir management.

Oil production

The determinants of oil production include supply capacity, the anticipated production level of competitors and the strength of oil demand as measured by the size of the expected market and oil prices. For an international oil company, exploiting oil in one country as opposed to another is not merely a reflection of geology and the marginal costs of production but also involves an assessment of country risk.

In the case of Saudi Arabia, when Exxon, Mobil and the other ARAMCO partners were taking the production decisions, investment and expansion plans were in part determined by the low marginal costs of oil production reflecting the scale of the oil resources, with the Ghawar onshore field the largest in the world. Favourable perceptions of political risk were also important given the regime's stability in comparison with those of neighbouring countries, notably Iraq. It would, therefore, be wrong to conclude that Saudi Arabia's growth as an oil economy was simply an accident of geology; it also reflected the consistent and reasonably efficient political and economic management of the kingdom.

Once ARAMCO was nationalised it was, of course, the government itself that took production decisions, which in practice meant the Oil Minister, although consultations took place with the King and other cabinet colleagues about significant decisions, given the wider importance of oil to the economy. In summary it could be said that day-to-day decisions were handled by the Oil Minister and ARAMCO, the former – especially when it was Sheikh Yamani – enjoying considerable discretion at OPEC meetings; however, strategic decisions on oil production involved the King and the Minister of Finance and, to a much lesser extent, the Minister of Planning.[7]

Figure 4.1 illustrates the rapid rise in Saudi Arabian oil production, which doubled during the 1960s, and rose consistently until 1974. With the 1975 recession in Europe and the United States that followed the oil-price shock of the previous year the demand for oil declined and the Saudi Arabian output level also fell for the first time. The resumption of economic growth in the major consuming countries resulted in Saudi Arabian oil output rising to record levels in 1976 and 1977, followed by a marginal decline in 1978, but it then rose to a peak in 1980 when additional oil was pumped to compensate for the shortfall in Iranian supplies during and after that nation's Islamic Revolution.

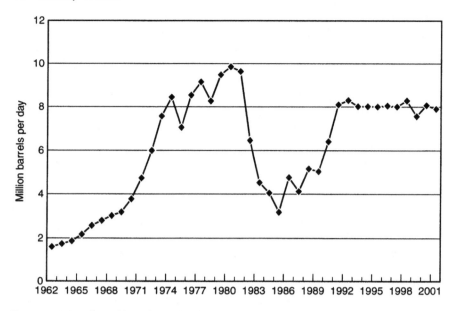

Figure 4.1 Saudi Arabian oil production
Sources: Saudi Arabian Monetary Agency *Thirty Seventh Annual Report*, Riyadh, 2001, p. 411 and *OPEC Annual Statistical Bulletin*, Vienna, 2002, p. 5.

Saudi Arabia is often described as the 'swing' producer in OPEC given its ability, once ARAMCO was nationalised, to vary production levels to satisfy market demands. The scale and modernity of its production capacity meant that output could be potentially varied from as little as three million barrels a day to a maximum of around twelve million a day. Unlike countries such as Iran and Nigeria, which were unable to sacrifice significant oil production because of their difficult budgetary position, Saudi Arabia and the other Gulf OPEC states were in a much more comfortable fiscal situation, at least until the 1980s.

Initially Saudi Arabia's role as a swing producer involved increasing production to compensate for shortfalls in Iran, as already indicated, at a time when the oil price was high. At this time Saudi Arabian and Western interests coincided: the increased production resulted in greater revenue for the kingdom yet at the same time moderated the price rise that would have driven the West into recession.

By the mid-1980s, however, Saudi Arabia's role as a swing producer to help the OPEC maintain prices resulted in real economic hardship. With the supply of oil from the North Sea and Alaska expanding, and OPEC reduced to the role of residual supplier, more substantial production cutbacks were implemented, as Figure 4.1 shows. With both oil production and prices falling, revenue declined sharply, and the government was running increasing fiscal deficits despite spending cuts. Tensions grew between King Fahd and the Oil Minister Sheikh Yamani over the policy of production cutbacks to limit price falls, and in 1986 the latter was dismissed to be replaced by Hisham Nazer, the Planning Minister.

Oil, gas and petrochemicals 45

Nazer focused on maintaining prices, but initially had to cut production even further than under Yamani, and by 1987 production was down to below 42 per cent of its 1981 peak. From its low point in 1987 it gradually revived, partly due to improved global economic conditions and the increasing demand for oil from rapidly growing Asian markets. The production level remained remarkable stable in the 1990s, indicating that Saudi Arabia was not prepared to play the role of swing producer to more than a marginal extent.

Oil pricing

Saudi Arabia is able to influence rather than determine the prices for its oil, which are ultimately the outcome of supply-and-demand forces in the global market. Oil policy decisions made in the kingdom or in consultation with other OPEC members can have some impact on oil supply, but demand is independently determined by global economic growth, the extent to which development and modernisation are energy-intensive or energy-saving and the pricing of energy substitutes. Oil is not homogenous, but there are many countries within and outside OPEC that supply oil of similar quality to that offered by Saudi Arabia. Consequently, the kingdom is much more of a price taker than a price maker, and although OPEC's role in determining prices should not be dismissed, it is clearly of less significance than in the organisation's 1970s heyday.

Despite the decreasing importance of OPEC, the kingdom exercises greater leverage over prices as a member than it would outside. Nevertheless the other OPEC members need Saudi Arabia much more than it needs them; indeed, without that country's participation the organisation would collapse. OPEC has been less of a cartel in recent years, as members have often persistently produced above their agreed quotas, but some observers – notably Ali D. Johany, possibly Saudi Arabia's most distinguished energy economist – have always been sceptical about OPEC's effectiveness as a cartel in any case.[8]

Figure 4.2 illustrates oil-price trends for Saudi Arabian medium crude oil during the period 1985–2001. Saudi Arabian medium-grade oil used to command a price premium of almost 1.20 dollars per barrel over Arab Heavy oil, but with improvements in refinery technology this was halved to sixty cents between 1991 and 2001.[9] The 1982–1984 price fall continued into 1985, after which prices mostly fluctuated in the 12–20 dollars per barrel range as Figure 4.2 shows. There was a brief rise after the Iraqi occupation of Kuwait, which was greater than indicated by the year-end data in the chart. The 1998 oil-price slump followed the previous year's Asia crisis and a fall in demand, although Iraq's re-emergence as a significant exporter under the oil-for-food programme was a contributory factor despite the remaining in place of the sanctions regime against Saddam Hussein. Improved Saudi Arabian relations with Iran, and an initiative by the kingdom, the Tehran government and Venezuela to cooperate more closely on oil production policy, caused oil prices to recover. The continuing 1990s boom in the United States also helped to increase oil demand,

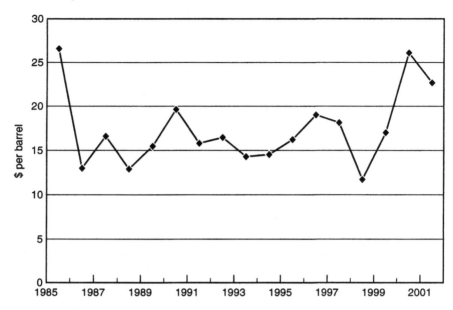

Figure 4.2 Price of Saudi Arabian medium

Sources: Saudi Arabian Monetary Agency *Thirty Seventh Annual Report*, Riyadh, 2001, p. 419 and *OPEC Annual Statistical Bulletin*, Vienna, 2002, p. 114.

as did the revival of the Asian economies. Although the US economy was subsequently to experience a downturn aggravated by the events of September 11, 2001, the uncertainties regarding a possible conflict between the that nation and Iraq kept buyers nervous and oil prices high.

Oil-export earnings are, of course, a function of the volume of production and the price level. During the period 1981–1986 it was falls in oil production that accounted for much of the decline in export earnings illustrated in Figure 4.3; and from then until 1992 it was the partial revival of production that mainly contributed to the rise in oil export earnings. For most of the remainder of the 1990s and into the twenty-first century it is price changes that largely account for changes in oil-export earnings, the production level being relatively stable, as discussed earlier.

Oil reserves, oil depletion and the future oil market

Saudi Arabia had proven crude oil reserves in 2001 of over 262 billion barrels, sufficient to sustain production for almost ninety years at eight million barrels a day. Figures for reserves have always been underestimated indeed – despite over sixty-five years of oil extraction – they have continued to rise. Yet admittedly, the increase in reserves has not been substantial in recent years, the last major upward revision being in 1988.[10] Nevertheless, as oil-production technology has advanced it has become possible to identify and extract oil from

Oil, gas and petrochemicals 47

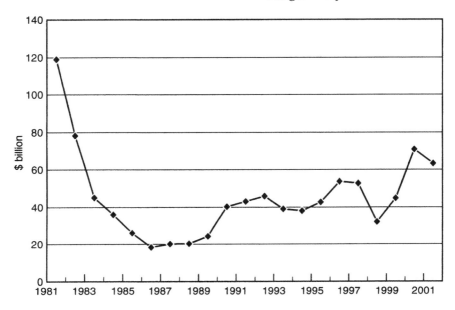

Figure 4.3 Saudi Arabian oil exports

Sources: Saudi Arabian Monetary Agency *Thirty Seventh Annual Report*, Riyadh, 2001, p. 419 and *OPEC Annual Statistical Bulletin*, Vienna, 2002, p. 114.

locations hitherto not considered either feasible or viable. Ultimately reserves are not only a matter of geology but, more importantly, of economics, as the higher the oil price the more worthwhile it is to exploit marginal fields.

Oil is, of course, an exhaustible rather than a renewable resource, but given Saudi Arabia's large proven reserves and ability to sustain current or even higher production levels for many decades, resource depletion should not be regarded as a serious problem or indeed the major motivation for economic diversification and the reducing of oil dependence. The main problem is likely to be the global demand for oil, not merely the Saudi Arabian supply: with technological change other fuels will come to be substituted for oil, as has already happened to a considerable extent, with most electricity no longer being produced from this source. Fuel oil consumption declined in the European Union, the United States and Japan by 18 per cent, 15 per cent and 8 per cent respectively over the decade 1991–2001. Even in China it has started to decline since its peak in 1997.[11] Petroleum consumption for vehicles and distillates have admittedly continued to grow, notably in the United States, but in the European Union such consumption fell during the period 1991–2001, as fuel management for vehicle engines improved significantly due to technology now being applied in North America and Japan.

There are lessons to be drawn from the precedent of coal: most coal resources will never be mined, and it is likely that most Saudi Arabian oil reserves will never be exploited. The slow but steady move from most global activity being

48   *Rodney Wilson*

based on the production of goods to the world's economy being largely service-based has profound implications for energy use and the oil-rich economies. The world's highest-income economies are not those with significant physical resources or heavy industrial capacity but rather those that have developed knowledge-based economies, with some of that knowledge being applied to energy-saving schemes.

In the longer term Saudi Arabia is likely to consume an increasing proportion of its own oil, although it is difficult to envisage exports being less dominant for several decades. The kingdom has not adopted a strategy of refining oil for export, largely due to the distances involved and the much greater transportation risks associated with refined products as opposed to crude oil. Hence most refined products are for the local market, the main one being diesel, followed by fuel oil, gasoline and naphtha, and then jet fuel and kerosene. Over half a million barrels of diesel are refined each day – double the 1984 amount – with fuel oil production amounting to 450,000 barrels a day, a decline of around 70 per cent since the early 1990s following the move to gas-generated electricity, even in Saudi Arabia. Gasoline production has expanded most rapidly to around 420,000 barrels per day, reflecting the steady increase in the number of cars in the kingdom that seems set to continue.[12]

As long as oil remains the most economic source of fuel for transportation, the demand for Saudi Arabian crude will remain; but in the longer term, with technological advance, this is unlikely to be the case despite the limited success in developing alternative fuel cell technology until now.

Contribution of oil to national economic development

Oil still accounted for 70 per cent of government income, 85 per cent of exports and 35 per cent of GDP in 2001. It is the GDP figure that has declined over the last two decades, indicating a considerable degree of economic diversification even if the non-oil sector remains largely dependent on oil developments.

In the case of Saudi Arabia there has been a consistent tendency to treat oil as a given parameter somewhat detached from the rest of the national economy. In other words, once a level of production deemed likely to be acceptable to other OPEC members is set, and the oil price is determined in international markets, either spot or on a contract basis, the resultant oil revenue accrues.

It perhaps ironic that the world's largest oil exporter has always played a largely reactive rather than a proactive role in the international oil market. The stress has being on tactics within and by OPEC, with the Oil Minister reporting to the King and Crown Prince rather than to other ministers. In particular, the Minister of Planning is regarded as having a less important and less prestigious position than the Oil Minister, and little contact takes place between civil servants in the two ministries. Hence development needs do not, and never have, determined oil policy; rather the development task is seen as the establishment of priorities for government spending over five-year periods on the basis of oil revenues that may or may not be realised.

Oil, gas and petrochemicals 49

The de-linkage of oil and development spending was less critical in the 1970s and early 1980s as oil revenues accrued to government reserves which acted as a buffer between revenue and expenditure. Reserves could be drawn upon if there was less oil revenue or added to when there was more. The problem by the late 1980s and 1990s, however, was that with sustained lower oil prices the government reserves disappeared and the state became a substantial net borrower from its own banks. There remained substantial Saudi Arabian asset holdings in the West – and, indeed, these grew during the 1990s – but they were privately owned, by businesses and families of high net worth, not controlled by the state.

Hence oil-price fluctuations have a more immediate impact on government revenues and the economy than in the past. In so far as there is an oil strategy it seems to be to maintain production levels with only marginal adjustments, in comparison to the policy of varying production levels much more dramatically in the Yamani era. Pricing policy since the late 1990s seems to be designed to hold prices within a reasonably wide band of between six and eight dollars per barrel, decreasing production marginally when the floor is reached and increasing it marginally when the ceiling is reached.

Staying within the band is a matter of tactics; but determining the position of the band is more a question of strategy. Once the strategy changes the target prices move, the range by 2002 being from 22 to 28 dollars a barrel. Saudi Arabian policy seems to be to emphasise its preference for stability in a market where prices inevitably fluctuate, often quite dramatically, in response to forces of supply and demand. In practice, neither the tactics nor the strategy may actually work, though that is no justification for not having a pricing policy, even if it is merely indicative.

In reality the Saudi Arabian economy retains a high degree of responsiveness to oil market developments, and it has not proved possible to break or even weaken the link. With production levels fairly constant, GDP still rises and falls in line with oil-price changes, and government expenditures are similarly constrained. In the absence of a significant cushion of reserves and government debt exceeding 95 per cent of GDP or 173 billion dollar in 2002, the lag between oil-price falls and the corresponding expenditure cuts is less than one year, with, for example, the oil revenue shortfall of 1998 when at one point prices fell to 10 dollars per barrel resulting in a two-billion-dollar cut in spending the following year.[13] This would have been even greater without the price recovery of the following year.

When oil prices fall it tends to be investment expenditure rather than government recurrent spending on salaries that is affected the most. Ironically, it is the investment in diversification and in achieving self-sustaining, non-oil-dependent development that suffers, while what can be classified as consumption through public sector wages is maintained. Regional redistribution suffers when oil prices fall, because the capital, Riyadh, as the centre of the state administration, is more dependent on recurrent government spending than more peripheral areas that tend to benefit from investment spending on infrastructure.

50 *Rodney Wilson*

The contribution of oil to development will inevitably diminish even further as oil production levels remain within the 7.5 to 8.5 million-barrel-per-day band rather than there being any attempt to ratchet up the level and face criticism from other OPEC members. Prices will continue to fluctuate, but are unlikely to be sustainable for any lengthy period of time beyond 28 dollars per barrel. There is no strategy in OPEC or in Saudi Arabia in trying to raise prices over time and having a gradually increasing upward target. Rather ministers have reconciled themselves to the objective of trend stability. This actually implies lower real purchasing power in the longer term as inflation diminished the real value of the US dollar in which oil prices are denominated, and as the dollar declines against stronger currencies, notably the euro.

Saudi ARAMCO has an excellent reputation in the kingdom as an employer, and though before nationalisation most of its staff were expatriates, with US citizens holding the majority of senior positions, even then it had a good record for training local people to undertake often complex and highly specialised work. By the 1990s most of its employees were local citizens, but as the total workforce in 2002 only amounted to 54,000, it accounted for less than one per cent of the total national workforce.[14] However, it does offer a wide variety of employment as it even maintains its own educational and health facilities; its workers, therefore, include teachers and physicians in addition to the expected geologists, engineers, computer and laboratory scientists, plant workers, harbour pilots and firefighters.

Gas development

Saudi Arabia has been producing gas in modest quantities since 1970, mostly as a by-product of oil production. The aim was to harness the gas previously flared off, most of the 1970s initial production being used in the oil industry itself. From the later part of that decade some gas was used as an energy source for domestic industries, and this has gradually increased, with over ten million barrels of liquefied petroleum gas and almost 206 million barrels of natural gas being consumed locally in 2000.[15]

The so-called 'gas initiative', launched in 2001, is seen as the key to future industrialisation in Saudi Arabia. The kingdom has the fourth largest proven reserves of gas in the world, estimated at 6.6 trillion cubic metres. Not surprisingly, Western oil companies are eager to get involved in the development and exploitation of these huge resources. Saudi Arabia is apprehensive about ceding control of basic resources, even though it lacks the finance and arguably the capability to develop them itself.

Consequently, in June 2001 a series of major deals were signed with international oil companies for the development of three gas projects in Saudi Arabia. The largest involved a consortium led by ExxonMobil and including Royal Dutch Shell, British Petroleum and the US company Phillips. This was to develop the South Ghawar gas fields as part of a fifteen-billion-dollar project, with the gas used as feedstock for industries in Jubail. It was envisaged that work

Oil, gas and petrochemicals 51

on this scheme would proceed first, especially given the success of gas developments in neighbouring Qatar. The second deal was for the development of gas fields on the Red Sea coast, with ExxonMobil also heading the project in collaboration with two other American oil companies, Occidental and Marathon. Gas from this area could serve industries in Yanbu. The third gas project was to be based in Saudi Arabia's empty quarter bordering the UAE and Oman. It was led by Shell, which had a 40 per cent stake, with TotalFinaElf of France and Conoco of the United States each having a 30 per cent stake.[16]

Total investment in the three projects was expected to exceed twenty-five billion dollar over a thirty-year period, with the oil companies working in partnership with Saudi ARAMCO. The exact form the partnership was to take and who was to play the leading role were not settled at the start as it was envisaged that due to the complexities involved such matters would have to be subject to detailed negotiation. In retrospect this lack of initial clarity seems unfortunate as it appears that some in Saudi ARAMCO were hostile to the structure agreed, and indeed the Oil Minister himself, Ali Naimi, was less than enthusiastic.

Many issues remained to be settled, including the price formula for the gas to be eventually produced, the tax liability of the international oil companies and the regulatory regime to govern their operations. Little progress has been made on any of these issues; indeed, there has been little specific discussion to reassure ExxonMobil or the other companies that they will get a reasonable rate of return on any investment. The very positive comments from Prince Abdullah Faisal bin Turki Al-Saud, governor of the Saudi Arabian General Investment Authority, regarding the participation of international oil companies in basic resource exploitation, were not echoed by key government ministers.

There were strong suspicions that Ali Naimi was stalling progress in order to protect the monopoly position of Saudi ARAMCO. That organisation is naturally reluctant to see other oil companies enter the kingdom, even for gas development. This could set a precedent for future involvement in oil development in competition with Saudi ARAMCO. Moreover, Saudi ARAMCO has itself already developed a master gas system without the involvement of foreign companies except on a contractual basis for a limited number of tasks of a technical nature. Its Hawiyah gas plant started processing in September 2001 and became fully operational in December 2001, the fourth major plant to open. Saudi ARAMCO's gas production already amounted to 3.5 billion cubic feet per day by 2002, and was planned to rise to 7.0 billion cubic feet per day by the end of 2003. Its directors argued that they could manage the gas expansion themselves with a much more limited involvement from foreign companies not necessitating a stake in ownership.[17]

Lee Raymond, head of ExxonMobil, had a meeting on February 20, 2002 with Ali Naimi and the Saudi Arabian Foreign Minister, Prince Saud Al-Faisal, in Los Angeles where the Prince was receiving medical treatment. At that meeting, in their review of the gas initiative it became clear that it would be the end of the year at best before the agreement, which was supposed to be concluded by March 2, 2002, had any chance of being finalised. It was also apparent that

52   *Rodney Wilson*

political developments since September 11 and the cooling of relations between Saudi Arabia and the United States were also affecting attitudes in the kingdom. There is a desire in Riyadh to have a greater diversity of both political and economic relationships rather than be too dependent on the United States and companies such as ExxonMobil. United States energy companies are in any case less respected since the collapse of Enron, in which many Saudi Arabian investors had stakes, to their bitter regret.

The failure of the gas initiative would be a major setback for economic diversification in Saudi Arabia, as the schemes involve not only the harnessing of gas but projects that include its use for electricity generation, water desalination and petrochemical production. This would further the development of downstream industries in Jubail and Yanbu, create much-needed employment for Saudi Arabian citizens and open up investment opportunities for local businesses. If the present negotiations fail and new bids are invited for a restructured scheme, the process is likely to take place over a much longer period of time and on a more limited scale.

Three major factors were responsible for the impasse. First, Western oil companies were expecting returns on their investments of up to 18 per cent per annum to reflect the risks involved, but on the most generous estimate the initial terms offered by the Saudi Arabian side were unlikely to result in the returns exceeding 10 per cent at best. Second, the areas offered by the government for gas exploration and exploitation were deemed by ExxonMobil and its Western partners to be too limited in size to produce the supplies needed for the electricity, desalinisation and petrochemical plants. The companies estimated that the fields offered were incapable of producing more than six trillion cubic feet, less than half the output they had originally envisaged.[18] Finally, there was considerable opposition from Saudi ARAMCO to Western oil companies becoming once again directly involved in resource exploitation in the kingdom, as although these projects involved gas rather than oil it was feared that their penetration could be merely the thin end of the wedge.

Crown Prince Abdullah wanted to see progress on the gas initiative as he realised that if it failed the new investment policy would be threatened and its credibility undermined. Moreover given Saudi Arabia's rapidly rising population, it is clear that the expansion of electricity generation capacity and desalinisation cannot be postponed or shelved, and that the further development of petrochemicals is of some urgency if other countries are to be prevented from building market shares. In addition, given the conflicting views within the Bush administration on Saudi-American relations, the Crown Prince recognises the need to encourage those who adopt a friendlier position towards the kingdom. Cementing relationship with business interests such as the Texas oil lobby and ExxonMobil can help in this process.

As a result the Foreign Minister, Prince Saud al-Faisal – rather than Ali Naimi – has been given responsibility for handling the negotiations. Both men accompanied the Crown Prince on his visit to the United States in May 2002, but it was the former who appeared more receptive to the points argued by Lee

Raymond, head of ExxonMobil. Although the returns on the gas-field developments estimated by the Western companies were only raised modestly in the so-called 'final offer' of September 2002 to between 10 and 12 per cent, a guaranteed rate of return of 15.5 per cent has been offered on the downstream elements of the scheme involving power generation, water desalinisation and petrochemicals. These higher returns are attractive to the Western companies; hence the major remaining issue is the quantity of gas needed for the scheme, a technical matter which should be capable of resolution.[19]

As Foreign Minister, Prince Saud al-Faisal has been able to see the gas initiative within the broader context of Saudi-American relations and his country's relations with the West more generally. He knows there is a great deal of domestic dissatisfaction – even anger – with some of the measures the United States has introduced since September 11, 2001, especially the fingerprinting and photographing of men and women with their heads uncovered that are required for visa applications. The interrogation of Saudi Arabian postgraduate students in the United States has also fuelled resentment. Threats to reciprocate and to introduce similar measures for US citizens entering Saudi Arabia – including oil-company employees – complicate matters.

Yet against these short-term difficulties the Prince has to balance the longer-term costs of not striking a deal with leading American oil companies, especially if gas is developed more rapidly elsewhere – notably in a post-Saddam Hussein Iraq – at the expense of Saudi Arabia. Other GCC countries – including Iran – are also pushing ahead with petrochemical developments, which could undermine the kingdom's position as a supplier. The electricity grids of the GCC countries are being interconnected, and in due course there will be links to Egypt, Jordan and even Turkey. Saudi Arabia has the potential to be a substantial exporter of electricity, but unless generating capacity is increased significantly it could just as easily become a net importer. The stakes with the gas initiative are clearly very high, and it will require political statesmanship to see beyond the present difficulties and realise the future gains.

The petrochemical industry

As already indicated, the major industrial diversification in Saudi Arabia has mainly been into petrochemicals, fertilizers and such energy-intensive industries as iron- and steel-making. The strategy was planned back in the 1970s, at the time of the oil-revenue boom, with the objective of creating an industrial base capable of bringing greater added value to the kingdom.

The establishment of SABIC, the Saudi Arabian Basic Industries Company, in September 1976 was seen as the key to these developments, the aim being to establish a series of joint ventures with foreign oil and chemical companies capable of providing technical and marketing skills, while the majority ownership would be Saudi Arabian. It was envisaged that the government would provide most of the capital but that SABIC would be incorporated to ensure proper financial reporting and transparency rather than being run like a

54 Rodney Wilson

government ministry. There was a desire to avoid the problems experienced by SAFCO, the fertiliser company set up by the Ministry of Petroleum which had proved to be an expensive, badly managed venture.[20]

A minority shareholding was offered to private equity investors from the start, and when the stock market was established SABIC became the largest quoted company not only in the kingdom but in the entire region, a prime position that was to last until the partial privatisation of the Saudi Telecommunications Company in December 2002. SABIC is actually structured as a holding company, with a series of multinational joint-venture partners involved in each particular project. These have included Mobil, Shell, Dow Chemicals, Mitsubishi and the Taiwan Fertiliser Company. By the 1980s SABIC had increased its stake in the joint ventures, the role of the joint-venture partners being downgraded to management and servicing-fee-based contracts rather than their having a direct share in the equity and hence the profits. This suited the foreign partners, as they reduced their risk profile and were yet assured of continuing involvement.

SABIC's industrial plants are located in the new industrial cities of Jubail on the Gulf and Yanbu on the Red Sea, enclaves somewhat removed from the country's chief major urban centres. Although SABIC is the kingdom's largest industrial company, it only employs 16,000, its activities being by nature capital-intensive. It accounts for almost one-tenth of Saudi Arabian exports, and its production exceeded 35 million metric tons by the end of 2000.[21]

A stark contrast exists between SABIC's largely efficient, sophisticated industrial plants and the much less efficient operation of many of the protected, subsidised import-substitution industries in the kingdom. The issue of economic dualism was discussed in Chapter 2, and the difference between SABIC's world-class facilities and those of other industries that conform more closely with Third World norms highlights this problem. No technological transfers have been made from SABIC to other industries, partly because of its specialised nature, and few demonstration effects in terms of the dissemination of management best practices.

The challenge in the decade ahead will be to encourage more linkages and spin-offs from SABIC to downstream industries capable of employing greater numbers. The HADEED steel company was initially geared to producing reinforcing rods and girders for the construction industry after its founding in 1983. By the 1990s it was producing rolled steel for the local and GCC engineering and manufacturing industries.[22] SABIC Polymers are a major exporter of polyethylene, including polypropylene, PVC and polystyrenes, with a production capacity of almost four million tons annually. They have diversified downstream into polyester fibres and filaments, textile-grade chips and PET packaging resins, as well as melamine.[23]

Although these downstream moves into plastics are welcome, there has been no attempt to move into textiles or clothing, ventures which might give rise to more employment opportunities. Saudi Arabia's wage costs are, of course, higher than those in East and South Asia where most of the global textile and clothing industry is located, but there may be niche areas offering scope for Saudi Arabian production, the challenge being to identify the appropriate differentiated product where costs are a less important price determinant.

With SABIC sales revenue worth around seven billion dollars annually and profits of almost one billion dollars, the company is able to sustain a substantial investment programme of its own. In some respects, however, it has outgrown the kingdom as it has moved from being a national to a multinational company. Its new technology centre is located in Houston, Texas, rather than in Saudi Arabia, a location determined by local synergies and the availability of highly specialised expertise.[24] In 2002 it acquired petrochemical facilities in the Netherlands and considered an acquisition in Italy that was finally abandoned on commercial grounds.

The danger is that as SABIC becomes more footloose and less closely identified with Saudi Arabia in the long term – despite its name – much of the downstream diversification will take place elsewhere, with the kingdom simply retaining its upstream, capital-intensive role.[25] Of course other players could enter the field locally, a process that has already started with the launch of the Saudi International Petrochemicals Company in which the Al-Zamel group is a major investor.[26] Yet this venture's initial capital of 133 million dollars is small by the standards of the petrochemical industry, and without the addition of more substantial investments it is likely to remain on the margins.

5 The banking sector and financial markets

Since the early years of economic development theory in the 1950s, there has been a good deal of debate about whether finance simply responds to the needs of enterprise or if the emergence of financial institutions is actually able to promote business and entrepreneurial activity.[1] In the former view, the role of finance is essentially a passive one, with banks and other financial institutions growing as the economy expands. In contrast to the demand-following view, the supply leading approach holds that the availability of substantial funding, perhaps at low cost, may stimulate entrepreneurial effort and encourage business ambitions. The top managers of financial institutions may themselves play an entrepreneurial role, perhaps because they are also company directors.[2] This was certainly experience in East and South-East Asia, one that proved successful in promoting high rates of economic growth, at least until the Asia crisis of 1997, which resulted in accusations of 'crony capitalism'.

Which approach is relevant to the banking experience of Saudi Arabia and the development of the kingdom's financial markets? It would be tempting to subscribe to the demand-following approach, with banks simply responding to the growth of the potential market for their services. However, the position is more complex: the market for banking services has always been subject to state controls, with the state determining the basic structural parameters leaving the banks and other financial institutions free for the most part to compete and expand within those parameters. State involvement has not been a matter of ideology, as there was no desire to nationalise the banking system as in neighbouring Iraq, Egypt or Syria. Rather, the state's injection of capital and acquisition of an ownership stake in the two of the largest banks – the National Commercial and the Riyadh – was to help the banks overcome bad debt problems and maintain the confidence of depositors.

In Saudi Arabia the shariah law nominally governs all aspects of commercial life, including financial transactions, but in practice banking operations are similar to those in Western countries, though there is a significant Islamic finance sub-sector which has existed informally since the origins of Muslim civilisation in the Arabian peninsula and formally since the 1980s. Unlike in Egypt, Western banks were not interested in securing a presence in the kingdom in the pre-oil era, as the size of the economy was very small and traditional

The banking sector and financial markets 57

money changers and moneylenders had captured what limited business there then was.

Early banking history

During the pre-oil period there were no banks in the territory occupied today by Saudi Arabia. The Ottoman Bank, a Franco-British institution which had expanded throughout the Arab world in the late nineteenth century and established a branch in Alexandria in 1867, did not see it as worthwhile to expand its branch network to the Heijaz or al-Hasa, the major centres of Ottoman commerce in the west and the east of the Arabian peninsula.[3] Barter and cash transactions prevailed, but supplier credits were normal in trade and money changers often provided loans on an informal basis. The latter were an established part of the souk economy, especially in the cities of the Heijaz, Jeddah, Mecca and Medina, where there was much demand from pilgrims performing haj to change coins and precious metals, mainly gold, into Saudi Arabian silver riyals.[4]

Ibn Saud, the kingdom's founder of the kingdom, was suspicious of banks and saw little need for such institutions, and the Wahhabis were both well aware of the prohibition of *riba* and hostile to the notion of foreign institutions serving local Muslims. By the early twentieth century there was in any case an expansion in the number of money changers in the Heijaz with an increasing volume of pilgrims visiting Mecca and Medina as transportation by road, rail and sea became easier and relatively cheaper. Most money changers operated from a single establishment, but some – notably the Mahfouz and Musa Kaki families – had several outlets in different geographical locations. Like many of the money changers and traders in the Heijaz, they originated from Yemen.

The kingdom's first foreign banking institution was Dutch and opened in 1928 largely to provide money-changing facilities for pilgrims setting out from Java in the then Dutch East Indies,[5] It was referred to as a trading company – the Netherlands Trading Society – rather than a bank as the King objected to that designation because of its *riba* connotations, though it actually performed a range of banking functions including trade-financing facilities.[6] The financing of imports from Britain and its empire was handled from the Jeddah office of the trading firm of Gellatly Hankey, which from the 1920s acted as agent for the British overseas banks.[7] In 1936 Bank Misr of Egypt applied for permission to open a bank in Jeddah to serve both Egyptian pilgrims and Red Sea trade, but its request was turned down due to suspicions among the ruling family regarding Egyptian intentions; it was felt that if a banking licence was to be granted for a substantial operation this should be to Saudi Arabian nationals.

In 1937 the Mahfouz and Musa Kaki families petitioned the King for permission to establish the first locally owned bank, with the result that the following year the Kaki Salih Company (later renamed the National Commercial Bank) opened for business in Jeddah, with 51.5 per cent of its capital owned by Bin Mahfouz and the remaining share by the Musa Kaki family. In many

58 *Rodney Wilson*

respects the new institution was similar to the traditional money changers with whom it competed, but as a formal bank it was able to issue letters of credit on behalf of Saudi Arabian merchants which represented guarantees to Western exporters that payments would be made, either by the importers or by the bank itself in case of default. Although the bank was unregulated, foreign banks, knowing it had the King's support, were prepared to accept its letters of credit on behalf of their exporting clients.

The government itself conducted much of its foreign exchange business through the Netherlands Trading Company, largely because it was able to secure longer deferred payments terms, as in the early years of oil production revenues were modest. In the late 1940s oil revenues increased considerably, and although some payments were received in the form of silver and gold there was an increasing supply of dollar notes. The French Banque de l'Indochine, which had extensive dealings in precious metals in South-East Asia, offered to exchange the dollar notes for gold sovereigns and silver riyals at favourable rates of exchange for the King.[8] The bank already had offices in Djibouti on the African side of the Red Sea, as well as in Lebanon and Syria, and in 1947 the King gave his permission – to its representative, Christian Delaby – for the opening of a branch in Jeddah the following year.[9]

Sheikh Abd Allah Sulayman, King Ibn Saud's Finance Minister, increasingly realised that this haphazard approach of relying on foreign banks for the government's own financing needs was unsatisfactory, but there was also a reluctance to favour one group of local financiers such as the Bin Mafouz family, over others. The main problem confronting the government was the variation in the price of silver, on which the riyal was based, with gold, on which the Saudi sovereign was based. Britain's ambassador advocated the setting up of a currency board similar to those existing in many British colonies, and a treasury official was dispatched from Whitehall to make the case for a Saudi dinar, to be at parity with the British pound, with the kingdom – like its neighbours, Iraq and Egypt – as part of the sterling area.

The King distrusted the British, and was not enthusiastic about either paper money or links to the sterling area that would have curtailed convertibility. He, therefore, turned to the Americans for advice as they provided much of the oil revenue and were already heavily involved in the kingdom. Arthur Young, a financial expert from California, was dispatched to Saudi Arabia in 1951 to head a mission on currency reform.[10] He recommended the establishment of a monetary agency, which would serve the government, regulate the banks, and issue a new currency, the Saudi riyal, to be linked to the dollar and hence directly to gold. This proved much more attractive to the King and Sheikh Abd Allah Sulayman than the British plan as sterling was not linked to gold and that currency had just been devalued (from 4 dollars to 2.8 dollars to the pound). The Saudi Arabian Monetary Agency (SAMA) opened in 1952 and functioned successfully along the lines envisaged by Young.

It is clear from these developments that the King was mainly concerned with not being exploited by foreign colonial interests, but also that a degree of

The banking sector and financial markets 59

practicality was involved when it came to securing deals with Dutch and French institutions plus a willingness to listen to American advice. Nevertheless, Islamic teaching on the *haram* nature of interest transactions was respected, and there was much debate on how the new monetary agency advocated by Young should be designated. Sheikh Sulayman indicated to Young that the King would need to be assured that the new agency would not deal in interest, and that the designation 'bank' could not be used.[11] Young suggested the term 'financial agency' but the King rejected this proposal, and in the end 'monetary agency' was agreed upon. Under Article 3.7 of the new agency's charter all paying or receiving of interest was prohibited[12] as was the issue of currency notes, though the latter was subsequently dropped.

The development of commercial banking

Despite Article 3.7, SAMA was concerned less with promoting Islamic finance than with the performance of normal central banking functions, notably providing the government – through Sheikh Sulayman – with advice on financing issues and acting as a regulator of the commercial banking system. The Kaki Salih Company changed its name to the National Commercial Bank and started to expand its branch network throughout the kingdom. The British Bank of Iran and the Middle East was allowed to open branches in Jeddah and Al-Khobar in 1952, and in 1957 a second locally owned bank, the Riyadh Bank, opened, introducing a degree of competition in the market for banking services.[13] Most depositors maintained current accounts with the banks that paid no interest, and borrowers paid arrangement fees for their loans and annual service charges that were, in practice, very similar to interest.

Ambitious merchants and minor members of the royal family increasingly put pressure on the commercial banks for loans, which it was difficult to refuse given the political influence wielded by such clients. There was also a reluctance to repay loans on time on the part of unscrupulous businessmen, some of whom cited the Islamic prohibition of *riba* to justify their delays and evasions despite the fact that they had been fully aware of the terms of the funding at the time the loans were taken out. The Riyadh Bank, as it attempted to build market share by gaining new clients, was especially subject to these pressures, and in 1964 it nearly became bankrupt.[14] The government was obliged to intervene to save the institution by injecting fresh capital and taking a 38 per cent equity stake so that provisions could be made for bad debt.

It was recognised that a more lasting solution was needed: if the banks were to be simply baled out of all difficulties, this would create moral hazards as there would be no incentive to be vigilant over lending policy. Consequently, the Banking Control Law of 1966 was passed precluding banks from lending to their own directors or auditors or from investing directly in company stock in excess of 10 per cent of the total shareholding.[15] There was a potential conflict between these provisions and the Islamic concept of *musharakah* participatory financing whereby a financier is able to form a partnership with an entrepreneur; but as

60   *Rodney Wilson*

neither the National Commercial nor the Riyadh Banks offered such Islamic facilities in any case, this legal safeguard was of no significance. Of greater significance for the banks was the requirement that they should deposit 15 per cent of their deposit liabilities with SAMA, funds on which they would earn no interest.[16] This provision was made in the interests of depositor protection rather than because of any Islamic considerations.

After the oil-price rises of the mid 1970s and the greatly expanded volume of funds in the Saudi Arabian financial system, pressure came from the foreign-owned banks to extend their branch networks, partly to serve the financial needs of the expatriate community and also to finance imports from their countries of origin. The government was reluctant to permit the expansion of foreign banks, one reason beings its concern about criticism from religious leaders on the issue of interest based institutions having an ever more visible presence in the heartland of Islam. The government's solution in 1976 was to pass the Bank Saudi-ization Act stipulating that the foreign banks had to incorporate within the kingdom and offer 60 per cent of their shares to local citizens.[17] Hence the First National City Bank became the Saudi American Bank, the British Bank of the Middle East the Saudi British Bank and the Banque de l'Indochine the Saudi French Bank.

Unlike the former foreign banks, the Saudi-ized institutions were allowed to extend their branch networks. As competition for deposits grew, savings accounts were introduced which paid a percentage return, although this was not described as interest. Savings accounts only accounted for less than 10 per cent of total deposits in 1978,[18] but by 1990 the proportion had increased to over half.[19] As a result, despite the nominal application of the shariah law, there was in practice little difference between the way the kingdom's banks operated and the methods employed by conventional Western ones. However, ownership was more concentrated, with for example, over 30 per cent of the shares in Al-Bank Al-Saudi Al-Hollandi being owned by three princes.[20]

Coexistence of conventional and Islamic finance

The government's own financial difficulties with declining oil revenues also resulted in a move away from Islamic finance and encouraged the emergence of conventional financing instruments. SAMA issued government development bonds in 1988 on behalf of the Ministry of Finance and National Economy. The return on these was theoretically linked to the profits on unspecified investment projects, but in practice directly linked to the returns on US treasury bonds, with a 0.2 per cent premium on two-year issues and a 0.5 per cent premium for longer issues. In November 1991 SAMA issued treasury bills with maturities running up to one year, which effectively paid interest, even though the term was not used because of Islamic sensitivities.[21] This westernisation of the Saudi financial system was far from what Ibn Saud would have envisaged or approved. The only real concession to Islamic finance by SAMA was to employ Umer Chapra, the well-known Islamic economist, as its financial advisor. In reality he spent most of his time on academic writing, and was rarely asked for practical advice.

The banking sector and financial markets 61

SAMA's attitude to Islamic finance was typified by the difficulties experienced by Al-Rajhi, the kingdom's largest money-exchange dealing and remittance transfer institution, in obtaining a banking licence. In 1983 Al-Rajhi sought a licence to become the kingdom's first designated Islamic bank as it wanted to diversify into accepting deposits and undertaking financing. The exchange and remittance businesses involved charging fees rather than interest, and the Al-Rajhis, being a devout family, wanted the new bank to avoid *riba* transactions. However, it was realised in SAMA that if Al-Rajhi was to be given a licence and designated an Islamic bank, this would imply that the other financial institutions were non-Islamic. SAMA, therefore, refused the application, but eventually in 1988, and after much lobbying, granted a licence on condition that Al-Rajhi refrained from using 'Islamic' in its title.[22]

Subsequently, the Al-Rajhi Banking and Investment Corporation became the world's largest Islamic commercial organisation with assets worth over 10 billion dollars. By 2000 it had become the most profitable bank in Saudi Arabia, with 363 branches, 457 cash dispenser machines, the largest branch network in the kingdom and 2,283 electronic point-of-sale facilities in retail establishments. However, within the country it is frequently alleged high profits reflect the lack of returns being paid to depositors, the implication being that devout Muslims wishing to avoid receiving *riba* are simply being exploited while Al-Rajhi makes a profit from financing. It is still not allowed to stress its Islamic character in its promotional material, although it has become increasingly involved with government. In 1999 it completed a 1.5 billion dollar contract for the finance and construction of 400 schools from the Ministry of Education and the General Presidency for Female Education, and in the same year it financed the Al-Shuaibaa electricity project in the Western Region for a similar amount.[23] The government's need for private finance, privatisation and public–private partnerships open up new possibilities for institutions such as Al-Rajhi, and it is possible to envisage a creeping Islamisation of government finance in Saudi Arabia even though there has been no actual policy decision by the state.

It is paradoxical that, although SAMA has a very cautious attitude towards the subject of Islamic finance within the kingdom, the Saudi Arabian government and some of the leading local businessmen have been keen to promote this type of financing elsewhere in the Islamic world. Prince Mohammed Bin Faisal was not allowed to open a banking network in his home country but proceeded to fund one internationally bearing his name that included the Faisal Islamic Banks of Egypt and the Sudan and Dar al-Maal al-Islami in Geneva, an institution with assets exceeding 3.5 billion dollars.[24] Similarly, Sheikh Saleh Kamel, founder of the Dallah Al-Baraka group, established banks and investment companies internationally, but these are not represented in Saudi Arabia, even though this is where the finance for all these ventures originates.[25]

The main Saudi Arabian government contribution to Islamic finance had been its sponsorship of the Islamic Development Bank (IDB). An agreement was reached by the finance ministers of the Organisation of the Islamic Conference in December 1973 to establish the Islamic Development Bank, which

62   Rodney Wilson

subsequently began operations in Jeddah two years later. By 2000 the paid-up capital of the IDB was almost 8 billion dollars, and it had approved trade-financing arrangements worth over 15 billion dollars and project finance valued at more than 6.5 billion, as well as 340 technical assistance operations.[26]

The IDB does not finance projects in Saudi Arabia, but the kingdom has benefited indirectly as almost one-third of the trade financing by the IDB has been for oil imports, with one of the original aims of the new institution being to assist poorer Muslim countries without oil resources to pay for their essential imports, especially since the oil-price rises of 1973–1974. In recent years trade financing has involved a diverse range of commodities including industrial intermediate goods (3.2 billion dollars), vegetable oil (900 million dollars), refined petroleum products (769 million dollars), fertilisers, phosphoric acid and potash (465 million dollars), rice and wheat (459 million dollars) and cotton (367 million dollars). All these figures refer to cumulative financing during the period 1975–1999. Project finance has become increasingly important for the IDB of late, with much of the funding provided through leasing (*ijara*), hire purchase (*ijara wa-iqtina*) and advance purchase financing (*istisna*). Almost one-third of project finance has been for public utilities such as power generation plants, electricity transmission, and water treatment and distribution facilities, with over 1.5 billion dollars being used in this way between 1995 and 1999. Social projects, including schools and hospitals, account for a further quarter of the total, with around 1.2 billion dollars disbursed between 1995 and 1999. Other project funding over the same period was for transport and communications (one billion dollars), industry (850 million dollars) and agriculture (800 million dollars).

Competition for bank deposits and lending

In Saudi Arabia most deposits are placed in current accounts that earn no return, and in some banks – notably the Al-Rajhi Banking and Investment Corporation – this proportion is much higher at over 80 per cent.[27] Competition for deposits seems to be less a matter of paying returns higher than other banks, than of projecting an image that reassures depositors about the safety of their assets and providing a range of useful services. Most clients use banks because they have to, rather than because they want: the government and most major public and private companies pay their employees' salaries directly into bank accounts. Thus for banks it is less a matter of enticing customers to use them than of ensuring they gain a share of a captive market.

Returns on savings and investment accounts are not emphasised in promotional literature or advertising, partly because of Islamic sensitivities concerning interest returns on the part of a significant part of the population. The proportion of funds placed in Saudi-riyal-denominated demand deposits actually increased over the 1996–2001 period from 40 to 45 per cent, while the proportion of time and savings accounts denominated in local currency stagnated at around one-third of the total.[28] Over 44 per cent of time and

The banking sector and financial markets 63

savings deposits are accounted for by official entities, generally state sector companies, as individuals and small businesses are more reluctant to deal in interest.[29] A significant proportion of deposits in the Saudi Arabian banking system are held in foreign currencies, usually dollars. These deposits amounted to one-quarter of the total in 1996, but by 2001 had declined to one fifth.[30] Companies accounted for most of them, which are maintained for payments purposes. Private individuals also hold some deposits denominated in dollars, both for foreign investment purposes and to finance travel abroad.

Where foreign currency deposits are in the form of savings or time deposits, lower returns are paid than on riyal deposits. This reflects the higher inter bank interest rates on riyals even though the riyal–dollar parity is fixed, as there is always a perceived risk of devaluation or depreciation. SAMA monitors and reports on inter-bank interest rates on Gulf currency deposits, including riyal deposits,[31] which demonstrates how far its stance on conventional banking instruments has evolved. Interest is not used for monetary policy purposes; instead, a fixed premium is maintained over dollar rates to maintain the exchange-rate parity.

Most Saudi Arabian banks are focused on retail business, which accounts for over half of total bank profits and, in the case of Al-Rajhi, almost all of its profits. The Saudi American Bank, the Saudi Dutch Bank and – not surprisingly – the Saudi Arabian Investment Bank derive most of their profits from corporate and investment banking.[32] Retail services include the provision of personal loans, with financing for cars and equipment, including household appliances, accounting for over one third of consumer credit by 2001. Over 10 per cent of consumer credit was for housing as there is a ten-year waiting list for subsidised housing loans from the state-owned Real Estate Development Fund. Almost 9 billion dollars in consumer credit was outstanding to Saudi Arabian banks by June 2001, of which 548 million represented very short-term credit card debt.[33]

Much Saudi Arabian bank funding is of government debt, which amounted by September 2001 to almost thirty-three billion dollars, of which over 90 per cent was accounted for by government bonds and the remainder by bills and credit to public-sector enterprises.[34] This exceeded the previous April 1999 peak, as the government debt built up once again with the decline in oil prices. Holding such a large quantity of government securities reduces the banks' ability to lend to the private sector: a process known as 'crowding out'. It also results in bankers having less need to manage commercial risk, reducing their role largely to the administrative one of government-debt funding. The extent of lending to government varies widely between banks, with Al-Rajhi, as an Islamic institution, being exempted from holding government bonds or bills. The part-foreign-owned joint-venture banks do not seem to be required to hold so much government debt, which results in the main burden falling on the National Commercial and Riyadh Banks, both of which are part-government-owned.

The relative size and performance of the banks in Saudi Arabia is shown in Table 5.1. The Al-Rahji Banking and Investment Corporation has the largest branch network and the highest return on assets but is fourth in terms of the size

64 Rodney Wilson

Table 5.1 Saudi Arabia commercial bank size and profitability, 2001

Bank	Branches	Assets $ billion	Net income $ million*	Return on assets %
Al-Rajhi	380	13.9	338	2.4
National Commercial	245	25.7	461	1.9
Riyadh	193	17.6	268	1.5
Arab National	114	9.7	97	1.0
Saudi British	71	11.4	170	1.5
Saudi American	63	20.4	448	2.2
Saudi French	56	11.1	167	1.5
Saudi Holland	37	6.5	99	1.5
Al-Jazira	13	1.4	11	0.8
Saudi Investment	13	4.0	65	1.6

Sources: Branch numbers: Saudi Arabian Monetary Agency, *Monthly Statistical Bulletin,* September 2001, p. 38. Assets, net income and return on assets excluding National Commercial Bank: National Commercial Bank, *Market Review and Outlook,* November 2, 2001, pp. 9–16. National Commercial Bank financial data: National Commercial Bank *Press Release,* November 10, 2001.

Note: * January–September 2001.

of its assets. The National Commercial Bank is by far the largest in terms of assets, with the largest net income – which indicates profitability – and the second largest branch network. The Saudi American Bank has been by far the most successful of the joint-venture banks, with its assets exceeding those of the Riyadh Bank and its net income the second highest in the kingdom.

Despite its size the National Commercial Bank was privately owned, largely by the Bin Mahfouz family who increased their majority stake over the decades from the 1950s onwards, to some extent at the expense of the Kaki family, the minority shareholders. Although Salim Bin Mahfouz had the confidence of King Saud and later of King Faisal, he gradually handed over control of the bank to his son Khalid, who assumed full charge in 1988.[35] Khalid became involved with the Bank of Credit and Commerce International, the institution closed for fraud and money laundering in 1991. He survived this crisis, even though the National Commercial Bank was obliged to write off significant amounts of bad debt, and failed to issue accounts for 1990 and 1991.[36] By 1997, however, the Saudi police and intelligence services had become suspicious of his involvement with dubious religious charities, and Islamic militants – including his brother-in-law, Osama bin Laden.[37] He was stripped of his Saudi Arabian citizenship while abroad. Nevertheless, he had already acquired Irish citizenship in 1990, under a dubious deal involving the sale of passports under former prime minister Charles Haughey that is being investigated by the Moriarty Tribunal[38] and the Flood Enquiry.[39]

In 1997 SAMA stepped in to urge major changes in the management and organisation of the National Commercial Bank. It became a joint stock company, and a new board of directors was appointed with Sheikh Abdullah Salim

The banking sector and financial markets 65

Bahamdan as chairman and managing director.[40] He had previously served with the bank but was regarded as highly professional, as was Abdulhadi A. Shayif, the new general manager. The Bin Mahfouz family was no longer represented on the board of directors. As new capital was needed, in 1999 the public investment fund took a 50 per cent stake in the bank, making it a semi-state-owned entity. Subsequently, 10 per cent of the shares were sold to the General Organisation for Social Insurance, another government-owned institution. The intention is to float the National Commercial Bank on the stock market once it has achieved several successful years of profitability. By 2001 the chairman was able to report a significant improvement in performance, although no date was fixed for its flotation.[41]

Corporate finance and investment banking

After lending to the government and consumers, the total outstanding amount advanced by Saudi Arabia's banks to private-sector businesses amounted in September 2001 to 40 billion dollars.[42] Most of this consisted of loans, advances and overdrafts, as bank holdings of corporate securities were minimal. Around 14 per cent of total lending was to manufacturing, 10 per cent to construction and the highest classified amount of 23 per cent to commerce, much of which was import financing. In 2001 the commercial banks settled letters of credit and bills received for import finance worth 2.4 billion dollars,[43] though in addition to this there is medium-term stock financing.

Banks in Saudi Arabia have largely concentrated on retail activity rather than investment banking, even though there are no regulatory or legislative restrictions on the undertaking of investment banking business.[44] This largely reflects market demand, as with the government itself playing such a dominant role in the economy the extent of private corporate activity has been limited. Traditional investment banking activity has involved mergers and acquisitions, initial public offerings (IPOs) of shares, and management of rights and corporate bonds issues, but the demand for this type of business in Saudi Arabia was extremely limited until the mid-1990s, chiefly because the local capital market was underdeveloped and most businesses were family-owned and controlled, with mergers and takeovers unknown.

The Saudi American Bank is the kingdom's leading institution in terms of investment-banking activity and capability. Although it is also a personal and retail bank, corporate finance has been significant from its inception in 1980 as it had the resources and expertise of Citibank, its part owner, to draw upon. The early emphasis was on building a relationship management team to work with corporate clients, both in the state and private sector. Team members acquired considerable knowledge of their clients business and specialisation in particular sectors was encouraged enabling the bank to play a proactive role in financial planning rather than being simply reactive.

In 1997, in anticipation of the economic reforms involving new investment laws and the reduction in protective tariffs necessary for accession to the World

66 Rodney Wilson

Trade Organisation, the Saudi American Bank adopted a new business model to serve its corporate clients. This involved the development of new banking products and the retraining of staff in investment services. A new corporate finance and equity advisory business was established comprising three divisions.[45] The merchant banking division handles mergers and acquisitions, IPOs and private equity placements. The structured finance division deals with securitisations and real-estate transactions, and is able to restructure balance sheets for both corporate and public-sector entities. The project finance division arranges finance for infrastructure projects and participates in syndicated finance for gas and petrochemical projects.

The Saudi American Bank's dominance of the kingdom's corporate market is illustrated in Table 5.2. The National Commercial Bank is excluded from the table as it is not a listed company and provides less detailed financial information, but it is probably the third largest provider of corporate funding after the Saudi American and Riyadh Banks. Unlike the other joint-venture banks, the Saudi American holds no government bonds, which accounts for much of the treasury assets listed in the table; hence it is able to focus more on the private business sector. This privileged position may be due to the influence of the Saudi American Bank's chairman, Abdulaziz bin Hamad Algosaibi, a leading businessman in the kingdom, and the ownership shares held by Princes Fahd bin Salman, Bandar and Turki as well as by three other more minor royals, each reputed to be worth at last three dollars.[46]

In 1976 the specialist Saudi Investment Bank – as its name implies – was established in to provide corporate banking services for the kingdom.[47] It is a much smaller institution than the Saudi American Bank, with assets of 3.7 billion dollars in 2002 compared with the latter's 21.6 billion. Its limited size has prevented it from playing a major role as an investment bank as envisaged by two of its international shareholders, JP Morgan (now Chase Manhattan International Finance), which holds a 7.5 per cent stake, and the Industrial Bank of Japan, with 2.5 per cent stake. Thought it sees its core strengths as being client relationships, risk management and productivity, in reality, despite its

Table 5.2 Saudi Arabia listed commercial bank assets, $ billion, 2001

Bank	Retail	Corporate	Treasury
Al-Rajhi	50,893	1,329	0
Riyadh	7,568	15,113	42,670
Arab National	7,912	8,857	19,610
Saudi British	4,649	9,212	24,933
Saudi American	30,702	45,724	0
Saudi French	1,918	16,677	22,659
Saudi Holland	2,608	9,222	12,252
Al-Jazira	1,371	2,401	1,353
Saudi Investment	3,753	11,129	0

Source: National Commercial Bank, *Market Review and Outlook,* November 2, 2001, p. 13.

The banking sector and financial markets 67

remit to deal with business as opposed to merely personal retail clients, it has drifted towards the latter because of a lack of focus and critical mass.

The Saudi Investment Bank has, therefore, repositioned itself in the market, thus enabling it to become a major player in a few key areas by undertaking three initiatives.[48] First, it entered a fifty–fifty joint venture arrangement with American Express to establish a new company with exclusive rights to promote and operate the American Express card business in the kingdom. The aim is to ensure the card is used more widely for corporate purchasing. Second, the bank entered a joint venture with the Japan-based Orix Leasing Group and the International Finance Corporation – a World Bank subsidiary – to found the Saudi Orix Leasing Corporation, the kingdom's first leasing company. The Saudi Investment Bank holds a 28 per cent stake in the new venture. Third, as the bank has only a limited branch network of seven branches in Riyadh and six elsewhere in the kingdom, it decided to focus on Internet banking through the provision of a site for American Express card applications and processing, investment and foreign-exchange dealing.

The stock market

Equity investments can contribute to economic development by the provision of risk capital. Stock prices are a measure of the financial health of quoted companies, and accountability to shareholders through a well-regulated market can provide a financial discipline for company managers. A company focus on adding shareholder value in the long term can improve efficiency and ensure companies remain competitive. There can, of course, be short-term conflicts between shareholders and other stakeholders in any company, notably employees. In the longer term, however, in a market system without government intervention, employment cannot be maintained and wages paid unless a business is perceived as viable by its shareholders.

Saudi Arabia has the largest stock market in the Middle East and the second largest in the Islamic world after that of Malaysia. The market's capitalisation was over 67.8 billion dollars by the end of 2000, as Table 5.3 shows, more than double the value in the early 1990s.[49] There are seventy-five quoted companies, most of which are substantial in size, averaging over 900 million dollars in 2000, much larger than in most other emerging markets and providing greater depth. The ratio of market capitalisation to GDP is around 40 per cent, indicating that the market still needs to grow considerably if it is to reach the position of countries such as Malaysia, where market capitalisation is over 80 per cent of GDP.[50]

The growth of the stock market has been hampered both by the government itself, which crowded out the private sector, and the 'family business' mentality which prevails in the kingdom.[51] Government finance was made available from the 1970s onwards for new manufacturing ventures through the Saudi Industrial Development at zero interest provided those seeking that finance were able to obtain counterpart bank funding for the other half of their borrowings.

68   Rodney Wilson

Table 5.3 Arab stock market indicators, 2000

	Market capitalisation $ billion	Number of listed companies	Average company size $ million	Share market depth* %	Share turnover** %
Saudi Arabia	67.8	75	905.3	39.2	25.6
Egypt	30.8	1,071	28.8	33.1	38.3
Kuwait	19.8	86	230.8	49.3	21.2
Morocco	10.9	54	201.4	31.7	11.1
Bahrain	6.6	41	161.6	90.7	3.7
Jordan	4.9	163	30.3	59.6	8.2
Oman	3.5	131	26.9	17.9	15.7
Tunisia	2.8	44	63.8	14.0	24.4
Lebanon	1.6	13	121.7	9.3	7.5

Source: Saudi Arabian Monetary Agency, *Thirty Seventh Annual Report,* 2001, op. cit., p. 111.

Notes: * Market capitalisation/GDP.
       ** Value of shares traded/market capitalisation.

This encouraged a reliance on debt financing as opposed to equity. By the time of the Fourth Plan, in operation from 1985 to 1990, efforts were being made to correct this bias, not least because the Saudi Industrial Development Fund had relatively less money to disburse with the decline in oil prices. The Fifth Plan, covering the period 1990–1995, stressed the importance of developing the local equity market to ensure that Saudi Arabian investors did not simply put their funds in Western markets, local land and real estate speculation and gold.[52]

The Saudi Arabian Basic Industries Corporation (SABIC) is the largest quoted company in the market, but banks are the dominant share group; although the largest bank, the National Commercial, is still not a quoted company. As Table 5.4 shows, it is the bank shares that have experienced the greatest capital gains during the 1990s, whereas shares in service companies – mainly

Table 5.4 Share price indices by sector

Year	1990	1995	2000	2001
Banking	1,900.93	3,278.40	7,229.53	7,326.53
Industry	1,428.13	2,497.80	3,514.01	3,218.86
Cement	947.22	1,371.60	1,735.29	2,408.99
Services	574.76	682.20	568.65	634.31
Electricity	539.52	425.60	705.05	756.03
Agriculture	1,011.05	689.40	457.50	447.26
Overall	979.77	1,367.60	2,258.29	2,311.44

Sources: Saudi Arabian Monetary Agency, *Thirty Seventh Annual Report, 2001,* op. cit., p. 335; Saudi Arabian Monetary Agency, *Monthly Statistical Bulletin,* September 2001, op. cit. p. 52.

Note: 1985=1000.

The banking sector and financial markets 69

distributors, agricultural companies and the electrical utilities – have languished below their 1985 levels. Industrial shares, notably those in SABIC and the Arab Fertiliser Company, have done better, and overall capital gains have kept pace with those on the world's leading stock markets.

Overall share performance in 2001 was better than in Western markets, which demonstrates to Saudi Arabian investors that at least during some periods it would be more profitable to deploy their funds at home rather than abroad. As Saudi Arabian private citizens have funds worth 700 billion dollars invested in Western markets – over ten times the capitalisation of the local market – the repatriation of even a small portion of these funds would drive up share prices in the kingdom.[53] Where investors place their funds depends on country-risk perceptions as well as anticipated returns. In Saudi Arabia price-to-earnings ratios are similar to those in Western markets, but it is largely aversion to risk that causes capital flight.

From a development perspective the issue of capital flight is a complex one. Controls on capital movements or coercion to bring funds back into the kingdom would be unlikely to be effective, and even if this occurred and repatriated funds were channelled into the local market the result would simply be a temporary and unsustainable boom in stock prices. Furthermore the funds invested abroad yield a significant income to those who own them, and in so far as this income is repatriated to cover living expenses in the kingdom, there are potential benefits for the local economy and even for employment, although most of these may be felt by expatriate workers rather than by local citizens.

One way of encouraging more local investment is by increasing confidence in the workings of the local stock market itself through sound regulation, transparency in corporate reporting and efficient, low-cost brokerage. Mindful of the problems that affected the unofficial Kuwait stock exchange, the Souk al-Manakh, which crashed when a speculative bubble burst in 1982,[54] dealings in the Saudi stock market have been closely monitored and controlled from its inception in 1983.[55] SAMA has supervised all share trading transactions since 1984, and in 1990 an electronic share information system was introduced which was maintained by SAMA and linked to the central trading units of the local commercial banks. The Ministry of Commerce undertakes the regulation of companies. It licences joint stock companies and gives permission for primary share offerings. Companies are required to submit their annual audited accounts to the Ministry, although this is more a matter of form for companies that are already quoted or those private firms not intending to seek a stock-market listing.

There was, however, concern about the relatively high costs of share trading, company disclosure and the division of regulatory responsibilities between the SAMA and the Ministry of Commerce. In 2001, to increase the efficiency of transactions, a new real-time trading network, the *Tadawul* system, was introduced which provides much greater capacity for electronic trading. At present the domestic Saudi Arabian banks, together with the Riyadh office of the Gulf International Bank, are the only licensed brokers. Nevertheless, the situation is changing under the Capital Markets Law of 2002 that provides for

70 *Rodney Wilson*

the registration of specialist brokerage houses. This will permit greater competition and lower transaction costs, though initially it is expected that the major local banks will establish broking subsidiaries to service their existing clients.

The Supreme Economic Council under Prince Abdullah reviewed the Capital Markets Law in 2002. It provides for a Capital Markets Authority that will take over regulatory responsibilities from SAMA and the Ministry of Commerce. Its functions will be similar to those of the United States Securities Exchange Commission, although the exact model adopted will more closely resemble the Malaysian Securities Commission which regulates the largest stock market in the Muslim world. Whether its remit will extend to bonds, as in Malaysia, is debatable, with shariah scholars in Saudi Arabia divided on the acceptability of the so-called Islamic bonds issued in Kuala Lumpur which provide an income stream unrelated to market interest rates at the time of issue.

Managed funds

Saudi Arabia has the largest mutual funds industry in the Middle East and Islamic world. The funds are offered by the kingdom's chief commercial banks to their existing clients, usually being cross-sold to depositors who are encouraged to take on equity exposure. The Islamic stress on participatory finance and the avoidance of *riba* or interest has caused those with savings to be more predisposed towards equity financing, and the higher potential returns usually gained over the medium to longer term for those taking some risks with their capital have also proved attractive. The National Commercial Bank pioneered mutual funds in the kingdom, offering the open-ended Al-Ahli Short Term Dollar Fund in 1979.[56] This fund, however, invests largely in time deposits with United States banks, dollar-denominated commercial paper and certificates of deposit thus its income is interest-derived and the only exposure is to default risk.[57]

The success of the banks in marketing mutual funds is illustrated in Table 5.5: by 2001 almost 175,000 Saudi Arabian residents had invested in this way. Until recently most of the funds invested abroad, mainly in equities in the United States, but the expansion and favourable performance of the local stock market has encouraged more domestic investment since 2000, a trend that has become

Table 5.5 Managed fund growth

Year	1992	1995	1998	2001
Number of funds	52	71	114	139
Number of subscribers	33,162	33,051	70,216	174,639
Foreign assets, $ billion	1.9	1.9	3.7	5.2
Domestic assets, $ billion	1.4	1.5	2.8	6.9

Sources: Saudi Arabian Monetary Agency, *Thirty Seventh Annual Report, 2001,* op. cit., p. 314; Saudi Arabian Monetary Agency *Quarterly Statistical Bulletin*, third Quarter 2001, p. 95.

The banking sector and financial markets 71

more pronounced with the large fall in stock prices quoted on the NASDEQ and the New York Stock Exchange, exacerbated by the events of September 11, 2001. By 2001 there were eleven equity funds investing wholly in Saudi Arabia, the largest of which was the Al-Ahli Saudi Equity Fund, first offered by the National Commercial Bank in 1992. Around 60 per cent of its assets are accounted for by bank stock, with industrial stock being worth one-fifth of the portfolio.[58]

The National Commercial Bank accounts for over half of the mutual fund market in Saudi Arabia – a position it has strived to hold on to – but the other major banks are striving to catch up: notably the Al-Rajhi Banking and Investment Corporation, which is the second largest fund provider, although its share of the market is only 11 per cent.[59] The latter, as an Islamic bank, solely offers funds that are acceptable in accordance with the shariah law. Investments are screened for compliance, companies involved in alcohol or pork production or distribution being excluded, as are conventional banks dealing in interest. The Al-Rajhi Local Share Fund has been the most successful domestic Islamic fund since its launch in 1992, which prompted the National Commercial bank six years later to launch the Al-Ahli Saudi Trading Equity Fund, also screened for shariah compliance. This fund cannot invest in shares in conventional banks, but ironically over 15 per cent of its portfolio is accounted for by investment in its banking rival, the Al-Rajhi Corporation.

Twenty-six Islamic funds were being offered in Saudi Arabia at the end of 2001 of which six, including the largest, were global ones mainly investing in the West.[60] There was one exclusively North American fund, the Al-Ahli US Trading Equity offered by the National Commercial Bank, and an exclusively European one, the Al-Ahli European Trading Equity, also offered by the National Commercial Bank. Three Asian Islamic funds are marketed to Saudi Arabian investors, their main focus being on Japan – and Hong Kong – quoted shares. Three so-called 'balanced' Islamic funds are offered, promising investors both income and capital growth, but these are also focused on the West as are the three small capital and technology funds. This leaves only seven Saudi Islamic funds concentrating on emerging markets, of which five invest within the kingdom. It is perhaps ironic that Islamic funds are more exposed in Western markets than conventional ones, although this can largely be explained by the predominance of shares in conventional banks in emerging markets that are excluded from shariah compliant portfolios because such banks deal in *riba*.[61]

Although much of the investment in Saudi Arabia goes abroad, there are important reasons – apart from patriotism – why many investors choose to invest at least some of their funds domestically. If investors have future-anticipated liabilities in riyals, then they will also want to have assets denominated in local currency. The banks or fund promoters also have an advantage in their local markets, as they are able to manage the funds themselves, given their knowledge of their own market, rather than relying on international banks or fund management groups.[62] Leading local Islamic funds in Saudi Arabia include the Al-Rajhi Local Share Fund, the Al-Ahli Saudi Riyal Trading Fund with assets exceeding 10.74 billion Saudi Riyals (2.86 billion dollars), Al-Ahli Saudi

72   *Rodney Wilson*

Trading Equity Fund marketed by the National Commercial Bank,[63] the Riyadh Equity Fund marketed and managed by the Riyadh Bank and the Al-Arabi Saudi Company Shares marketed by the Arab National Bank.

Non-interest Islamic funds accounted for 43.2 per cent of all mutual fund investment in Saudi Arabia by March 2001, and these funds are increasing rapidly in importance and may account for over half of the total by 2003.[64] As total mutual fund investment in March 2001 was 10.7 billion dollars, this meant Islamic funds were worth 4.62 billion dollars. Within the National Commercial Bank the trend towards Islamic funds is especially marked, with a 57 per cent increase in assets managed in accordance with shariah law in 2001 while assets in conventional funds fell by 32 per cent over the same period. Islamic mutual funds in the National Commercial Bank alone amounted to 4.73 billion dollars by the end of 2001: more than the total for all banks in the kingdom the preceding March. Islamic funds account for three-quarters of all National Commercial Bank mutual funds.

In the case of the National Commercial Bank funds, the Al-Ahli Saudi Riyal Trading Fund, established in 1995, aims at capital preservation while producing regular income based on the mark-up from *murabaha* transactions, largely in metals and soft commodities, with an annual fee of only 0.75 per cent and a modest minimum investment of 10,000 Saudi riyals (2,667 dollars). Returns are paid annually directly into investor's bank accounts. Although non-interest based, returns fell from 4.81 per cent in April 2001 to 3.96 per cent in June, and by February 2002 were down to under 3.5 per cent year on year.[65] For those with larger amounts to invest the Al-Ahli Saudi Riyal *Murabaha* Fund, established in 2000, has a lower annual management fee of 0.5 per cent and the advantage of monthly income payments. However, the minimum investment is 250,000 riyals (66,667 dollars) and the minimum amount for subsequent transactions and redemptions 50,000 riyals (13,333 dollars).[66] Returns are marginally higher than those in the Al-Ahli Saudi Riyal Trading Fund.

The objective of the Al-Ahli Saudi Trading Equity Fund is to produce capital growth through investment in Saudi-listed stock – mostly in industrial and cement production – with this actively managed fund applying a higher management charge of 1.75 per cent annually, but with a relatively modest minimum investment of 5,000 riyals (1,333 dollars). The Al-Ahli Saudi Trading Equity Fund has over 30 million riyals (8 million dollars) under management, making it the largest local equity fund in the kingdom, although its size is modest compared to that of Islamic global funds. It has produced a return of 22 per cent since its inception in 1998, and a return of 23.4 per cent for 2001, a remarkable performance given the impact of the events of September 11, 2001.

This performance can be compared with that of the much larger Al-Ahli Global Trading Equity Fund, the largest Islamic equity fund in the world, with over 640 million dollars under management. The value of units in the fund has doubled since inception in January 1995, although there was a loss of 20.9 per cent in 2000 and a marginally smaller loss in capital values in 2001. The last profitable year was 1999 when the units increased in value by 27.3 per cent.[67]

The banking sector and financial markets 73

In Saudi Arabia, users of Islamic finance are usually from the richer sections of society, including members of the royal family, but the stress is more on legal compliance rather than social purpose. There is little difference between the ways conventional and Islamic finance are employed in the kingdom. Mutual funds could make a significant contribution to development finance, and the encouragement of such investments is preferable to speculation in land for capital gains. However, a disproportionate amount of the funding remains outside the kingdom, in Western markets, and much of that within the kingdom is deployed in short-term trading funds, usually simply financing imports as opposed to longer-term equity investment in utilities or manufacturing.

Finance and development

Saudi Arabia has a sophisticated financial system which serves the retail market well but is less geared to the needs of business except with respect to import finance, foreign exchange, money transfers and treasury services. As already indicated, however, there is only a limited investment banking capability, partly reflecting the absence of merger and takeover activity in the kingdom and the very limited number of initial public offerings and rights issues on the local stock exchange. During the oil-revenue boom of the 1970s the government crowded out the commercial banks' finance by providing subsidised credit through state agencies such as the Saudi Industrial Development Fund and the Real Estate Bank, but in recent years the main problem has been the need for the commercial banks to fund government debt, thus reducing their capacity to lend to the private sector.

Yet finance is arguably not the main constraint on development; rather it is the government itself. Banks and the local equity market could provide more project finance for the expansion of utilities and even government services if privatisation was allowed to proceed at a faster rate. In 2000 the private sector still accounted for only 32 per cent of total GDP and around 58 per cent of non-oil GDP.[68] Rather than the government struggling to finance the expansion of the electricity supply and desalinated water, this could be left to the private sector while the state concentrated on the funding of education, health and increasing the effectiveness and capability of the armed services. Investment in relation to GDP has been falling in most years since the early 1980s, a trend that can only be reversed by faster economic restructuring.

Saudi Arabia's banks are technologically advanced, with sound information technology systems, Internet banking services, cash dispensers and point-of-sale-card acceptance throughout the kingdom and abroad.[69] They provide a good level of retail service for their clients and have built up strong brand and customer loyalty.[70] Yet it would be a mistake to be complacent about the Saudi Arabian banking system and the workings of financial markets, as despite its modernity by Middle Eastern standards there are serious shortcomings. One issue is the limited size of the major banks, which lack the resources and institutional capacity to fund their own large-scale projects in petrochemicals, oil

74 *Rodney Wilson*

and gas. Recourse has to be made to major multinational banks for such financing, although the joint-venture partners of the Saudi-ised banks, which already have a substantial stake in the kingdom, are very willing to be involved.

In order to provide a substantial local investment banking capability one possibility would be to merge the National Commercial Bank with the Riyadh Bank, in which the Saudi Arabian government also owns a stake, in this case 29 per cent. This would create by far the largest bank in the Middle East and be a real force on the international banking scene.[71] There is no Arab bank in the global largest one hundred banks by assets, profits or even employment, yet size matters in the banking industry as much as in manufacturing to benefit from economies of scale. Ultimately the local market for financial services in Saudi Arabia will be opened up to external competition, which means domestic banks may have to merge to survive.[72]

The family-business culture that permeates much of Saudi Arabian society results in an unwillingness to expand rapidly through both external debt and equity financing. There are over 10,000 private companies registered in Saudi Arabia,[73] including 1044 owned by members of the royal family,[74] but only 75 listed companies quoted on the stock exchange at the end of 2000. There is a reluctance to seek stock market listings, as by bringing in outsiders families lose control of businesses they have built up with future generations in mind. There is also natural caution about encumbering family businesses with bank debts, the preference being to seek capital injections from family members if these have the resources available. Such prudence is to be commended, but it inhibits small and medium-sized firms from increasing their capacity and thus from creating the additional employment the kingdom so badly needs.

6 International trade and GCC economic relations

Saudi Arabia is the largest exporter and importer in the Arab world, the second largest exporter in the Islamic world after Malaysia and its fifth largest importer after that country, Turkey, Indonesia and the UAE. In global terms the kingdom ranks as the twentieth largest exporting country, with exports worth over 68 billion dollars in 2001, and the thirty-ninth importer with imports worth just over 32 billion dollars in 2000 according to data from the World Trade Organisation.[1]

Despite its regional and global significance Saudi Arabia's share of trade has diminished since the 1980s, largely, though not exclusively, reflecting oil revenue trends. In 1980 the kingdom accounted for 5.36 per cent of global exports, but this had fallen to 1.11 per cent by 2001.[2] Similarly, Saudi Arabia's share of the global market for imports fell from 1.45 per cent in 1980 to 0.50 per cent by 2001.[3] At regional level the United Arab Emirates overtook Saudi Arabia in terms of imports in 1998, and since then the gap has widened, with the UAE imports worth approximately 36 billion dollars by 2001, almost 4 billion more than those of Saudi Arabia. Imports should not simply be regarded as an illustration of commercial success; indeed, they become a problem if there is a serious trade deficit. This is not the case with Saudi Arabia or its Gulf Co-operation Council (GCC) neighbours however; rather, it is indicative of relative development performance and, arguably, shortcomings in trade policy.

In contrast to the UAE and other GCC countries that opted for outward-orientated economic policies, Saudi Arabia, partly because of its larger economic size, has adopted, at least to some extent, an import-substitution policy. The benefits of this policy can be questioned in Saudi Arabia as they have been in some of the other large Arab countries, notably Egypt, Syria and Iraq, which have also experienced slow or even negative economic growth to which inward looking, nationalistic economic policies have arguably been a contributory factor. Rather than governments playing a restrictive role as in Saudi Arabia, a more effective approach might be to adopt policies that enable markets to function more effectively. The restrictive role has involved tariffs to protect industrial ventures catering for the local market, the enforcement of exclusive agency arrangements for imports and discriminatory government purchasing favouring local suppliers. An enabling approach might involve encouraging increased competition amongst local businesses to create cost and product

76   *Rodney Wilson*

advantage, and allowing foreign owned firms to enter the kingdom to exploit its mineral resources by adding value that can help exports.

In order to assess the kingdom's trade prospects it is helpful to identify the underlying economic rationale for its trading regime and its contribution to both social and individual welfare. Is trade merely about extending the consumer choices of Saudi Arabian families, or about widening development options for the possible benefit of the kingdom as a whole? Has the open-economy approach facilitated or retarded the efforts to achieve greater economic diversification? International trade also has implications for regional economic policy, notably the position of Jeddah and the Hejaz relative to Riyadh and the Najd. The internal dynamics of trade are often ignored, but in geographically large countries with distinctive regional characteristics such as Saudi Arabia, commerce affects regional balances.

Export and import trends since the late 1960s are analysed and the impact of export earnings instability on imports is assessed. The composition and sources of Saudi Arabian imports are examined, notably the changes in manufactured imports and the extent of the kingdom's dependence on imported foodstuffs. In most years Saudi Arabia has enjoyed a trade surplus, which has often been substantial, but the overall balance of payments position is frequently much less favourable once payments for services, remittances and capital flows have been taken into account.

The data analysis paves the way for the consideration of trade policy choices. Gulf and international trade policy issues are considered, especially Saudi Arabia's position as the largest economy in the GCC as this regional grouping has moved from being a free trade area to a customs union. The wider international context is also important, not least because the five other GCC states – though not Saudi Arabia – are members of the World Trade Organisation (WTO). The kingdom has aspired to joint the WTO since the organisation's inception and a joint working party to study the issues was first established in 1993. Progress in the negotiations has been painfully slow, however, and significant obstacles remain to the country's accession to the WTO. What are the causes of this lack of progress and what is the outlook for the kingdom's membership bid?

The economic rationale for Saudi Arabian trade

Economic theory can help explain the nature of international specialisation and exchange between countries as well as the direction of trade, or in other words why particular countries trade largely with particular partners. In terms of economic theory the composition of Saudi Arabia's trade could be categorised as a 'vent for a surplus', with international markets providing the outlet for the export of surplus oil in return for a diverse range of import supplies of manufactured products and foodstuffs not available locally.[4]

Saudi Arabia, with its large, low-cost oilfields, has a competitive advantage, but not an absolute advantage as defined by Adam Smith in the eighteenth

International trade and GCC economic relations 77

century or a comparative one as defined by David Ricardo in the early nineteenth. These concepts imply a form of specialisation brought about by a country's abandoning lines of output that it is less efficient at producing in favour of those types of production where it enjoys a greater relative efficiency.[5] In the case of Saudi Arabia there was no need to sacrifice non-oil production to concentrate on oil as there was no opportunity cost. Thus instead of a trade-off between oil and non-oil production – as theories of international trade based on specialisation imply – Saudi Arabia has experienced a positive relationship between the two. As the oil economy has flourished with increases in oil revenues the non-oil sector and imports have been buoyant, while during periods of falling oil revenues imports have been static or even in decline.

Production technology models of international trade such as those associated with Raymond Vernon[6] have at best limited relevance for Saudi Arabia, as although oil is by nature a high-technology industry the technological advantages are firm rather than country-specific, and Saudi ARAMCO and the Saudi Arabian Basic Industries Corporation (SABIC) have the financial resources and international partners to acquire the technology they need. Of greater potential relevance, at least for imports, are explanations of trade based on consumer preferences for differentiated products. Such models are intended to apply primarily to trade between developed countries and are sometimes referred to as country-similarity theories whereby countries trade primarily with others whose production structures and levels of development are similar to their own.[7]

In the case of Saudi Arabia the tastes and preferences of a significant proportion of consumers have been influenced through so-called international demonstration effects by the consumption habits of their counterparts in the industrialised world. Advertising and marketing have developed brand awareness, especially regarding clothing, vehicles and household equipment, with marked changes in consumer culture taking place over the last two decades, especially among the younger generations. Consumer preferences are increasingly expressed through brand rather than country preference, with price being less important than quality.

Apart from such items as defence equipment, most Saudi Arabian imports are consumer-determined, and even for industrial supplies the emphasis of purchasers is on the commercial value of the imports and not on political considerations such as the country of import origin. By contrast, in countries such as Egypt or Syria there was – and still remains – a much greater political input into import determination, with most imports being acquired by state sector companies and through government-to-government bilateral deals affecting procurement policy.

Strategic trade theory, which ascribes a role for government in export promotion, has arguably some relevance for Saudi Arabia. Oil exports could be analysed using game theory, with prisoners' dilemmas arising where there are too many oil producers exporting, each one spoiling international markets for its rivals as over-supply adversely affects prices. The original strategic trade model,

78   Rodney Wilson

as developed by Brander and Spencer,[8] could controversially be reinterpreted as applying to Saudi Arabia's petrochemical exports since the latter were the result of an industrial targeting policy.

A fuller explanation of Saudi Arabia's potential competitive advantage in industries such as petrochemicals can be provided using Michael Porter's diamond model.[9] The four determinants stressed by Porter are factor conditions, related and supporting industries, demand conditions and firm strategy, structure and rivalry. For petrochemicals the factor conditions include capital availability and an increasing pool of both local and foreign expertise on the industry. The related and supporting industries include oil and gas and externalities from existing petrochemical plants. The demand conditions refer to the local and international market for petrochemicals and the firm strategy, structure and rivalry related to the aims and organisation of SABIC and its position with respect to foreign competitors.

Regional implicational of international trade

Saudi Arabia's economy has been open since its inception, and with the development of the oil industry from the 1930s there was a pragmatic view of trading, with the revenues from oil exports used to finance imports, as there were no domestic supplies of most manufactured goods. Much of the economy of the Najd was largely subsistence-based before oil, but even there centres such as Hofuf in the eastern Al-Hasa region were significant for trade, as in this oasis the trade routes from the Ottoman territories to the north met those leading to the trading centres of the Gulf. In the Hejaz to the west Mecca, Medina and the port of Jeddah were important regional trading centres before the time of the Prophet, and with the advent of Islam and the consequent significance of the haj, trade and the pilgrimage traffic became interwoven.

Given that in Islam trade is viewed as a productive activity, it would seem appropriate that a kingdom whose ruler is designated custodian of the two holiest sites for Muslims should be heavily engaged in it. Even before the discovery of oil the merchants of the Hejaz made their livelihoods through trade, both during the years of the Ottoman Empire, and within the independent kingdom of the Hejaz from 1918 until 1932. The Hejaz has always flourished as part of a larger entity, however, and looked outwards rather than inwards; and from 1925 onwards the leading merchant families of Jeddah favoured a closer association with the ruler of the Najd, Abdul-Aziz ibn Saud, as this promised to boost the city's role as a trading centre. In 1932 the sultanate of the Najd was merged with the kingdom of the Hejaz to form the kingdom of Saudi Arabia with Jeddah as its commercial centre.

The discovery of oil in 1938 in the Eastern Province helped cement the kingdom together both economically and politically and resulted in a great expansion in Jeddah's role as the gateway by sea to the wider kingdom, and hence in its commercial activity. Although Riyadh was to become the political capital – and the largest city in the kingdom, with over four million inhabitants –

International trade and GCC economic relations 79

Jeddah's population has increased to three million, most of whom are involved in commerce rather than administration. It is in Jeddah that the private sector is most developed and where the great merchant families of the kingdom continue to be based. As privatisation gathers momentum and government patronage over economic activity becomes reduced, it is Jeddah, with its long trading tradition, which stands to gain most.[10]

Almost 95 per cent of Saudi Arabia's trade is transported by sea, with eight major commercial and industrial ports handling the trade.[11] Jeddah Islamic Port is by far the most important, accounting for around two-thirds of the goods entering the kingdom. The largest port in the Middle East and the major port on the Red Sea, it has much greater handling facilities than Aden, Port Sudan, Suez and Massawa in Eritrea combined. Its total capacity exceeds two million twenty-foot equivalent units (TEU), the usual measure of port size. In 2002 capacity was expanded by one-fifth, and the new north terminal has four berths with 1,000 metres of quayside and 900,000 square metres of land for container storage and handling. Jeddah Islamic Port handles 1.5 million containers per annum and has the facilities to dock and unload ten large container vessels simultaneously.

Although the Saudi Arabian government retains its ownership of the kingdom's ports and the Saudi Ports Authority maintains a supervisory role, the management of all the facilities, including those at Jeddah Islamic Port, has been handed over to private companies under twenty-year concessions, with the Gulf Stevedoring Company running the north terminal at Jeddah and the terminals at Damman, the kingdom's second largest port. A joint venture company owned by the Dubai Port Authority and the Saudi Maintenance Corporation manages the south terminal at Jeddah. This has resulted in a marked improvement in operational efficiency, with the tonnage handled per shift increasing by over 62 per cent over the 1998–2002 period largely as a result of new information technology systems for stock control and flow management. The ports in Jeddah and Damman have achieved world-class levels of efficiency, which has attracted ever more business.

Most of the goods entering through Saudi Arabia's ports, unlike Dubai, are destined for local consumption rather than for re-export. Re-exports were worth around 500 million dollars in 1999 and 2000, less than one per cent of total exports.[12] Jeddah played a major role historically in the trade of the Red Sea, but the volume of commerce between Asian and African ports is minimal compared to the volume and value of trans-Gulf trade, especially between Dubai and Iran. To a large extent this reflects the relative decline of the Sudanese economy, the loss of Ethiopian access to the Red Sea with Eritrean independence and the break-up of Somalia as feudal warlords took over control and the state dissolved. Nevertheless in 1999 a bonded and re-export zone was established at Jeddah Islamic Port which is managed under a twenty-year lease by the Saudi Trade and Export Development Company, its main function being to provide container services for breaking-bulk cargoes, warehousing, vehicle storage and the assembling and repackaging of goods.[13] The Saudi Trade and Export Development Company is majority-owned by four local merchant families.

No customs duties or demurrage is applied to goods stored in the zone, although these are applied when goods are distributed within the kingdom, as was the case during the initial phase of the project. A revival in neighbouring African economies is the main prerequisite for re-exports to take off.

In order to preserve regional balance part of the port area of Damman in Eastern Province has also been designated a bonded and re-export zone with the Saudi Development and Re-Export Services Company also awarded in 1999 a twenty-year lease to manage the facility.[14] In practice the scope for re-exports is more limited in Damman, as Dubai has a large share of the Iranian business, and there is little rationale to justify transit trade to other GCC destinations in the Gulf such as Kuwait. Jebel Ali, the main port for Dubai, also has the advantage of being a duty-free zone allowing the tariff-free entry of input supplies, which facilitates manufacturing, unlike Damman and Jeddah, which merely have bonded warehousing facilities.[15] Economic development in Iraq and a revival of its Gulf trade could help Damman as it has deep-water berths which Umm Qasr still lacks, but this is problematic without progress towards establishing a variable and stable government in Baghdad. In practice, as with Jeddah, most transhipment is to other destinations within Saudi Arabia rather than abroad.

Analysis of exports and import trends and assessment of stability

Over the long term the value of Saudi Arabia's imports has been linked to its oil exports and hence international prices and export volumes. As Figure 6.1 shows, with the oil boom of the 1970s and early 1980s imports increased rapidly as oil exports rose, but there was a lagged effect, as the value of exports peaked in 1981 at over 405 billion riyals (108 billion dollars) while imports peaked in 1982 140 billion riyals (37 billion dollars).

After 1982 imports declined as government spending plans were cut back because of lower oil revenues, although imports have never fallen below their

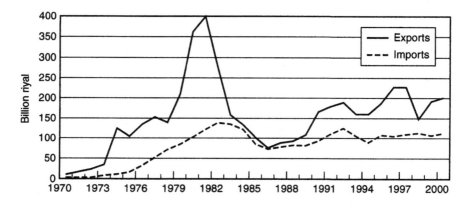

Figure 6.1 Balance of trade

Source: SAMA, *Thirty Seventh Annual Report* 2001, p. 371.

International trade and GCC economic relations 81

1978 level in nominal terms. It was only in 1992 with the temporary oil-price rises following the First Gulf War and the disruption of Iraqi supplies due to United Nations sanctions that imports rose again to almost 125 billion riyals (33 billion dollars) a figure that was only surpassed in 2001 following an oil-price recovery from the slump of 1998.

Although Saudi Arabia's aggregate trade cannot be separated from the vagaries of the international oil market, and exports inevitably remain unstable given the dominance of oil, imports have exhibited greater stability since the early 1990s. This largely reflects their changing composition, with recurrent demand from the private sector increasingly driving imports rather than government development expenditures. There has been a degree of stability in import composition as Table 6.1 shows, but food imports are increasing in relative value as a result of the rising population and greater consumption of livestock products, despite increasing grain production related to agricultural development in the kingdom.

Textiles and footwear have declined in relative value, reflecting the sourcing of these goods from low-cost Asian suppliers even for designer labels rather than from the West, although British clothing retailers retain valuable franchised outlets in the kingdom.[16] Gold imports experienced a one-off rise in 1990 as a result of the uncertainties at the time of the Gulf War. Although it is not apparent from the table, there has been a rise in the share of vehicles and transport equipment since the mid-1980s when these typically accounted for around 14 per cent of imports. By the late 1990s this proportion had risen to over 18 per cent, most of which is accounted for by imports for the private sector.[17]

Although exports are dominated by crude oil, petrochemicals are becoming increasingly important. In 1984 chemical products accounted for only 1 per cent of total exports and exports of plastic products were negligible. By 1990 chemicals accounted for 3.4 per cent of the total and plastics 2.2 per cent, and by 2000 the figures for chemicals had risen to 6.4 while plastics remained at around 2 per cent.[18] By 2010 as gas resources are developed it is possible that the industries this supports, together with petrochemicals, could account for up to one-fifth of Saudi Arabia's exports, which will bring some degree of diversification.

Table 6.1 Commodity composition of Saudi Arabian imports

Commodity	1985	1990	1995	2000
Foodstuffs	15.1	14.1	16.3	17.9
Textiles and footwear	9.7	9.7	8.5	6.6
Base metals	12.0	8.7	10.3	7.8
Gold and jewellery	3.8	6.8	4.0	4.0
Machinery	20.8	16.4	21.9	22.0
Vehicles	14.1	20.4	14.4	17.7

Source: SAMA, *Thirty-Seventh Annual Report* 2001, pp. 373–375.

Trade surpluses and payments deficits

Although Saudi Arabia usually enjoys a substantial trade surplus, its overall balance of payments position is much less favourable when payments for services, the remittances from foreign workers in the kingdom and capital movements are taken into account. In 2000, according to WTO statistics, Saudi Arabia was ranked fortieth in terms of earnings from commercial services, with an income of 4.8 billion dollars,[19] most of which was accounted for by the earnings from overseas investments held by private citizens and repatriated to the kingdom. As most of these earnings are held offshore in dollars rather than converted into riyals repatriated income represents only a small portion of the earnings from the assets of held by Saudi Arabian nationals in the West that are estimated to be worth over 700 billion dollars.[20] The WTO recorded Saudi Arabia's total payments for commercial services at 10.9 billion dollars in 2000, much of which was accounted for by remittances, which implied an overall deficit in commercial services of over 6 billion dollars, the largest in the region apart from that of the UAE which is even more dependent on migrant workers and has a lower proportion of investment income repatriated.

As Figure 6.2 shows, there is a close relationship between receipts from services and investment income in Saudi Arabia, with both rising in the 1970s as revenues from oil were invested at least partially in overseas assets rather than being entirely absorbed domestically. By the mid-1980s receipts from both services and investment income reached their peaks, followed by a period of decline lasting until the 1990s and a subsequent, more modest, rise.

What the chart does not show is the changing ownership of foreign assets and hence the income recipients. In the 1970s it was the government itself that was

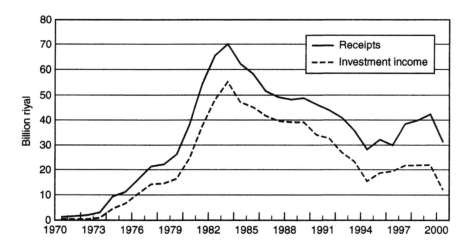

Figure 6.2 Receipts from services and investment income

Source: SAMA, *Thirty-Seventh Annual Report* 2001, pp. 390–393.

International trade and GCC economic relations 83

the major owner of foreign assets, mainly in the form of United States treasury bills and other liquid assets, often comprising Western sovereign debt. These government assets were run down as budgetary deficits grew in the 1980s with falling oil revenues but difficulties in curtailing current government spending on the wages and salaries of public-sector workers. The deficits were covered, at least in part, by the liquidation of state overseas asset holdings.

However, private wealth overseas continued to grow, partly because of new capital flight from the kingdom in response to regional and domestic political uncertainty and a poor domestic investment climate. The chief source of private capital accumulation, however, has been the capital gains on overseas asset holdings and reinvested income. Unlike the government, which held mainly debt instruments, private investment has largely been in Western equities and property which experienced substantial capital gains in the 1980s followed by some losses in the early 1990s as Western equity – and, to a lesser extent, property – prices fell, before the markets resumed their upward movement prior to the 2001 stock-price crash. It was only subsequently that significant private-wealth holdings began to be repatriated, partly in response to the events of September 11, 2001 and its consequences for Saudi Arabia's relations with the United States.

The composition of overseas payments has changed considerably since the 1970s, when it was dominated by payments for government services, as Table 6.2 shows. At that time the government was embarking on its most ambitious development plans and required substantial foreign technical assistance, all of which had to be paid for through consultancy contracts, engineering payments and other transportation – and industry-related service items. These foreign payments for government services peaked in the early 1980s, after which they were scaled back, partly as a consequence of the completion of major infrastructure projects but also because of the kingdom's increasing services expertise. Payments by the private sector for foreign insurance and financial services have become more significant in relation to government payments, though they exhibit similar trends, as Table 6.2 illustrates.

Remittances have increased steadily since the 1970s as greater numbers of foreign workers have been employed in the kingdom, their number exceeding

Table 6.2 Overseas payments and remittances from Saudi Arabia, SR billion

Item	1975	1980	1985	1990	1995	2000
Freight & insurance	1.9	15.3	11.8	9.7	9.1	9.4
Oil sector	5.7	23.0	6.4	4.5	8.2	11.1
Private services	6.0	22.3	38.3	37.9	23.4	31.6
Government services	28.5	71.1	55.2	52.9	40.1	54.0
Remittances	1.9	13.6	18.8	42.1	62.2	57.7
Total	44.0	145.3	130.5	147.1	143.0	163.8

Source: SAMA, *Thirty Seventh Annual Report* 2001, pp. 390–393.

84 *Rodney Wilson*

five million by the 1990s. Remittances have increased in importance relative to other overseas payments, and were by the late 1990s the largest single item on the services account of the balance of payments. This negative outflow of funds increases the case for employing more local citizens rather than foreign workers, although progress has been slow on this to date. The employment of local nationals has increased most rapidly in the public sector, while in the private sector it has lagged. The increase in the numbers of foreign workers has, however, slowed down, and the numbers are expected to stabilise over the next ten years. There has also been some replacement of more expensive expatriate labour from neighbouring Arab countries with cheaper labour from South Asia and the Philippines. This has reduced the value of remittances from their peak in the mid-1990s, with the saving amounting to around 10 per cent of the total. The savings in wage costs has also helped to make the local private sector more competitive, as with the economy – including the services sector – being opened up increasingly to international competition wage costs matter more than ever before.

The overall balance of payments accounts must of necessity balance with the trade surplus in the case of Saudi Arabia being reduced or eliminated by the services sector debit and transfers such as remittances. Capital movements include portfolio investment flows by Saudi Arabian investors and foreign direct investments by foreign companies in the kingdom and by Saudi Arabian companies (such as SABIC), abroad. These are usually negative, indicating a net capital outflow, as Table 6.3 shows.

Government transfers are also included on the capital account, including contributions to international agencies such as the United Nations and IMF, as well as contributions to regional institutions such as the Jeddah-based Islamic Development Bank, the Abu Dhabi-based Arab Monetary Fund and the Riyadh-based GCC. Contributions to the Arab League are minimal. Bilateral aid has been and remains of significance, notably to countries such as Syria and Yemen, although this has fallen relatively since the oil boom period of the 1970s and early 1980s. The capital account also included official financing operations by SAMA to balance overseas payments. SAMA has substantial official holdings of foreign government securities that were worth over 30 billion dollars in 2000, which it increases in periods of surplus and reduces to cover deficits as and when required.[21]

Table 6.3 Balance of payment accounts of Saudi Arabia, SR billion

Item	1975	1980	1985	1990	1995	2000
Visible trade	83.1	250.0	25.5	85.1	90.9	190.8
Services and transfers	−32.8	−107.8	−72.3	−100.6	−110.8	−132.5
Capital movements	−50.3	−142.2	46.8	15.5	19.9	−58.3

Source: SAMA, *Thirty Seventh Annual Report* 2001, pp. 390–393.

The trading partners of Saudi Arabia

The kingdom's direction of trade is largely determined by commercial rather than political considerations, with exports destined for markets where there is the most demand for oil and petrochemical products, and imports sourced from suppliers that are competitive in terms of both price and quality. Political lobbying can help secure contracts from the Saudi Arabian government, but the state itself is a less important source of procurement than in the 1970s and 1980s outside the area of defence contracts, as private companies and local distributors account for most import purchases. Their main concern is consumer tastes and preferences, since their profits as merchants depend on their ability to retail the goods effectively.

Not surprisingly Saudi Arabia, as the world's largest oil-exporting country, has the world's number one oil-importing country, the United States, as its largest single market. Oil exports to the United States alone are worth around ten billion dollars annually, but this varies considerably with oil price fluctuations. The European Union (EU) collectively is the second largest export market for the kingdom for oil, and its leading market for petrochemicals, with Rotterdam being the major destination for Saudi Arabian crude, much of which is subsequently refined before being re-exported from the Netherlands to Germany. France is the second largest European Union destination, followed by Italy, exports to the United Kingdom being for less important as the country still has its own North Sea oil.

Within Asia, Japan and South Korea are the major markets for Saudi Arabian crude oil: again, hardly surprisingly as Japan remains the world's second largest industrial economy with no oil resources of its own. South Korea's oil imports have increased because of its heavy industrial base, and it is Saudi Arabia's third largest oil export market if the European Union countries are treated separately. Singapore is also of major significance as a refining centre for Saudi Arabian crude, its role in Asia's oil trade being analogous to that of Rotterdam in Europe, with most of the refined oil subsequently exported. The other Asian market of increasing significance for oil is India, whose imports from Saudi Arabia compare with those of France. As Figure 6.3 shows, the United States, the EU and non-Islamic states in Asia account for around three-quarters of Saudi Arabian exports.

Despite rhetoric about an Islamic common market in the context of the Organisation of the Islamic Conference and attempts at Arab regional integration under the auspicious of the Arab League, Saudi Arabia's exports to the Islamic countries represent only around 11 per cent of the total, and exports to other Arab League states apart from the GCC less than 3 per cent of the total. The only Islamic oil markets of significance to Saudi Arabia are Indonesia, Pakistan and Turkey. Bahrain, Kuwait and the UAE are significant as markets for non-oil exports, while Morocco is the only other Arab market of any importance, the oil for Egypt merely being trans-shipped through the Suez–Mediterranean pipeline.

86 *Rodney Wilson*

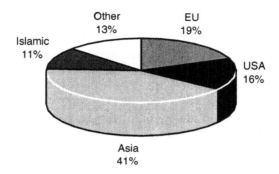

Figure 6.3 Destinations for Saudi Arabian exports, 2000
Source: SAMA, *Thirty Seventh Annual Report* 2001, pp. 382–383.

The sources of Saudi Arabia's import supplies are comparable with its export destinations, with the United States as the largest single supplier accounting for around one-fifth of the total, and the European Union collectively over one-third of the total as Figure 6.4 shows. Within the European Union, Germany is the chief supplier, followed by the United Kingdom and France, while Japan is the leading Asian supplier with around 10 per cent of the Saudi Arabian market for imports. South Korea's share of Saudi Arabia's trade has fallen since 2000 with increased competition in the market for electrical goods and declining prices.[22]

Defence equipment, oil industry supplies and aircraft are the major United States exports to the kingdom, with Germany and Japan being major sources of vehicle and equipment imports. United States exports seem to have fallen in the aftermath of strains in Saudi Arabia–United States relations since September 11, 2001, but this appeared to be a result of a consumer campaign to boycott American products because of its alleged support for Israel rather than a consequence of a change in official purchasing policy.[23] For the United Kingdom, the Al-Yamanah defence contract for the supply and servicing of Tornado strike

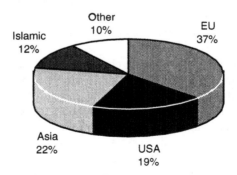

Figure 6.4 Sources of Saudi Arabian imports, 2000
Source: SAMA, *Thirty Seventh Annual Report* 2001, pp. 378–379.

International trade and GCC economic relations 87

and Hawk trainer aircraft continues to be important. The life of the Tornado aircraft has been extended to at least 2010, but BAE Systems are hoping to sell its new Eurofighter aircraft, Typhoon, to the Royal Saudi Air Force to boost the GCC defence capability and secure British jobs and defence export earnings.[24]

The GCC and regional trade

Although the overwhelming proportion of Saudi Arabia's trade is with the West, for non-oil trade the neighbouring countries of the Gulf Cooperation Council have become more significant since the 1990s. Outside the GCC Indonesia and Malaysia are the main Islamic developing countries from which imports are sourced, imports from Mediterranean Arab countries being minimal despite the efforts of regional institutions such as the Arab League to promote Arab trade. The Arab Free Trade Agreement of 1998 under which tariffs were supposed to be reduced by 10 per cent per annum to facilitate the creation of a free trade zone by 2007, was not implemented because of long lists of exemptions granted to protect local industries.[25] The GCC, however, unlike other inter-Arab economic groupings, has been relatively successful as a trading bloc, even though its largest member, Saudi Arabia, has only enjoyed marginal economic benefits from its participation. As with other regional groupings such as the European Union, the Association of South-East Asian Nations (ASEAN) and the North American Free Trade Agreement (NAFTA), the benefits have to be seen in wider geopolitical and strategic terms rather than simply as financial gains.

The GCC was founded with the signing of the Unified Economic Agreement in 1981 which provided for free trade between its six member states, Saudi Arabia, Bahrain, Kuwait, Oman, Qatar and the UAE. Iraq and Yemen were not included as they were republics with very different political regimes, and in the case of Iraq a centrally controlled economy as opposed to a market system. Though the GCC has its headquarters in Riyadh, there is a balance between its members and the organisation was never seen as a means of asserting Saudi Arabian hegemony over the region.

Saudi Arabia's main GCC trading partner is the UAE, with Dubai serving as a major centre for goods re-exported to the kingdom. Traders in Dubai can often obtain discounts for bulk purchases and then split consignments between GCC markets and Iran. Transhipment via Dubai also has advantages where products or equipment have to be modified for GCC markets, and it is more economic to undertake such work on a large-scale basis rather than at different entry points. Often this is tied to the servicing of equipment that is undertaken by expatriates based in Dubai but serving the entire Gulf market. As a result of such business the Dubai re-export zone with its bonded warehouses has become the largest in the Middle East and Western Asia, its role being comparable to that of Singapore. As Saudi Arabia's own re-export facilities in Jeddah and Damman are much younger ventures, they are not well positioned to take business away from established centres such as Jebel Ali with over two decades of experience, logistical advantages and an environment that attracts specialised workers.

88   Rodney Wilson

As Table 6.4 shows, Saudi Arabia has a substantial trade deficit with the UAE, as its own exports consist largely of grains and processed foodstuffs and construction and oil industry supplies, with the latter coming mostly from the Damman Industrial Estate. Saudi Arabia is Abu Dhabi's leading supplier,[26] and the GCC free trade zone has given its manufacturing industry an advantage in the UAE market, even thought the scale and scope of the kingdom's non-oil industrial sector is limited. An example of Saudi Arabian exports to the UAE is high-capacity electrical cabling. In 2002 Riyadh Cables, the largest manufacturer of power cables in the GCC, set up a joint venture with Emirates Holdings for the sale and distribution of cables to Abu Dhabi.[27] The interconnection of the electricity grids in the Gulf is bringing in useful orders for Saudi Arabian suppliers, not only for international links but also for domestic grids. Exports of dates and date products to other GCC states are of limited significance, but the Al-Hasa region, as the leading date producer in the region, has the potential to serve the entire GCC market.[28]

Kuwait is Saudi Arabia's second largest GCC market for non-oil exports, with oil-industry supplies and equipment being the major products. Unlike the UAE and Bahrain, where trade deficits are recorded, Saudi Arabia enjoys a surplus in its non-oil trade with Kuwait. The deficit with the UAE and Bahrain largely results from the re-exports from these countries to Saudi Arabia rather than from goods originating in the GCC. Overall the pattern of non-oil trade between Saudi Arabia and the other GCC states is interesting as an indicator of future trading strengths since it reflects a competitive advantage as opposed to simply a 'vent for a surplus' as is the case with the kingdom's oil trade.

The regional dimension of Saudi Arabia's trade is likely to become more significant as a result of the GCC agreement on a customs union and single currency that was signed by ministers from six Gulf countries meeting in Muscat on December 31, 2001.[29] The twenty-second GCC summit was the most important since the signing of the original agreement in 1981, as this has now been replaced by a much more ambitious programme aiming to make the Arabian peninsula the region's chief economic power, with a gross domestic income likely to dwarf those of its neighbours including Israel, Iran and Egypt. The economic integration of the six GCC countries – Bahrain, Kuwait, Oman,

Table 6.4 Saudi Arabia's non-oil trade with GCC countries, SR million, 2000

	Imports	*Exports*	*Trade balance*
UAE	8,920	3,261	−5,029
Bahrain	1,960	910	−1,050
Kuwait	881	1,749	868
Qatar	595	709	114
Oman	494	412	−82
Total	12,220	7,041	−5,179

Source: SAMA, *Thirty Seventh Annual Report* 2001, p. 172.

International trade and GCC economic relations 89

Qatar, Saudi Arabia and the UAE – has the potential to create an economic giant in western Asia and transform the region from its position on the periphery into the economic hub of the Middle Eastern Arab World.

The timetable for the GCC's transformation from a free trade area to a customs union was brought forward from January 1, 2005 to January 1, 2003 as a result of the Muscat agreement. Bahrain had already proposed 2003 at the meeting three years earlier, but the UAE was opposed to early implementation as its tariff levels were lower than those proposed for the customs union of 5.5 per cent for basic commodities and 7.5 per cent for luxury goods, which included most consumer durables and cars. However, rather than continuing the lengthy process of agreeing what goods should be classified as 'luxury', the GCC ministers in Muscat agreed on a single-tariff rate. This was set at a mere 5 per cent as a concession to the UAE, with commodities such as foodstuffs and energy remaining tariff-free.

Saudi Arabia had already been paving the way for the agreement by reducing its 12 per cent tariff level to 5 per cent in 2001,[30] although the 20 per cent level designed to protect local producers from international competition was retained.[31] An exception was made for goods originating in the GCC produced by firms owned by local nationals, but in May 2001 this requirement was dropped and in its place a regulation introduced that there should be 40 per cent GCC value-added in order to qualify for preferred tariff rates.

Since January 1, 2003, as a result of the Muscat agreement, goods entering Dubai and re-exported to Saudi Arabia and other GCC states have not been subject to any further tariffs, effectively creating a single market comparable to that of the EU. The entry point into the GCC is determined solely by commercial and logistical considerations such as port fees and transportation charges. As there is an excellent network of highways linking the GCC states, cross-border road freight transport has increased considerably, with containers from the EU arriving through the Suez Canal in Jeddah and then been sent by road to Riyadh and the Gulf, while Jebel Ali near Dubai serves as the major entry point for containers from East and Southeast Asia.

The issue of how to distribute the revenue from the common external tariff amongst GCC member states was successfully negotiated in May 2002. The income from the 5 per cent common tariff was estimated at four billion dollars a year, with member states benefiting according to their share of GCC imports, but without an allowance for re-exports within the region, the benefit accruing at the ultimate destination. This formula benefits Saudi Arabia as it receives between 45 and 47 per cent of the total tariff revenue, with the UAE receiving between 20 and 23 per cent.[32]. The GCC plans were approved by the Saudi Arabian Council of Ministers in July 2002.[33]

The GCC single market

In addition to the single market for goods there is also a single market for labour and capital. No work permits are required for GCC nationals working in each

90 *Rodney Wilson*

other's countries, although these are required for foreign workers from South Asia or the Mediterranean Arab countries. In practice, however, there has been relatively little mobility, due partly to a reluctance to relocate but also to educational differences. Work began in 2001 on a joint GCC educational curriculum designed to replace the various national curricula in existence that were based on old Egyptian and Jordanian models. In the past many teachers in the GCC had come from these countries, but now most are GCC citizens. The joint curriculum will bring a mutual recognition of qualifications at all levels. Universities in the GCC are already organise many joint conferences, usually discipline-based, with academics from departments in particular fields debating their research and teaching methods. This wider interchange is much more fruitful than what would be possible within individual GCC countries.

Capital also moves freely between GCC states, and since last year locally owned banks in one GCC country have been free to open banks elsewhere in the region. Bahrain's Gulf International Bank was the first to take advantage of this, with the opening of a branch in Riyadh. Companies quoted in one GCC stock market can now cross-list on others, which improves access to capital, without undermining share prices. Citizens of any GCC country can establish and own retail businesses in Saudi Arabia providing they become local residents; and if the business capital exceeds 26,000 dollars the trader is obliged to subscribe to the chamber of commerce in the place where the business is located.[34]

The GCC's single market will be enhanced by the adoption of a common currency for the region. At the meeting in Muscat GCC ministers agreed that a new common currency would be introduced on January 1, 2010 replacing the Saudi Arabian and Qatari riyal, Omani rial, UAE dirham and Kuwaiti and Bahraini dinar. Like these existing national currencies the new common currency will be freely convertible into dollars, euros and yen, and is likely to emerge as the major currency of the Islamic world. The expectation is that the new currency, designated a dinar, will be exchanged on a one-for-one basis with the Islamic dinar, which is used as the Islamic Development Bank's unit of account. The existing Islamic dinar trades at parity with the IMF's Special Drawing Right, which is in turn valued on the basis of a weighted basket of the dollar, euro and yen. As most the GCC countries' trade is based on these currencies an SDR peg seems appropriate to replace the current dollar ones.

A common currency for the Gulf will mean that stock market prices can be more easily compared, which will enhance the prospects for stock-market integration and development. Saudi Arabia's new Tadawul real-time trading system has been successfully operating since October 2001, with all the kingdom's banks linked into the system so that they can provide speedy and efficient brokerage facilities. Compatible systems are likely to be introduced by other GCC countries, which should facilitate cross-border trading. Currency union should also assist the expansion of derivatives markets, most likely to be located in Bahrain. This may extend to oil and gas options and futures, especially if the price of Gulf oil is denominated in the new dinars rather than in dollars.

International trade and GCC economic relations 91

In Muscat GCC ministers also discussed common defence matters and external political issues of mutual concern. Looking to the future, increasing reliance on the GCC itself for defence rather than the United States is seen as vital to the region's interests. Ministers agreed that defence cooperation and intelligence-sharing should be strengthened, and the decision was taken to establish a Joint Defence Council and formulate a joint strategy on terrorism. A new GCC combined defence force of 25,000 men is to be established by 2004 under joint GCC command.[35] Comparability of weapons systems remains a difficulty, but in the future consultation over the procurement of military equipment is recognised as essential.

In their discussions on relations with neighbouring states at the Muscat summit ministers had already noted with satisfaction the resolution of boundaries between Saudi Arabia and Yemen, the only Arabian peninsula state not a GCC member. At the December 31, 2001 meeting it was agreed that Yemen should be invited to participate in a number of GCC forums as a prelude to its eventual membership. Since then, Yemeni ministers have attended meetings of the GCC health and labour councils, and to increase public visibility, that country has been allowed to participate in the GCC football championships.

The pace of integration within the GCC appears to have quickened considerably, spurred on by the events of September 11, 2001 and their implications for regional security. The completion of the GCC customs union in 2003 also paves the way for progress on the much-discussed free trade agreement between the GCC and the European Union. The EU saw a common GCC external tariff as a necessary precondition for wider trade liberalisation and the establishment of a EU office in Riyadh. Free trade would result in the elimination of EU tariffs on Saudi Arabia's petrochemical exports as well as on aluminium exports from Bahrain and Dubai and possibly help to reduce the region's substantial trade deficit with the EU.[36]

WTO accession

Saudi Arabia has aspired to become a member of the World Trade Organisation since that organisation's inception in 1993 as this would bring substantial benefits to the kingdom, not least in easing access for petrochemical exports to Western markets and in reducing the price of imports as those trading with the country could then obtain finance on more favourable terms because of greater certainty over trading rules. Yet there has been a reluctance to make concessions likely to undermine local interest groups, not least in the fields of telecommunications and banking services. The kingdom's negotiators also see it as unfair that those Arab countries, such as Egypt, which were already GATT (General Agreement on Tariffs and Trade) signatories, were admitted to the WTO almost as a matter of course despite their having much more restrictive trading systems than those of the kingdom, which has always been a relatively open economy. Saudi Arabian negotiators feel that the 'goalposts' are constantly being moved without justification and that the WTO rules for accession are far

92   Rodney Wilson

from clear.[37] However, some Saudi observers have expressed concern about the skills and understanding of their own negotiating team.[38]

A working party of Saudi Arabian and WTO officials has been labouring on the kingdom's accession since July 21, 1993,[39] but progress has been slow on securing agreement on agricultural subsidies, pre-shipment inspections, trade-related intellectual property rights (TRIPs) and sanitary and phyto-sanitary measures (SPS). At the full meeting of the working party in October 2000 limited progress was made, but despite negotiations being resumed in earnest following the fourth WTO Ministerial Council Meeting in neighbouring Qatar (November 9–13, 2001), talks seem to have stalled. WTO accession in the short or even medium term still seems unlikely, despite the fact that the other five GCC countries are already members.[40]

Bilateral-market access agreements are seen as an essential prerequisite to WTO entry, as these ensure the support of WTO members. So far Saudi Arabia has secured such an agreement with Japan – which supports the kingdom's entry – and the EU has also taken a supportive stance despite the kingdom's insistence that it would not be able to open its market to goods deemed offensive to Islam (such as alcohol or pork products) of which the EU is the world's largest supplier.[41] The re-entry of United States oil companies into the Saudi Arabia energy sector would help to ensure support from the Bush administration, even if there are continuing reservations about the failure to open up the oil sector completely or to allow access to international banks and telecommunications companies. The strains in US–Saudi Arabian relations since the events of September 11, 2001 have undoubtedly held back entry, which is impossible without strong American support. The Saudi Arabian ban on companies that have forged certificates of origin to disguise goods originating in Israel has not helped, even though most of these were Jordanian and Cypriot rather than American.[42]

It is recognised in the kingdom that the WTO affects Saudi Arabia even though it is not a member, as the organisation has 141 members controlling 85 per cent of world trade.[43] With the admission of China into the WTO in 2001 Saudi Arabia has become one of the four largest economies still excluded from it. Despite domestic opposition a number of measures are being instigated to facilitate membership, most controversially the creation of specialised commercial tribunals to replace the shariah religious courts for settling trade disputes.[44] Saudi Arabia's trading partners have long complained of the lengthy delays in resolving disputes, and the uncertainties of the shariah court system. Privatisation of the telecommunications industry and the opening up of the banking system would facilitate membership, although Saudi Arabian negotiators point out that Kuwait was admitted to the WTO with a banking system under protected majority local ownership similar to that in the kingdom.

Some observers argue that Saudi Arabian products should be able to compete in the local market after WTO entry without significant protection, as the infant industries of the 1970s and 1980s have now matured and proved their commercial viability.[45] Furthermore, the competitiveness of the petrochemicals industry might be improved by WTO membership, as the tariffs that the European Union unilaterally imposes on Saudi Arabian petrochemical exports could be challenged under WTO rules and the issue referred to an arbitration panel that might well rule in kingdom's favour. At present, by being excluded from the WTO Saudi Arabia does not have access to such arbitration. These gains for industry are likely to offset any losses suffered by local vested interests by the further opening of the economy, and in the long run a competitive environment both locally and internationally should serve the interests of Saudi Arabia's consumers.

7 Employment issues

Until the mid-twentieth century the territories that today comprise Saudi Arabia were sparsely populated, with coastal settlements and small trading towns in the interior and some agricultural settlements – such as the Hofuf oasis of Al-Hasa – in the east and the mountainous region of Asir in the south-west. Before oil the entire population of the area was less than one million; by 2000, though still sparsely populated, Saudi Arabia had one of the highest rates of population increase in the world. This had inevitable consequences for employment, with a great deal of media comment, official documentation and even more academic writing regarding the issue in terms of job creation and the need for a so-called Saudi-isation of the workforce, a process that refers to the replacement of expatriate workers by local citizens.

Employment issues are, however, more complex in societies undergoing profound change such as Saudi Arabia. Government-inspired job creation programmes can actually have the effect of undermining employment as opposed to helping reduce unemployment by creating distortions in labour markets. Furthermore, jobs should not be seen merely as ends in themselves, a means of keeping younger people occupied and out of trouble. Rather, for jobs to be meaningful they should enhance the supply capacity of the economy and contribute to sustainable higher living standards for the employees, their dependents and society as a whole. It is not clear that the administrative posts created by the government for local citizens in the oil-boom years achieved these objectives, not least because the net productivity of state-sector employees is arguably rather low. The employees themselves are not to blame for any deficiencies; it is more a matter of organisation and training.

Here demographic trends are examined first, as these have implications for future conditions in the labour market. To what extent is the population explosion largely a consequence of improved health facilities and declining infant mortality rates? How long will the gap be until the decline in death rates results in a fall in birth rates? Rather than simply looking at whether population growth is a cause of unemployment, is it perhaps pertinent to consider reverse causation? Does unemployment result in falling birth rates because the young cannot afford to get married?

Employment issues 95

Furthermore, before rushing into doubtful policy prescriptions to reduce unemployment, it is necessary to identify the nature of that unemployment. Is it cyclical, somehow connected with oil revenue fluctuations, which might suggest the solution may lie with macroeconomic demand management? Alternatively, is unemployment in Saudi Arabia a consequence of structural factors such as the regional or occupational immobility of labour? If there are inefficiencies in the kingdom's labour markets, with, for example, frictional unemployment, this implies that the solution lies with long-term economic reforms.

The issue of Saudi-isation is also complex, as although the simplest solution to unemployment amongst local citizens might appear to be to replace all the foreign workers with Saudi Arabian nationals, this could actually exacerbate the problem. Private-sector companies might become less competitive if required to pay the higher wages Saudi employees expect and if obliged to improve working conditions, which adds to costs. In this case private-sector expansion might slow, with both local and foreign workers suffering as a result. There may, of course, be other economic reasons for reducing the numbers of foreign workers, not least to save on remittances. Social and political factors may also favour the long-term employment of more indigenous labour and a reduced dependence on foreigners. At professional and managerial level the extent to which nationalistic labour policies work in an at least partially global labour market can also be questioned.

The demographic transition

The population of Saudi Arabia has been rising since the 1960s at the highest rate in the Islamic world apart from that of neighbouring Yemen. By 2000 the population numbered over twenty-two million, and demographers estimate that by 2020 it will exceed 33.4 million. Almost three-quarters of Saudi Arabian nationals are under thirty years of age, and over 57 per cent under the age of twenty.

The fertility rate remains high, despite the decline from 6.6 births per woman in 1990 to 5.5 births per woman in 2000.[1] This fertility rate still greatly exceeds that of neighbouring countries such as Iraq, with 4.4 births per woman, Jordan with 3.7 or Bahrain and the UAE with 3.3 births per woman.[2] Only neighbouring Yemen has a higher fertility rate, with 6.2 births per woman, and a larger indigenous population of seventeen million compared to around 16.2 million in Saudi Arabia (excluding foreign residents) as Table 7.1 shows. The kingdom's population is nevertheless expected to exceed that of its northern neighbour Iraq by 2010.

Over one-quarter of the Saudi Arabian population is accounted for by foreign residents, mostly migrant workers from South Asia and the Philippines, the latter accounting for around 250,000 annual arrivals, while over one million travel between South Asia and the kingdom annually.[3] There are in addition at least 600,000 workers in Saudi Arabia from neighbouring Yemen and around 400,000 from Egypt. The replacement of foreign nationals by local citizens has resulted

96 Rodney Wilson

Table 7.1 Population growth and composition

	1995, million	*2000, million*	*Annual growth %*
Total	18.80	22.01	3.1
Saudi	13.59	16.21	3.5
Non-Saudi	5.21	5.80	2.1

Source: SAMA, *Thirty Seventh Annual Report 2001*, p. 274.

in a more modest increase in the male expatriate population, which rose by around 0.4 per cent per annum during the period 1992–1999.[4] With few Saudi Arabian women entering the workforce, however, the number of expatriate women rose rapidly over the same period, at over 3.1 per cent per annum. The Central Department of Statistics in the Ministry of Planning carried out a demographic sample survey in 1999 which indicated that the country had 3.35 million male expatriates and 1.67 million female ones, a giving a total of 5.02 million, lower than the estimate given in Table 7.1.

As in other developing countries, in Saudi Arabia large families were largely a reflection of high infant mortality rates as parents had many children in order to ensure that at least some survived. With greatly improved health provision there has been a substantial decline in infant mortality rates in the kingdom, from 32 per thousand live births in 1990 to 19 per thousand live births in 1999, much lower than in neighbouring countries such as Iraq, where infant mortality exceeds 100 per 1000 live births. The trend in Saudi Arabia is similar to the UAE, where the infant mortality rate has fallen to eight per thousand live births, comparable with that of the healthiest countries in the world.

Empirical evidence suggests there is a demographic transition in most countries, with declines in birth rates lagging behind falls in infant mortality rates.[5] It is during this period of demographic transition that population increases most rapidly before the rate of growth declines and the population eventually stabilises. Saudi Arabia has been going through this period of transition since the 1970s, and it may last until 2020 or beyond. One consequence has been an enormous increase the in numbers in education, with, by 2000, over four million attending school, almost 400,000 in higher education and over 50,000 in technical education.[6]

Another consequence – though with a longer time lag – is a large increase in the number of those entering and trying to enter the workforce, with, by 2000, those born in the 1970s oil-boom years starting to seek employment. To a considerable extent the Saudi Arabian economy has been able to absorb this increase, with the number of local nationals in employment increasing from around 1.2 million in 1969 to almost 3.2 million by 1999.[7] Despite this success in increasing employment for local nationals, around 15.3 per cent of the population of working age remain unemployed according to reliable estimates,[8] although the country has no official figures for unemployment. Ali Al-Namiah, the Minister of Labour and Social Affairs, has estimated the number of Saudi Arabian job seekers at 3.2 million out of a population of nationals of 9.7 million

Employment issues 97

of working age,[9] giving an unemployment rate of over 30 per cent, but this is probably an exaggeration as some of the job seekers may be working informally while seeking better positions.[10]

Unemployment

The absence of official unemployment data is not part of a political cover-up to disguise weaknesses in the economy, as some critics of government policies assert, but mainly a consequence of the difficulty of devising accurate measures.[11] There are no specific unemployment benefits in Saudi Arabia as employment for those local citizens already in the state sector is virtually guaranteed, with redundancy being regarded as politically and socially unacceptable. Government employees retire at fifty-five – early by Western standards – and sickness benefits are available to those who become ill, which restricts the numbers in the unemployment category. Most unemployed are young school leavers who have never had a job rather than those who have been in employment before. Many of the unemployed have studied at college or university, although a high proportion of those without work have dropped out and failed to complete their studies.

In the absence of unemployment compensation schemes numbers cannot be estimated through benefit claimants. Random-sample surveys are the most usual method of calculating unemployment rates in Western countries, but this implies that unemployment is to some extent a matter of self-perception. In Saudi Arabia, school leavers living with their families do not regard themselves as unemployed even when not working, and indeed some – though a minority – are simply taking time off before continuing in some form of education. Similarly, the many dropouts from the university system may be hoping to re-enrol at some point in the future. Others regard themselves as being engaged in looking for work, even if in practice their efforts to find employment may be somewhat half-hearted. Still others are either waiting for military service or resting and recovering from it, as although the kingdom has no conscription there is substantial mobility in and out of the army in particular. All these factors make asking direct questions about unemployment a somewhat meaningless exercise.

Women play only a minor role in the workforce, with job opportunities largely restricted to the more educated, who take teaching posts. Girls leaving school are often engaged in household tasks, including the care of younger siblings, and do not, therefore, perceive themselves as unemployed; indeed, they may feel they have much busier lives than their unemployed brothers. Unemployment, in so far as it can be identified in Saudi Arabia, is thus essentially a male phenomenon.

The unemployment figure of 15 per cent has been estimated from Central Department of Statistics data on the size and growth of the workforce since 1994, when the natural rate of unemployment was assumed to be 4 per cent, the rate which corresponds to the full employment equilibrium when there is no cyclical unemployment as a result of favourable oil prices. By projecting

98 Rodney Wilson

population figures forward for those reaching working age and taking Central Department of Statistics data for the growth of the workforce, the unemployment rate for 1999 was calculated as 12 per cent and that for the end of 2001 as 15.3 per cent.[12] The problem with this methodology is that the 4 per cent figure for 1994 may not have been accurate, although Manpower Council estimates of 350,000 unemployed Saudi citizens in 1999 corresponds with the 12 per cent figure.[13] If the total workforce of Saudi and non-Saudis is included the unemployment figure falls to 7 per cent, as non-Saudis are in the kingdom to work and most are obliged by law to leave when their permits expire.

Recent estimates highlight the problem of unemployment amongst young Saudi Arabian males. Ministry of Planning data used in association with Central Department of Statistics data show unemployment amongst Saudi Arabian males at 11.9 per cent in 2002, the figure of 15.3 per cent previously cited reflecting the higher level of unemployment among females, as this was already 15.8 per cent by 1999. Unemployment amongst Saudi Arabian males in the 20–24 age group stands at 26.5 per cent, however, before tapering off to 0.9 per cent for the over 30 age group.[14]

As many foreign workers do not leave when their permits expire – especially those from Yemen and the Sudan and central African states – they become either a disguised class of unemployed, or more usually illegal workers in the so-called 'informal' workforce, which is not included in the statistics. This implies that the actual workforce is larger than the recorded one, further reducing the unemployment percentage. Increasingly there are also local citizens working on a casual basis and not included in the official statistics. These include women undertaking piecework at home on an informal subcontracting basis to boost household income as they have few opportunities in the official workplace. It also includes young men undertaking jobs that the older generation of Saudi citizens would have found demeaning such as cleaning, the collection and disposal of waste and catering work. Although of low status, such jobs at least ensure that young men have some form of independent income. These jobs are usually casual, which those who undertake them prefer as, because of the stigmas associated with such occupations, they do not wish their families, especially their parents, to regard this employment as permanent.

For employers the advantage of informal work is that it enables them to avoid the cost of work permits in the case of foreign nationals, even though they risk prosecution for the illegal hiring of workers. Furthermore, in the case of local nationals they avoid having to hire workers protected from dismissal and the need to pay wage rates that potentially make their businesses uncompetitive. Saudi Arabian informal employees would of course prefer better pay and conditions, but most regard it as better to have some income, even if it is insecure, rather than none at all.

Traditional family structures in Saudi Arabia ensure a degree of economic protection for the young unemployed, as parental responsibilities are taken seriously, with daughters being cared for until marriage and sons provided with a basic financial safety net as long as they acknowledge their family obligations.[15]

Employment issues 99

In many respects the family and extended kinship system is a great strength of Saudi Arabian society, although most of the young unemployed would like to be more financially, and indeed socially, independent like their counterparts in other societies. Those helping on an informal basis within family businesses often get little pay; indeed they may get less than the hired employees, and benefits in kind such as free lodging and food within the family home do not allow for much financial autonomy.

In Saudi Arabia the young unemployed typically live with their parents, and there are no street children or unemployed drifters seeking jobs in distant cities or regions.[16] As the kingdom is highly urbanised, with over 85 per cent of the population living in cities and towns, most unemployed seek jobs in their immediate locality. The extent of regional differences in unemployment is unclear as there are no statistics on this, but it seems likely that unemployment is higher in smaller towns than in Riyadh, the location of the largest number of government jobs, or Jeddah, where private-sector commerce is strongest. In so far as those from other towns seek jobs in Jeddah and Riyadh they usually do so through family contacts, residing with uncles or cousins during periods of temporary employment or job search.

Labour market trends

The demographic developments in Saudi Arabia are having major consequences for the growth of the workforce. As the situation reached a critical point in the late 1990s, with increasing awareness of the damaging social consequences of unemployment, much attention has been paid to the workforce issues in the Seventh Development Plan covering the period 2000–2004.

As Table 7.2 shows, the problem is an immediate one. The development planners anticipated a lower rate of increase in the population below working age reflecting some slowing in population growth, but as those born in previous high-growth periods reach working age it is this section of the population that shows the most rapid increase. Optimistically the planners projected an even faster growth in the population actually in the workforce, the assumption being that the private sector and the replacement of foreigners by nationals would deliver an average annual increase in the workforce of 4.7 per cent. How this is to be attained is not spelt out in the Seventh Development Plan, which contains

Table 7.2 Labour-force projections for Seventh Development Plan

	1999 *000*	*2004* *000*	*Increase* *%*
Population below working age	5,996	6,815	2.6
Working age population	9,662	11,705	3.9
Total population	15,658	18,520	3.4
Population in work force	3,173	3,990	4.7

Source: Ministry of Planning, *Seventh Development Plan 2000–2004*, p. 162.

100 Rodney Wilson

ambitious targets but little reference to the mechanisms required to ensure these are met.

A central assumption is that the participation rate, calculated as the population in the workforce as a proportion of the working age population, will increase, thus lowering the dependency ratio, as Table 7.3 shows. Superficially the dependency ratio for Saudi Arabia does not appear especially high when compared with other developing countries, although it is high in comparison to the European Union and the United States, where the rate is below 50 per cent. The dependency rate is projected to decrease – this being the population below working age as a proportion of the working-age population – regardless of whether they are actually in employment. Although this could be rejected as a real measure of dependency, as many unemployed are actually engaged in casual or informal work, the notion of a dependency ratio as measured by the planners arguably has some validity, even though this case is not argued in the Seventh Plan.

Although the planners in Saudi Arabia stress the role of the private sector in increasing employment for local citizens and reducing unemployment there is no analysis of the workings of the labour market in the Seventh Development Plan. How responsive is the demand for labour to the expected wage rate, and is the wage at the rate that would bring demand and supply into equilibrium in the job market? Are labour markets in Saudi Arabia excessively fragmented, with insufficient occupational and geographical mobility? Are the labour markets for Saudi Arabian and foreign workers completely segmented so that little competition exists between the two groups? Although answers may not be readily available given data limitations, there is little evidence that the fundamental questions are really being asked.

The type of rigidities that exist in the Saudi Arabia labour market are demonstrated by the difficulties that British Aerospace (BAE Systems) has had over its offset contracts for Tornado Aircraft and the servicing of other military equipment in the kingdom. BAE Systems faced losses on its worldwide operations, and in 2002 it wanted to cut costs through a redundancy programme while striving to raise the productivity of those workers who remained. It attempted to apply these cutbacks to its operations in Saudi Arabia, with local staff expected to share in the job reductions. New working arrangements were to be introduced for staff remaining with the company, with these involving longer standard working hours and a reduction in the amount of overtime working for which additional bonuses had been paid. The reduction in overtime effectively meant a pay cut for Saudi employees.[17]

Table 7.3 Participation rates for workforce

	1999	2004
Dependency ratio, %	62.1	58.2
Participation rate, %	32.8	34.1

Source: Ministry of Planning, *Seventh Development Plan 2000–2004*, p. 162.

Employment issues 101

The Saudi Arabian workers complained that they had not been consulted about the proposed changes to working arrangements, and that these were being introduced to force employees into resigning. The local Saudi staff refused to sign the new employment contracts, which, they asserted, were contrary to the kingdom's law. Yahya Al-Fifi, one of those refusing to sign and leading opposition to the new contracts, was dismissed in July 2002. Subsequently, the workers formed a Labour Committee of Saudi Workers and took their case to the Ministry of Defence in Riyadh. The Ministry took up the workers' case with the United Kingdom's Ministry of Defence As a consequence of this lobbying, BAE Systems backed down and agreed to maintain existing work schedules and workforce levels, although there is an ongoing review of every post in Saudi Arabia. BAE Systems is appealing to the kingdom's Higher Labour Committee against a verdict by its Preliminary Committee stating that no punitive action should be taken against Saudi Arabian employees. The dispute remains to be resolved, but the Labour Committee of Saudi Workers has set a precedent for groups of local employees. Although trade unions are not permitted in Saudi Arabia, the Labour Committee is performing virtually the same role with considerable success.[18]

Structure of employment

The capital-intensive nature of the oil industry means that there are relatively few workers employed in the sector despite its importance for government revenue and export earnings. There are fewer than 100,000 employed in the oil and gas industry, which accounts for a mere 1.4 per cent of the total workforce, as Table 7.4 shows. The growth of jobs in the oil and gas sector is also low, which implies that over the longer term the industry will account for a diminishing proportion of the total workforce, and even the ambitious schemes

Table 7.4 Structure of the labour force by economic activity, 1999

	Employees, 000	Ratio, %	Annual growth, %
Agriculture	558	7.8	0.9
Mining	13	0.2	2.2
Oil and gas	99	1.4	0.9
Manufacturing	589	8.2	2.3
Utilities	93	1.3	1.7
Construction	1,110	14.2	1.5
Trade	1,037	14.4	0.7
Transport	299	4.2	0.7
Finance and real estate	2,217	30.9	0.3
Community and personal services	335	4.7	2.3
Government services	916	12.8	0.3

Source: SAMA, *Thirty Seventh Annual Report* 2001, p. 279.

102 *Rodney Wilson*

to exploit local gas and promote gas exports will not contribute significantly to employment.

Agriculture accounts for a much higher proportion of the workforce, especially in the traditional farming areas of Asir Province and Al-Hasa, but much of the modern irrigated agriculture is also highly capital-intensive and makes only a modest contribution to employment. Production of wheat and barley was deliberately reduced during the 1994–1999 period to cut grain surpluses and the cost of government subsidies. Milk and poultry production were expanded considerably, both of which are more labour-intensive, and production of fruit and vegetables was also increased. There was much overgrazing by sheep and goats, however, and by 1999 there were over 4.5 million grazing animals in the kingdom despite an estimated capacity to feed only 1.7 million animals on the grazing ranges, with locally produced fodder supporting a further two million. Random overgrazing has resulted in serious soil erosion, but much of this is the responsibility of the nomads, who are not included in the workforce statistics.[19]

Manufacturing employed almost 590,000 workers in Saudi Arabia accounting for over 8 per cent of the workforce as Table 7.4 shows. Over half of these employees are engaged in small establishments, with factories employing over ten employees accounting for 287,000 workers in 1999. As Table 7.5 shows the largest numbers were employed in machinery and equipment workshops, usually undertaking servicing and repairs, while the chemical and petroleum industry accounted for 68,000 employees, excluding those in crude-oil production. Non-metallic industries and food processing for the local and GCC markets accounted for most of the remaining manufacturing employment.

The cost of job creation in factories in Saudi Arabia is high, this being calculated from the total investment financed by the Saudi Industrial Development Fund and the commercial banks divided by the number of jobs

Table 7.5 Factory employment

	Factories	Investment, SR million	Employment 000	Investment per job SR 000
Foodstuffs	497	16,446	40.1	410
Textiles and clothing	135	3,015	16.8	179
Carpentry	135	2,093	11.8	177
Paper and printing	187	4,998	14.6	342
Chemicals and petroleum	643	150,553	68.5	2,198
Non-metallic metals	560	25,370	51.7	491
Base metals industries	74	5,709	9.3	614
Machinery and equipment	814	20,736	69.0	300
Other industries	56	1,081	5.1	212
Cold storage	22	262	0.7	374
Total/*Average*	3,123	230,263	287.6	*801**

Source: Ministry of Planning, *Seventh Development Plan 2000–2004*, p. 217.

Note: * Average investment per job for whole economy.

Employment issues 103

within each activity. The overall average is raised considerably by the high investment costs in the chemicals and petroleum sector, the more modest cost of job creation being in textile and clothing factories and wood and furniture workshops, where it is below 180,000 riyals (48,000 dollars) per employee. This includes the cost of both Saudi and non-Saudi jobs, but it is likely that the cost of the former is higher.

The employment and replacement of expatriate labour

The largest sources of employment in Saudi Arabia are construction, retail trade and finance and real estate. Although over one million workers are employed in construction and a further million in retail trade, as Table 7.4 showed, the majority are non-Saudi Arabians. Most construction employment involves housing and commercial projects for the private sector, as the major infrastructure schemes funded by the government have been undertaken at a slower pace in recent years reflecting constraints on the state budget. For the housing and commercial projects large numbers of unskilled and semi-skilled workers are required, most coming from the Indian subcontinent. They are paid relatively modest wages for the long hours they work, but this keeps construction costs low and results in building work being considerably cheaper to carry out in Saudi Arabia than in Western countries. Few Saudi Arabian nationals – even the unemployed – are interested in jobs in the construction industry.

Given the increasing size of the Saudi Arabian market for consumer goods there has been a substantial expansion in retailing in recent years, which has created many employment opportunities. As all establishments have to be owned by local nationals, this ensures that large numbers of Saudis are absorbed; indeed, more are engaged in retailing than in any other private-sector activity. This partly reflects the large number of small retail establishments and the lack of concentration of ownership, although some owners have chain stores. In order to boost the employment of local nationals the government has decreed that one-third of the workforce in retail establishments should be Saudi Arabian, but this is widely ignored. In the cheaper shops in the downtown areas that cater for migrant workers and local citizens with limited amounts of disposable income, most employees are from South Asia and, to a lesser extent, Yemen. In the more expensive stores, often run on a franchising basis and selling branded products, many of the sales staff are from Egypt, Lebanon, Jordan and Palestine, although Saudi Arabian nationals are increasingly employed. In such upmarket establishments where quality matters it is important to have sales staff who know the products and are able to converse with the customers; therefore, a knowledge of Arabic as well as English is important. Generally this sector of the market, especially establishments in the major shopping malls, adhere to the requirements for employing local nationals.

The commercial banks are the most progressive segment in terms of employing local nationals, and many have spent substantial amounts on training programmes. Banking is arguably one of the most interesting career

104 *Rodney Wilson*

opportunities for Saudi Arabian graduates, as pay and working conditions are generally attractive. Not surprisingly, there is increasing competition for jobs in banking amongst local nationals, and the banks are in a position where they can choose the most highly motivated and adaptable among them. Academic performance is important, but employers see university degrees as a screening device rather than necessarily of much relevance to the actual employment. This is similar to the experience of graduates in Egypt.[20] Elsewhere in the private-services sector the major hotel chains increasingly employ local nationals on their reception desks and to handle billing and financial controls, although most of the service staff such as cleaners are from South Asia and the Philippines.

The Ministry of Planning projections in the Seventh Development Plan indicate the extent to which the private sector will be expected to account for the major job-creation effort during the period leading up to 2020. As Table 7.6 shows, the demand for labour by the private sector is expected to grow by a further 50 per cent within this period with the number of non-Saudi Arabians employed expected to decline by over one-third. If the target of employing over 8.2 million local nationals in the private sector is to be achieved by 2020 it will require both a huge training effort and the ability of businesses to maintain and enhance competitiveness while restructuring their workforces completely. The experience of the commercial banks, which by 2000 already employed a majority of local nationals, shows what can be achieved, but it will require a change of business culture and employer attitudes towards local nationals.

In the overall workforce (as Table 7.7 shows), there are almost 3.2 million jobs for Saudi Arabian citizens, of which around 2.4 million are in the private sector. As the ministries and state sector organisations already have a high proportion of local citizens employed, and as government expenditure is constrained by budgetary considerations, the prospects for increasing employment in government are very limited. Most of the recruitment of local nationals by 2010 will simply be to replace retiring employees, the

Table 7.6 Manpower demand and supply projections, thousands

	1999	2004	2020
Demand			
Government	916	932	984
Oil and gas	99	100	127
Private	6,161	6,472	9,635
Total demand	7,176	7,505	10,746
Supply			
Saudi population	15,658	18,530	29,717
Saudi labour force	3,173	3,990	8,263
Demand/supply balance			
Non-Saudi labour	4,003	3,515	2,483

Source: Ministry of Planning, *Seventh Development Plan 2000–2004*, p. 162.

Employment issues 105

Table 7.7 Structure of the Saudi Arabian labour force, 1999

	Employees 000	Employees %
Total labour force	7,176	100.0
Saudi	3,173	44.2
Non-Saudi	4,003	55.8
Government employment	916	100
Saudi	716	78.2
Non-Saudi	200	21.8
Private sector	6,260	100.0
Saudi	2,423	38.7
Non-Saudi	3,837	61.3

Source: SAMA, *Thirty Seventh Annual Report* 2001, p. 274.

majority of whom will be Saudi Arabians recruited in the oil boom years of the 1970s and early 1980s. Hence it is the private sector that will have to account for most new job creation, not least as the scope of the public sector itself is likely to be reduced with privatisations. Many of the public-sector jobs are in education and health care, although most of the nursing staffs are expatriates, given the supposed unsuitability of such employment for Saudi Arabian women. In single-sex schools there are, however, guaranteed jobs for women who are local citizens. Increased private provision of education, especially at college and university level, may also increase the scope for local nationals in the private sector.

The major factor deterring private sector employers from taking on more Saudi Arabian nationals is their relatively high cost. Wages for Saudi Arabian citizens average three times that of non-citizens with the same level of education, as Table 7.8 shows. This increases expenses for private sector businesses and makes them uncompetitive. A tighter immigration policy might reduce the differentials, and more expensive work permits would result in a greater preference for local nationals. However, this would also add to business

Table 7.8 Average monthly salaries, 2000 (SR)

Education level	Local nationals	Foreign employees
Illiterate	3,155	1,136
Read and write	3,450	1,260
Primary school	4,600	1,378
Intermediate school	5,437	1,587
Secondary school	7,200	2,580
College leaver	6,810	2,880
University graduate	10,893	5,581
Post graduate	21,112	10,856
Average	7,043	2,354

Source: Central Department of Statistics, Riyadh, 2002.

106 *Rodney Wilson*

costs, which would not matter if the only competition was domestic, but in an open economy such as that of the kingdom there is also the need to compete with other GCC suppliers as well as those from further away. The GCC customs union includes the UAE, where there is a liberal policy on work permits and very competitive wage costs. As there is free trade with Saudi Arabia this increases the pressure on the kingdom's employers to keep costs down. One solution would be for the private sector to employ more Saudi Arabian women, as their wages average only half those of their male counterparts.[21]

Education and training issues

Saudi Arabia invests substantial amounts in education provision, averaging around 5 per cent of GDP during the 1990s, although this is lower than in 1986 when spending amounted to 6.7 per cent of GNP. By 2000 the kingdom, with its youthful population, had over 4.5 million pupils and students in education, 25,000 schools and over 300,000 teachers.[22] Illiteracy rates are now very low and compare favourably with those of Mediterranean Arab countries and developing countries generally with around 17 per cent male illiteracy and 34 per cent female illiteracy in the over-15 age group.[23] Most of the illiterate are older people rather than the young, as adult literacy programmes have only a limited impact. Female illiteracy is falling rapidly and, with the majority of the primary school age group being educated, the major challenge is to extend education to Bedouin children whose families are reluctant to settle in one location.

Children often start school at a later age than they should, or leave earlier; hence the 1998 enrolment figure of 61 per cent of the relevant age group underestimates the proportions that have had some schooling. The proportion going into secondary schools has risen rapidly, with 43 per cent of the relevant age group enrolled, but there is a high dropout rate and absenteeism, especially on the part of boys. Although there are gender imbalances in literacy, these no longer exist in either primary or secondary school as 48 per cent of those enrolled in primary schools and 44 per cent of those in secondary school are male.[24]

In addition to the substantial investment in primary and secondary education the Saudi Arabian government has also spent large amounts in expanding universities. As a result over the period 1990–1999 the number of students increased from 132,827 to 371,522.[25] This expenditure is likely to increase over the next decade, although it is likely that as in the UAE there will also be substantial private provision. Under the Seventh Development Plan covering the period 2000–2004 the number of male students in higher education is projected to increase from 122,000 to 200,000 (64 per cent growth) and that of female students from 141,000 to 280,000 (99 per cent growth).[26]

In 1998/99 Saudi Arabia had 52,148 students graduating of which 28,228 were female and 23,920 male. This pattern of females representing the majority of graduates applies in all GCC countries, the gender disparities being particularly marked in Bahrain, Kuwait, Qatar and the UAE. There is a serious problem of male academic underachievement at all levels in Saudi Arabian

Employment issues 107

education and that of the GCC as a whole, but the problem seems especially acute at university level. The difficulty appears to arise from a lack of commitment by male students to their studies, peer-group pressures to socialise, poor family support and a general lack of interest in learning. Many enter university because of the absence of employment possibilities but do not regard degree qualifications as especially useful for finding employment as the governments themselves now recruit few graduates, apart from for teaching, which is increasingly dominated by women.

Student–staff ratios are high in Saudi Arabia, imposing considerable burdens on university teachers who are relatively underpaid and not especially well regarded. There were 18,925 academic staff during the 1998/99 academic year, with a staff–student ratio of 1:19.63. Pay compares unfavourably with salaries in the civil service and banks, and many university staff in subjects such as economics or management regard their university jobs as part-time occupations, as they seek remuneration in business and commerce.

In Saudi Arabia the largest number of students are taking undergraduate degrees in Islamic studies, with engineering, sciences, education, the humanities and medicine being ranked the next most popular subjects. Women predominate in Islamic studies and education, while men do so in engineering, sciences and medicine, and to a lesser extent in humanities. Young men are often sceptical about the value of degrees in Islamic studies, and indeed there is increasing resentment about the role of the ulema in higher education.[27] Women are, however, increasingly attracted to Islamic studies, partly because fewer opportunities are available to them in the workplace but also due to the increasingly influential Islamic feminist movement. This movement has spread rapidly within the secondary schools and universities, originally nurtured by lecturers influenced by Egyptian ideas on women's Muslim rights but now propelled forward by charismatic leaders.[28] Table 7.9 shows that women's colleges will continue to play a major role in the future. The curriculum of these

Table 7.9 Planned student numbers during Seventh Development Plan

	Male	*Female*	*Total*
King Saud University	47,700	22,300	70,000
King Abdul Aziz University	33,600	26,400	60,000
King Faisal University	10,800	7,200	18,000
King Fahd University	9,000		9,000
Islamic University	6,000		6,000
Iman University	58,500	11,500	70,000
Umm Al-Qura University	24,400	15,600	40,000
King Khalid University	13,500	3,500	17,000
Girls Colleges		200,000	200,000
Technical Colleges	95,636		95,636
Vocational Centres	82,893		82,893

Source: Ministry of Planning, *Seventh Development Plan 2000–2004*, p. 264 and p. 271.

108 *Rodney Wilson*

colleges is nevertheless biased towards arts and Islamic studies rather than the sciences. King Fahd University, the main centre of excellence for science and engineering, has no female students.

Women in the workforce

Although state spending on girls' education is valuable as an end in itself, the returns are lowered by the minimal participation of Saudi Arabian women in the formal workforce. The belief remains widespread that a wife neglects her duty of taking care of her husband and children if she decides to take up employment outside the home.[29]

Yet many Saudi Arabian women are marrying later than previously, largely because of the limited availability of eligible men whose families can afford the high cost of the dowry or bride price. Some parents are demanding more than 200,000 riyals (53,000 dollars) from prospective husbands. The average dowry by 2002 amounted to 50,000 riyals (13,300 dollars) for virgins to between SR 20,000 and 30,000 riyals (5,300 dollars and 8,000 dollars) for divorcees and widows. Rising dowries could be taken as a sign of a shortage of eligible women driving up the price, but this is unlikely to be the case in Saudi Arabia, where by 2001 there were an estimated 1.52 million unmarried women of marriageable age, including almost 400,000 in the Jeddah and Mecca region alone.[30] A more likely explanation for rising dowries is the generous spending that parents have lavished on their daughters and the expectation that there should be some return so that expenditure can be sustained on younger siblings. Furthermore, educated daughters can make a valuable contribution to the household even if they are not participating in the formal workforce, not least as younger children benefit from contact with knowledgeable older sisters rather than unqualified Filipina or Sri Lankan housemaids with at best a limited knowledge of Arabic.

A mere 5.8 per cent of the 3.38 million Saudi Arabian women aged between nineteen and forty-nine are in formal employment, one of the lowest proportions in the world.[31] Social custom precludes women from entering many types of employment; most of those in employment working as kindergarten and primary school teachers at girls' schools. Work is sexually segregated in Saudi Arabia, with men – usually expatriates from South Asia – serving as secretaries for male managers rather than women as in the West. Saudi Arabian women are unable to become nurses in hospital wards with male patients, and even in banks they are not permitted to work in the same offices as men or to deal directly with male clients. As women cannot drive, getting to work presents a problem, with women teachers having to rely on male relatives or paid male drivers to transport them to their schools.[32] All this adds to the cost of being employed and deters women from entering the workforce.

The social constraints facing Saudi Arabian women are apparent from many studies, including the interviews conducted by Mai Yamani for her profile of Saudi Arabian youth.[33] Hekmat Al-Orabi of King Saud University undertook a detailed survey covering 1,225 respondents of the attitudes of Saudi Arabian

Employment issues 109

women towards participating in the labour force.[34] This showed that women able to obtain higher monthly incomes were more likely to be employed, although there was a negative relationship between family income and female employment. Marital status and the number of small children also exerted a negative effect, as might be expected, and level of education had a positive effect.

Competition from migrant labour has a negative effect on wages in less skilled occupations and deters women with lower levels of education from entering the workforce. Yet there are some occupations where, even if the pay was higher, Saudi Arabian women would not contemplate being involved. Such work includes domestic service. A detailed study of Sri Lankan housemaids working in Saudi Arabia and other Gulf states showed that such women earned little by the time they had paid the agencies that recruited them, although they were able to use retained earnings to improve their social standing in their country of origin.[35]

Over 90 per cent of the 230,000 working women in Saudi Arabia are employed in the public sector. As the private sector is expected to be the major source of employment in the future for both local males and females, women's attitudes toward potential jobs in business are clearly important. Abdullah Al-Shetaiwi undertook a study of the employment issues facing qualified Saudi Arabian women working or seeking to work in the private sector.[36] Of the 800 business managers contacted 220 responded to the survey of their attitudes to women employees; and of the 700 women contacted 207 women employees and 145 unemployed women responded. Over four-fifths of the business managers who responded saw the need for women to participate in private sector employment, even though a mere 2.5 per cent of their workforce were Saudi women and 9.8 per cent foreign women.[37]

Abdullah Al-Shetaiwi found that most women who worked in the private sector in Saudi Arabia were in small companies with local nationals working in administrative, supervisory and professional jobs, while expatriate women worked in technical and vocational positions. Most women worked full-time despite the lack of childcare places provided by the businesses. Over nine tenths of respondents identified the difficulty in females moving from one city to another as the chief obstacle to women's employment. This was not surprising in view of family ties and the prohibition on women driving. Business managers identified the mixed working environment in some private sector job categories as a significant deterrent to the employment of local women. The negative social attitude to women working outside the home was also seen as a deterrent to employing women, as were the extended holidays that some sought because of their family obligations.[38] Business managers also saw the need for higher-quality women's education and training as important if more local females were to be recruited, and most felt that the lack of part-time work was a deterrent to some women seeking employment.

The survey of women in the labour market undertaken by Abdullah Al-Shetaiwi showed – rather surprisingly – that a majority of those employed were married, whereas a majority of the unemployed were single. It was evident

110 *Rodney Wilson*

that work was not a prime concern in educational choices, as over 70 per cent of women had chosen subjects likely to convey a high social status after graduation, whereas only 16 per cent had considered the market needs of the private sector. Most women in Saudi Arabia, like their male counterparts, expressed a preference for public-sector work, and most wanted employment in order to fulfil cultural and social needs rather than to support personal or family financial needs.[39]

8 Employment conditions in SABIC

Abdullah Al-Salamah

In 1999 the Ministerial Oil Committee carried out a review of foreign energy investment policy with the aim of developing a new oil and gas strategy. Subsequently, the Saudi Arabian authorities informed international oil companies that they were interested in investments and joint ventures in natural gas, power, refineries and petrochemical projects. Of particular interest was the production and industrialisation of natural gas.

To what extent is there a conflict between this desire to encourage foreign investment and the policy of Saudi-isation of the labour force? Much can be learnt from the experience of the Saudi Arabian Basic Industries Corporation (SABIC), as its companies in the fields of petrochemicals, fertilisers and steel products involved foreign direct investment.

This research involved a survey of 312 SABIC employees – both Saudi Arabian and foreign – to gauge their attitudes to pay, promotion and training.[1] The employees surveyed worked for joint ventures involving American, Japanese, South Korean and Taiwanese companies. Local nationals appear to have benefited from the training programmes offered by SABIC under the government's Saudi-isation policy, and the majority were satisfied with the training they received.

Industrialisation and job creation

For over thirty years Saudi Arabia's economic policy has been designed to promote economic diversification, and industrialisation has been seen as a key element of this policy. Diversification has two industrial strands: first, the development of import substitution industries, geared primarily to the domestic market, and second energy and petroleum-related industries orientated largely to export markets in those fields where Saudi Arabia enjoys a potential competitive advantage. The SABIC joint-venture companies are in the latter category, which implies that they have to strive to achieve international standards of efficiency and productivity. This has implications for SABIC's recruitment policy as well as for pay and employment conditions within the companies.

There can be no featherbedding with the SABIC companies involved in job creation for its own sake. Although the issue of indirect subsidies through input

112 *Abdullah Al-Salamah*

costs is complex, there are increasing international pressures from trading partners to ensure there are no 'unfair' subsidies that might assist SABIC's competitive position to the detriment of rival companies from other countries. This has been an issue with the European Union for more than a decade as far as access to Saudi Arabian petrochemicals is concerned, and it has also been an issue in the kingdom's bid for membership of the World Trade Organisation.

SABIC has been central to the kingdom's industrialisation effort since its establishment in 1976 as a public shareholding company, with the government holding 70 per cent of the shares and private Saudi Arabian citizens and other Gulf nationals the remaining 30 per cent. The Minister of Industry and Electricity at that time, Dr Ghazi A. al-Gosaibi, chaired the SABIC board, with Abd al-Aziz al-Zamil serving as chief executive officer.[2] No foreign ownership was allowed in SABIC, though it was set up as a public shareholding company, thus enabling it to enter into joint-venture arrangements with major multinational companies from the United States and the Far East. SABIC, however, was to maintain a majority ownership stake in the joint ventures and exercise effective control.

For the ambitious projects in petrochemicals, fertilisers and iron and steel making it was recognised that the technical expertise of multinational companies would be invaluable, not to mention their management skills and marketing contacts. ARAMCO (the Arabian American Oil Company) provided a precedent for this. It was also felt that the joint-venture partners could provide valuable training for Saudi Arabian workers, and that this skills acquisition would be extremely useful in the long run as knowledge became diffused within the kingdom. From the very start of the ventures in the late 1970s Saudi Arabian engineers received training in the United States.[3]

The new cities of Jubail and Yanbu, where the SABIC industries are located, had originally been identified as growth poles for petrochemicals. Jubail enjoys proximity to the crude oil and gas fields of the Gulf, and Yanbu is the Red Sea terminal of the gas pipeline from Eastern Province.[4] It was the Bechtel Corporation of the United States which in 1973 designed the master plan for Jubail that led to the establishment of the Royal Commission for Jubail and Yanbu chaired by the then Crown Prince, Fahd.[5]

It was recognised from the start that the SABIC industries would be very capital-intensive and would create only a limited number of jobs in relation to the funds invested. However, wage costs are relatively high in Saudi Arabia, and those for the petrochemical industry were estimated to be 40 per cent higher than those for comparable jobs during the 1980s in Houston, Texas.[6] Furthermore, the cost of training one Saudi Arabian employee averaged 70,000 dollars according to SABIC sources, and by the end of 1992 the company had spent over 300 million dollars on training.[7] The kingdom had clearly no wage-cost advantage, but industries which were energy-intensive were seen as potentially viable.

By 1990 there were 14,553 SABIC employees, 8202 of whom were Saudi Arabians.[8] Since then the number of employees has risen to 20,000, two-thirds of whom are local citizens. A further 20,000 are employed in industries in the kingdom which use SABIC products, and perhaps 30,000 are employed as a result

Employment conditions in SABIC   113

of spending by SABIC and its employees on local goods and services. The revisions to the foreign investment laws in 2000 were designed to help encourage more foreign investment in downstream processing industries capable of using SABIC products and activities capable of increasing the ability of local suppliers to benefit from expenditure multiplier effects from SABIC and its employees.[9]

The survey

The work was undertaken in Jubail, with six SABIC companies was included: the Saudi Petrochemical Company, the Eastern Petrochemical Company, the Al-Jubail Fertiliser Company, the National Methanol Company, the Saudi Iron and Steel Company and the National Plastics Company. These account for around half of the SABIC workforce.

A pilot survey of fifty respondents was undertaken in 1992, and the main survey the following year. Questionnaires were distributed randomly to 900 employees, of which 333 were completed. Of these twenty-one were discarded either because they were only partially completed or the answers were inconsistent. There were thus 312 valid questionnaires, which meant a response rate of 34.7 per cent. The responses were analysed using SPSS (the Statistical Package for Social Sciences). Tests for statistical significance were carried out using the Kruskal-Wallis technique, which is an appropriate non-parametric method for ranked data.

Profile of the respondents

In order to make comparisons between employees from different backgrounds, the respondents were divided into three groups: Saudis, expatriates from developed countries, and workers from developing countries. Of the 312 respondents interviewed 171 – almost 55 per cent of the sample – were Saudi Arabian citizens. Those from developing countries included a majority from South Asia (sixty-seven), most of who were from Pakistan and India, and a minority from the Arab world (eleven), most of whom were from Egypt and Jordan.[10] Employees surveyed from developed countries came from the United States (eleven), Europe (twelve) and Japan (one). Table 8.1 shows the educational background of each group, with those from developing countries the most educated in terms of paper qualifications.

Not surprisingly there was a larger number of Saudi Arabian employees with only primary education (15.7 per cent) than from the other groups. One way in which SABIC had increased the number of Saudi Arabian nationals was by recruiting security staff, low -level technicians and administrative staff such as messengers from the local population. Most of those who had only secondary education but no further or higher education were also Saudi Arabian citizens. These more highly qualified employees tended to work as middle-rank administrators or as higher-level technicians. Graduates occupied senior administrative positions and worked as engineers, but as Table 8.2 shows, it

114 *Abdullah Al-Salamah*

Table 8.1 Educational level of SABIC employees surveyed

	Saudi Arabian	Developed country	Developing country	Row total
Elementary	27	0	1	28
Secondary	75	3	9	87
College	12	11	12	35
Bachelor of Science	31	5	56	92
Bachelor of Arts or Social Science	22	0	16	38
Higher degree	4	5	23	32
Total	171	24	117	312

Source: Survey of SABIC employees.

Table 8.2 Occupation of SABIC employees surveyed

	Saudi Arabian	Developed country	Developing country	Row total
Technician	75	4	23	102
Engineer	21	8	40	69
Administrator	46	3	15	64
Financial Officer	14	4	7	25
Security	13	1	0	14
Other	2	4	32	38
Total	171	24	117	312

Source: Survey of SABIC employees.

was in the latter field that citizens of Saudi Arabia were heavily out-numbered by non-citizens.

In Saudi Arabia, as in other Arab countries, families are especially important as a social unit, and, therefore, their views towards the suitability of particular jobs for family members weigh heavily with employees and potential employees. Certain jobs may be seen as honourable and highly respected, others less so, and family pressures are felt more acutely than is the case in more individualistic societies. SABIC employees were asked about their families' attitudes towards their jobs and, as Table 8.3 shows, the majority believed their families were satisfied.

Over 90 per cent of employees from Saudi Arabia and developed countries were married, and over 80 per cent of those from developing countries.[11] The majority of Saudi Arabian employees (86 per cent) had their families living with them in Jubail, as had almost 70 per cent of employees from developed countries, but in the case of employees from developing countries only 41 per cent lived with their families while in Jubail. Nevertheless this absence from families did not seem to be a cause for concern amongst employees from developing countries as the majority believed their families were satisfied with this situation, as Table 8.4 shows. As these employees sent back remittances to

Employment conditions in SABIC 115

Table 8.3 Families' acceptances of employees' job

	Saudi Arabian	*Developed country*	*Developing country*	*Row total*
Very satisfied	31	1	15	47
Satisfied	70	13	64	147
Less satisfied	41	6	32	79
Dissatisfied	18	3	4	25
Very dissatisfied	10	0	2	12
Total	170	23	117	310

Source: Survey of SABIC employees.

Table 8.4 Families' acceptances of time employees spend with them

	Saudi Arabian	*Developed country*	*Developing country*	*Row total*
Very satisfied	8	5	16	29
Satisfied	44	10	45	99
Less satisfied	58	1	15	74
Dissatisfied	43	6	17	66
Very dissatisfied	17	1	21	39
Total	170	23	114	307

Source: Survey of SABIC employees.

their families in their home countries, this may explain this acceptance of such separation. Living costs are generally lower in the developing countries from where these employees originate, and it is cheaper for them to live in accommodation for single people in Saudi Arabia while their families remain in their home countries.

Training

In-house training is an essential prerequisite not only for increasing the proportion of Saudi Arabian citizens in the workforce but also for ensuring that where foreigners are employed they can be used effectively.[12] As the largest industrial enterprise in the country, and the largest single employer, SABIC has to devote substantial resources to training. Its highly technical activities mean that job-specific skills have to be acquired by the workforce at all levels, and the joint ventures with major multinational companies means that international best practice can be introduced to ensure employees are well equipped for their work.

All the SABIC companies offer training courses, though not all employees were aware of what was on offer. Almost 96 per cent of respondents from Saudi Arabia and twenty-three out of the twenty-four respondents from developed countries were aware of the courses, but over 10 per cent of employees from developing countries had no knowledge of the training provision.

116   Abdullah Al-Salamah

Almost one-quarter of Saudi Arabian nationals had been on seven or more training courses, compared to 8 per cent of those from developed countries and only 3 per cent of those from developing countries, as Table 8.5 shows.[13] Almost two-thirds of employees from developing countries had not been on any training courses, and of the remainder most had been on only one or two courses. This is not surprising as training is directed at local nationals who, it is hoped, will have long-term careers with SABIC rather than as workers on contracts with only temporary work permits to remain in the kingdom. Most training is in-house in Jubail, but some takes place in other centres in the kingdom, and some is held in the home countries of the SABIC joint venture partners, the United States, Japan, South Korea, Taiwan and Germany. Saudi Arabia nationals and those from developed countries were the most likely to have been on courses outside the kingdom.

Over 90 per cent of Saudi Arabian respondents said that training was important, with almost 45 per cent seeing it as very important. Three-quarters of employees from developing countries also viewed training as important, while those from developed countries were more sceptical, with two-thirds of them regarding training as unimportant, as Table 8.6 shows.

Although most Saudi Arabian employees viewed training as important, there was much dissatisfaction with SABIC's training policy. The majority (88 per cent) of Saudi Arabian respondents were below forty years of age and had hoped that by joining SABIC they would receive training likely to further their careers and enhance their pay and promotion prospects.[14] Over 45 per cent were either dissatisfied or very dissatisfied with the company's training policy, largely

Table 8.5 Number of training courses attended

	Saudi Arabian	Developed country	Developing country	Row total
None	23	10	74	107
1–3	69	10	36	115
4–6	38	2	3	43
7 and over	41	2	4	47
Total	171	24	117	312

Source: Survey of SABIC employees.

Table 8.6 Importance of training to employees

	Saudi Arabian	Developed country	Developing country	Row total
Unimportant	12	16	31	59
Of some use	30	6	10	46
Important	53	1	56	110
Very important	76	1	20	97
Total	171	24	117	312

Source: Survey of SABIC employees.

Employment conditions in SABIC 117

because there were no guidelines for those responsible for training and because opportunities for training varied considerably among the different SABIC companies. As most of these respondents had been on training courses their views deserve to be treated very seriously.

Some argued that the time allocated for training was unsatisfactory, either because it was insufficient or because it was scheduled at inconvenient times, or both. This timing may reflect an employer's view that training is an extra, a type of luxury, which has to be fitted in around more pressing work commitments. If employers are only paying lip-service to training rather than regarding it as an essential means of raising productivity, then participants will not treat training programmes very seriously. There was some evidence from informal comments that this was the case.

Amongst employees from developed countries there was even more dissatisfaction with training policy, with 62 per cent dissatisfied, and nobody very satisfied. Fewer from developing countries were dissatisfied, but this probably reflected their lower expectations and the lower standards of training they had experienced in their home countries in the past.

Despite the reservations about company training policy there was general satisfaction with the skills acquired through training with over 13 per cent of Saudi Arabian respondents very satisfied and over 80 per cent satisfied to some extent, and almost 93 per cent of workers from developed countries satisfied.

Table 8.7 Satisfaction with training policy

	Saudi Arabian	*Developed country*	*Developing country*	*Row total*
Very satisfied	7	0	3	10
Satisfied	40	5	16	61
Less satisfied	47	4	47	98
Dissatisfied	47	9	33	89
Very dissatisfied	30	6	16	52
Total	171	24	115	310

Source: Survey of SABIC employees.

Table 8.8 Satisfaction with skills acquired through training

	Saudi Arabian	*Developed country*	*Developing country*	*Row total*
Very satisfied	21	1	5	27
Satisfied	59	7	26	92
Less satisfied	45	5	15	65
Dissatisfied	14	0	2	16
Very dissatisfied	12	1	2	15
Total	151	14	50	215

Source: Survey of SABIC employees.

118   *Abdullah Al-Salamah*

Only those who had received training answered this question, which may partly explain the higher degree of satisfaction, but the findings show that SABIC training policy is perhaps more useful than many of its critics suggest.

Salaries

Remuneration was, not surprisingly, very important for the overwhelming majority of respondents, both Saudi Arabian and foreign. For those from developed countries one of the attractions of working in Saudi Arabia is the possibility of earning a salary on which no income tax is payable either locally or in their home countries, provided they are classed as non-residents in the case of the latter. Most expatriates and migrant workers are attracted to Saudi Arabia because there they can earn a much higher net income than in their countries of origin, and perhaps accumulate savings and investments.[15] These are typically used to finance the purchase of property in their home country, or to fund retirement or major family expenditures.

Salaries are relatively less important for Saudi Arabian nationals than for foreigners, as only 62 per cent of the former said they were the most important factor in taking a job with SABIC compared to almost 80 per cent of workers from developed countries and 87 per cent of those from developing countries. Nevertheless, for Saudi Arabian citizens SABIC salaries are around one-third higher than for those in government departments, though many see this as compensation for having to live in Jubail rather than in a major urban centre such as Jeddah and Riyadh, close to family and friends. Jobs with SABIC are viewed as secure as employment in government departments; hence this pay differential is not viewed as compensation for uncertainty.

Saudi citizens are paid more than workers from developing countries in equivalent jobs but often less than the salaries paid to expatriates from developed countries in highly specialised or technical occupations. As Table 8.10 shows, the pay rises for Saudi Arabian workers were generally higher than for the other two groups, with 36 per cent enjoying a pay increase of from 6 to 10 per cent in the year prior to the survey, compared to one quarter of foreign workers.

There is a potential conflict between having higher relative pay increases for Saudi Arabian nationals and the policy objective of increasing the proportion of

Table 8.9 Importance of salaries as a job attraction

	Saudi Arabian	Developed country	Developing country	Row total
Very important	106	19	102	227
Important	55	5	10	70
Less important	8	0	3	11
Unimportant	1	0	2	3
Total	170	24	117	311

Source: Survey of SABIC employees.

Employment conditions in SABIC 119

Table 8.10 Percentage pay increase

	Saudi Arabian	Developed country	Developing country	Row total
Over 11%	1	2	1	4
6–10%	61	6	30	97
1–5%	100	12	58	170
None	6	4	27	37
Total	168	24	116	308

Source: Survey of SABIC employees.

Table 8.11 Satisfaction with salaries

	Saudi Arabian	Developed country	Developing country	Row total
Very satisfied	20	2	6	28
Satisfied	55	12	45	112
Less satisfied	62	5	35	102
Dissatisfied	34	5	31	70
Total	171	24	117	312

Source: Survey of SABIC employees.

local citizens in the workforce. Tighter restrictions on work permits for foreign workers may not work if there are strong market incentives against employing Saudi Arabian citizens. It is not always easy, however, to separate cause from effect. Even where there are unemployed or underemployed local citizens there may be shortages of skilled and specialist workers in companies such as SABIC. In these circumstances salaries for such occupations may be bid up if fewer work permits are issued, but only relatively few Saudi Arabian workers may benefit. Fortunately such local salary pressures will only have a marginal effect on SABIC's international competitiveness, as in such capital- and energy-intensive activities, salaries represent only a relatively small proportion of total costs.

Most Saudi Arabian nationals and those from developed countries are satisfied with their salaries, as Table 8.11 shows, but over half of those from developing countries are either less satisfied or dissatisfied. This undoubtedly reflects the lower salary levels of those from developing countries, and perhaps their resentment when they contrast their remuneration with that of Saudi Arabian nationals and employees from the West.

Promotion opportunities

There is widespread dissatisfaction with promotion opportunities within SABIC, especially amongst foreign employees, with those from developed countries being the most dissatisfied.[16] Over 83 per cent of respondents from developed countries indicated their dissatisfaction, compared to 47 per cent from

120   *Abdullah Al-Salamah*

Table 8.12 Satisfaction with promotion opportunities

	Saudi Arabian	Developed country	Developing country	Row total
Very satisfied	6	1	4	11
Satisfied	31	1	27	59
Less satisfied	66	2	31	99
Dissatisfied	68	20	55	143
Total	171	24	117	312

Source: Survey of SABIC employees.

developing countries. The latter had perhaps lower expectations concerning promotion than employees from developed countries given their level of skills and their position in SABIC

Preference is given to suitably qualified and experienced Saudi Arabian nationals with respect to promotion, but it was notable that even amongst the local citizens surveyed there was considerable dissatisfaction. Surprisingly, a lower proportion of respondents from Saudi Arabia were either very satisfied or satisfied (21 per cent), compared to those from developing countries (26 per cent). Almost 40 per cent of Saudi Arabian respondents were less than satisfied, with a similar proportion dissatisfied.

Inevitably in any organisation it will be a minority that actually achieve promotion to the highest ranks, and in a corporation such as SABIC, involved in highly complex processes, only those with exceptional organisational and technical skills can aspire to reach the top. Personal ability ceilings may explain some of the dissatisfaction, rather than simply company policy. Where those occupying senior positions are relatively young, then more junior employees may have longer to wait for promotion, which may also be a source of frustration in SABIC. Those who have acquired technical skills and attended management training courses are often disappointed when they see no immediate benefits in terms of career prospects despite having fulfilled all the prerequisites. There has been some movement of the most able employees from SABIC to ARAMCO, the Arabian American Oil Company, where there are arguably greater opportunities for advancement.

Management decisions and labour relations

Frustrations over promotion prospects do not appear to impact too adversely on employees' satisfaction and respect for management decision-making, although there is some criticism. Over 58 per cent of respondents from developed countries were satisfied with management decision-taking, and over 71 per cent of those from developing countries. Respondents from Saudi Arabia tended to be more critical, with only 45 per cent satisfied with management decision-making, while 30 per cent had some reservations and one-quarter expressed dissatisfaction.

Employment conditions in SABIC 121

Table 8.13 Satisfaction with management decision-making

	Saudi Arabian	Developed country	Developing country	Row total
Very satisfied	12	3	20	35
Satisfied	66	11	64	141
Less satisfied	51	5	24	80
Dissatisfied	42	5	9	56
Total	171	24	117	312

Source: Survey of SABIC employees.

Table 8.14 Satisfaction with how managers/supervisors deal with employees

	Saudi Arabian	Developed country	Developing country	Row total
Very satisfied	31	2	31	64
Satisfied	60	9	57	126
Less satisfied	48	5	18	71
Dissatisfied	32	8	11	51
Total	171	24	117	312

Source: Survey of SABIC employees.

Some of this dissatisfaction stemmed from a feeling that was too little consultation with employees. Saudi Arabian respondents were particularly unhappy about this, with almost one-quarter registering dissatisfaction and 30 per cent satisfied to only a limited extent. Foreign workers were less concerned about being consulted by management, perhaps because they were on temporary contracts and so had less of a stake in the organisation. Saudi Arabian workers were also less amenable to accepting the suggestions of managers and supervisors, though over 40 per cent did so with no reservations and a further 40 per cent did so with some reservations.

A majority of Saudi Arabian employees were satisfied with the way in which they were treated by management, with less than one-fifth dissatisfied, as Table 8.14 shows. Employees from developed countries appeared to be more dissatisfied, with one-third responding negatively. The responses of those from developing countries were in line with those from Saudi Arabia, with less than 10 per cent being dissatisfied.

There is only limited labour market flexibility in Saudi Arabia, with relatively few local citizens moving from one employer to another, especially in the case of government service and partially state-owned companies such as SABIC, where those recruited believe they have jobs for their entire working lives. Indeed, Saudi employees are rarely dismissed or declared redundant, and those who do change jobs or leave before retirement age do so of their own free will.[17]

Western expatriates and workers from developing countries are on fixed-term contracts with their employers which are usually honoured and rarely terminated

122 *Abdullah Al-Salamah*

before their time by the Saudi authorities or companies without good legal reasons. Such contracts can be extended and renewed, but as work permits are issued for particular companies or branches of government they cannot be transferred to other employers. There is no market in work permits, and foreign employees are not free to change jobs within the kingdom. Indeed some employers are reluctant to allow foreign employees to leave before the end of their contracts, although this cannot be enforced.

The low degree of satisfaction with procedures for job termination and transfer by expatriates from developed countries and workers from developing countries probably reflects these national restrictions within the kingdom rather than specific dissatisfaction with SABIC, which has only limited freedom for discretion. Of greater interest is the dissatisfaction of Saudi Arabian employees, since only one-third were either very satisfied or satisfied – as Table 8.15 shows – while almost one-quarter were either dissatisfied or at best only partially satisfied (44 per cent). It may be that at least some local employees would welcome increased job flexibility.

Working arrangements and time management

Plants such as those run by SABIC have to operate continuously throughout the day and year to ensure an adequate level of cover at all times.[18] All employees are unable to take holidays and leave at the same time, and the day and night have to be covered through shifts. Despite this necessity there was general

Table 8.15 Satisfaction with procedures for job termination and transfer

	Saudi Arabian	Developed country	Developing country	Row total
Very satisfied	5	2	6	13
Satisfied	49	7	49	105
Less satisfied	74	9	43	126
Dissatisfied	39	6	13	58
Total	167	24	111	302

Source: Survey of SABIC employees.

Table 8.16 Satisfaction with holidays and leave

	Saudi Arabian	Developed country	Developing country	Row total
Very satisfied	22	1	14	37
Satisfied	62	16	67	145
Less satisfied	49	1	22	72
Dissatisfied	38	6	14	58
Total	171	24	117	312

Source: Survey of SABIC employees.

satisfaction with holiday and leave arrangements, as well as with working hours and shifts. Employees from both developed and developing countries preferred to work long hours with relatively short breaks while in the kingdom, provided they could have lengthy periods of leave enabling them to return to their home countries for holidays. Saudi Arabian employees were generally less satisfied as some felt there was insufficient leave and there was concern about the need to work during religious holidays. However, less than one-quarter were dissatisfied, though over a quarter believed the holiday arrangements were not entirely satisfactory.

A higher proportion of all categories of respondents were very satisfied with the working hours, especially those from developing countries who were willing to work long hours to maximise their earnings. However, Saudi Arabian respondents appeared to be less satisfied than foreign employees, the issues being the length of the working day and the inflexibility of the working hours.[19]

Those who apply to SABIC for employment know that shift working will be involved and, as Table 8.18 shows, the vast majority of workers from developed countries and those from developing countries were satisfied with the timing of their shifts. There was more dissatisfaction amongst Saudi Arabian workers, partly because they had heavier family commitments which could be affected by the need to work unsociable hours.[20]

Working conditions in large industrial complexes are inevitably varied because of the nature of the chemical processes carried out. The SABIC facilities are modern and compare with the best in Europe or North America.

Table 8.17 Satisfaction with working hours

	Saudi Arabian	Developed country	Developing country	Row total
Very satisfied	34	7	39	80
Satisfied	60	13	70	143
Less satisfied	40	1	5	46
Dissatisfied	35	3	2	40
Total	169	24	116	309

Source: Survey of SABIC employees.

Table 8.18 Satisfaction with scheduling of shifts

	Saudi Arabian	Developed country	Developing country	Row total
Very satisfied	16	3	25	44
Satisfied	32	11	53	96
Less satisfied	44	4	7	55
Dissatisfied	16	1	1	18
Total	108	19	86	213

Source: Survey of SABIC employees.

124 Abdullah Al-Salamah

Being located in a harsh desert region, with extremes of temperature, presents challenges, but most working areas are air-conditioned and shaded from the sun. There are adequate canteens and areas for relaxation in most of the facilities, and the working environment has been designed to ensure it is as pleasant as possible. Productivity is usually higher when workers are satisfied with their working conditions, and absenteeism less frequent.[21]

The majority of workers are satisfied with working conditions at SABIC, especially those from developing countries who have worked at similar facilities in their home countries where conditions are often much less satisfactory.[22] Proportionately more of those from developed countries were less satisfied or dissatisfied, and around one-third of Saudi Arabian workers felt that conditions could be better, while around one-fifth were dissatisfied. Clearly there is still scope for improving working conditions despite the generally high standards.

In chemical and petrochemical complexes there is always a risk of accidents, gas leaks and fires being the main potential hazards. SABIC has an excellent safety record and clear emergency procedures. Designated employees are given training in first aid, and instruction in the use of fire extinguishers and other types of safety equipment. Where incidents occur, detailed reports have to be prepared leading to appropriate measures being taken to prevent them from happening again. One of the Saudi Arabian respondents alleged that there were some inaccuracies in safety reports and that not all accidents had been recorded, although this could not be verified.

Table 8.19 Satisfaction with working conditions

	Saudi Arabian	Developed country	Developing country	Row total
Very satisfied	14	3	23	40
Satisfied	66	11	71	148
Less satisfied	57	5	16	78
Dissatisfied	34	5	7	46
Total	171	24	117	312

Source: Survey of SABIC employees.

Table 8.20 Satisfaction with safety and accident prevention

	Saudi Arabian	Developed country	Developing country	Row total
Very satisfied	48	6	48	102
Satisfied	64	13	59	136
Less satisfied	41	3	8	52
Dissatisfied	18	2	2	22
Total	171	24	117	312

Source: Survey of SABIC employees.

Over three-quarters of all respondents were either very satisfied or satisfied with safety and accident prevention measures, with those from developing countries being the most satisfied.[23] Of those who were dissatisfied the majority were Saudi Arabian employees, with just under 10 per cent. Although there can be no room for complacency over safety issues, the survey results reflect very positively on the accident prevention measures undertaken by the SABIC companies.

Conclusion

Saudi Arabian employees saw salary levels as important in attracting workers, but this fact was emphasised to a greater extent by Western expatriates and employees from developing countries. A higher proportion of Saudi nationals were satisfied with their salaries, which was not surprising as their pay had risen more rapidly than that for foreign workers. However, fewer Saudi Arabian nationals were satisfied with their promotion opportunities, and almost one-fifth were very dissatisfied. More Saudi Arabian than Western employees were satisfied with management methods, which in the joint ventures tended to be more authoritarian than those used by the Western parent companies.

Overall it seems that the joint-venture companies were willing to carry out their statutory obligations, especially with respect to training, but that Saudi Arabian nationals were disappointed that the training they had received had not been of more help in terms of career advancement. Workplace tensions and conflicts may increase if Saudi Arabia opens up its economy to increased foreign investment as a result of accession to the World Trade Organisation. It may prove more difficult to Saudi-ise in an industrial environment that is subject to intense global competition.

9 The role of the private sector

Monica Malik

This chapter is based on research that considered private-sector-led development as an alternative strategy for economic growth and development in the context of the Saudi Arabian economy, through the views of the private sector. Thirty leading Saudi businessmen were interviewed during 1999, and their responses provide the key findings of this investigation. Since the mid-1980s Saudi Arabians have expressed a desire for the private sector to play the leading role in the economy, with the government playing a supportive one by providing a positive environment for private-sector activity. Up to the present the government has played the central role in the economy as the oil revenue has accrued directly to the authorities. The research focused on analysing the potential for private-sector development.

In order to comprehend whether the private sector is capable of creating self-sustained growth there is a need to understand how the private sector contributes to the economy and whether its growth is independent of the state. It is also necessary to examine whether the requisite business environment is in place for development led by the private sector.

The relationship between the private sector and the state

A good state–private sector relationship is central to the economic development of the country. This includes such factors as whether the private sector is involved in long-term policy formulation and if it is able to set its own agenda. The relevance of this research is to analyse what is undoubtedly one of the most important elements of Saudi Arabia's economic development drive for the future: private-sector development. The perceptions of this sector will illustrate the potential for economic development, the role that the private sector can play in the economy and the nature of the relationship between it and the state.

In addition, noting the importance of the state as the main agent of development, the research examined the quality of state intervention, based on interviews conducted with those in the private sector. The research attempted to place Saudi Arabia in the context of the theory suggested by Peter Evans on the state and its relationship with the economic structure.

The role of the private sector   127

Evans[1] suggested that there were three types of state: first, the predatory state where there are high levels of unearned income due to rent-seeking behaviour throughout the state structure; second, the intermediate state where there are inconsistencies in the state's behaviour, as for example where there are patches of predatory and corrupt behaviour but also areas of efficient behaviour. Finally, there is the developmental state where development is central to the goals of the state.

Evans suggested that certain factors are important for the developmental state. First, autonomy to carry out its policies, as the type of rule often aids autonomy. Cammack[2] noted that strong authoritarian rule was central to the success of economic development in East Asia. Second, strong links with the private sector and other sectors are needed for the transformation of the economy[3]. Roumasset[4] placed strong emphasis on the role of partnerships with the financial sector

Ability of the private sector to initiate development

When the government wants the private sector to take the lead in the economy or during a process of economic liberalisation when the state is being rolled back, there needs to be a strong, independent and efficient private sector in place. Thus much of the work of the World Bank and the International Finance Corporation is based around the strengthening of that sector.

The interviewees' general perceptions are that the capabilities of the private sector have to be strengthened before it becomes able to take the lead in the economy and that the business environment has to be improved. Many of the interviewees also recognised the central role still played by oil revenue in driving the economy and the private sector, which also indicated a failure on the part of the government to diversify. The level of development of the private sector is a result of government policy.

Many of the interviewees felt the private sector was taking up the challenge and had started to restructure and reorganise itself in order to compete internationally; also, that some of the dead wood in that sector had been removed as a result of the 1980s recession. The private sector has gained in strength and in independence from the government. Despite this improvement in its ability to stand on its own two feet, there is still a certain amount of reliance on the government and independence has gone only so far. One interviewee noted that had the low oil prices of 1998 and early 1999 continued the private sector would been unable to survive the recession.

The sector is still dependent on government subsidies (though indirect), support, spending and – in some cases – contracts. Also mentioned, as a form of protectionism, is the phenomenon of agencies: Saudi companies have often flourished merely because of their role as sole agents and distributors. The foreign partner profits as it gains access to the Saudi market and the government through the Saudi partner. Due to the fact that agencies are often sole agents and distributors they are often able to set monopolistic prices. For example, one of

128 *Monica Malik*

the interviewees stated: 'If you call IBM in Saudi Arabia you will see that they set their own prices. It is much cheaper if you have a credit card to buy an IBM over the phone from America and get it delivered.' In addition it was mentioned that not only is it possible to charge higher prices but also this allows the possibility of greater inefficiencies. For instance, the servicing of vehicles is often of a poor standard and the quality of electronics comparatively low.

Successful private-sector development depends on key services being provided by the state: notably an effective bureaucracy, an adequate infrastructure and a clear legal and regulatory system. When answering the question, 'Is the private sector is ready to take the lead in the economy?' only three of the thirty interviewees replied that it was and that the environmental preconditions for this had been met. Later in the interviews, when asked specifically about such areas as the provision of infrastructure and the legal and educational systems, the responses were even more negative. The majority felt either that the private sector was not mature enough or that the environment was unsuitable for private-sector development. Despite these hindrances the private-sector businessmen felt capable of playing a greater role in the economy than at present and that privatisation was one way in which they could contribute to development.

The interviews conducted also indicated that despite the continuing importance of government expenditure for the health of the private sector, that sector had gained a degree of independence since the recession of the 1980s. It was also less dependent on government contracts, and the role of subsidies had been reduced. The majority of interviewees agreed with the policy of privatisation as a means of increasing the sector's role within the economy and of improving their own capabilities, while noting that many uncertainties existed. First, the fear of job losses within the state-owned enterprises might prevent privatisation from taking place. Second, questions were raised concerning the ability of private-sector managers to make their own decisions after privatisation. Some interviewees noted that the importance of privatisation was not merely to change ownership from public to private but also to change the way the company was being run.

The efficiency of the private sector

One of the basic assumptions supporting private-sector development as opposed to its state-led equivalent is that it is efficient and able to combine a number of inputs to achieve the best possible product or service in the cheapest possible way. First, all the interviewees who drew a comparison between the levels of efficiency in state organisations and the private sector judged the latter to be the more efficient of the two. However, some interviewees pointed out that the private sector was only slightly more efficient than the government. Second, the majority of interviewees felt that the Saudi private sector was not competitive internationally and that its efficiency was not comparable to that of the international private sector. This is especially important given the fact that

The role of the private sector   129

Saudi Arabia is negotiating its accession to the World Trade Organisation, which will mean the removal of certain forms of protection and the sector's being forced to compete internationally. On the subject of Saudi Arabia's future WTO membership, there was a great deal of uncertainty as to how the opening up of markets would affect the sector. Its ability to compete internationally was seen as critical to its survival, and there was a need for it to make use of the transitional period to reorganise itself and prepare for the competition.

Despite noting these points, the interviews indicated that efficiency within the private sector varied considerably, with those areas still dependent on protection and subsidies – such as agriculture – arguably the least efficient. Many interviewees pointed out that subsidies merely continued to promote dependence within farming rather than nurturing this activity until it became capable of supporting itself. As a result companies involved in agriculture fail to mature or to gain in efficiency. All the interviewees who spoke on this issue stated that subsidies for agriculture could not continue indefinitely and should be withdrawn. Some mentioned the fact that agricultural subsidies no longer benefited the Bedouin people: they went to high-income farmers as opposed to those using traditional methods.

Some interviewees felt that tariffs and subsidised loans from the Saudi Industrial Development Fund protected some forms of manufacturing excessively. The subsidies are ill-conceived and inflexible as they relate mainly to start-up capital and cease to be flexible once an industry reaches maturity. The subsidies have no social aims, nor do they result in the establishment of self-sufficient new industries; instead they create inefficient companies dependent on government handouts for their survival.

The size of a company can be important. Some interviewees mentioned that small companies did not have to worry about management systems and economic planning. The larger the company, the greater the tendency towards inefficiency: some of the larger ones functioned like bureaucracies. They mentioned that it was all too easy for firms to flourish while remaining inefficient due to the easy profits to be made through the absence of taxation, the availability of loans and the lack of competition. Also, within a captive market luxury products could be sold without the need to carry out promotion, which could mean that companies failed to become competitive and efficient and thus to grow.

If a Saudi company has a foreign partner, the Saudi partner gains efficiency and good management from the partnership. Other benefits noted were brand loyalty, production, marketing and technology transfer. Foreign partners were also seen as crucial in the implementing of projects and the setting up of system.

Problems of management capability

The majority of interviewees felt that only a small number of companies generally were highly sophisticated and well developed in terms of management capabilities and techniques, and that the number was particularly small in Saudi Arabia. Saudi businesses were seen as traditional in nature; they did not consider

130 *Monica Malik*

long-term goals and strategies but instead looked to the short term. Respondents also suggested that the private sector did not consider the business and the process as a whole. When thinking of entering a new area or investing in something new, businesses did not consider whether this would add to their other interests or what they themselves could bring to the venture. The businessman merely saw each new opportunity as a means of making a profit, without considering the finer points. Another example given was that a firm might have a large foreign treasury operation, but if that treasury was not up to scratch then it was of very little use.

Respondents suggested that Saudi Arabian companies were slow to change and had poor planning. Very few conducted feasibility studies, and also there were no proper recruitment systems. In addition, there was a lack of accountability within the companies. One of the important preconditions for efficiency is that people have to be accountable at every level and to remain focused on the goals set. As mentioned above, the planning and setting of goals were found to be weak, and when the desired results were not obtained no one was made accountable for this failure. The Saudi businessman was not seen as entrepreneurial in nature, and most respondents suggested there was still a trading- and agency-based mentality rather than a manufacturing capability. In short, management had not matured.

Family business is currently the subject of much debate within Saudi Arabia. As many of the top private companies are family-owned their performance and continuity affect the entire national economy. All the interviewees felt that succession was an area of difficulty for some family-owned firms, especially those now in the third or fourth generation. They specifically identified the key issues affecting family-owned businesses as being the size of the family, whether or not the owner had left a succession plan, whether they knew how to delegate responsibility to the children, and whether the management of the company was kept separate from its ownership.

A further area raised by the interviewees was the impact of family-owned businesses on efficiency, an important point given the fact that many of the leading private-sector companies belong to this category. One possible solution is for the companies to go public. Many of the interviewees suggested that there were other options, and that going public was not the first solution for a family-owned business as this would create a sense of losing something that belonged to the family as a whole. Such firms needed to address these issues of continuation, whether through the formulation of succession plans or by separating management from ownership. The responses showed that the private sector needed to improve its capability and managerial abilities and to respond to challenges such as joining the WTO.

The respondents suggested that inefficiency and a lack of managerial development came about because success was often due not to entrepreneurial capability but to certain other factors. Some interviewees mentioned the links with agencies and royal families. This can be illustrated by the following quote from the one of them:

The role of the private sector   131

'The major and successful members of the private sector have made it because of government largess – contracts, connections, etc. The trick is when someone is rising in the private sector is to see who is behind it. For example, two families in the Eastern Province became very rich and their wealth grew very quickly. This was because of their close links with the government and with the Governor of the Province. You always have to look at the name behind the name. The question is why don't the Princes do it themselves – because they are not successful that way.'

The respondents mentioned that each region had certain well-established families that were well known, so people who look to do business in these areas will continue to deal with them. Thus, once a name has been built up either through its links with agencies, the royal family or the government, it builds up momentum and continues to grow.

Perceptions of the business environment and legal system

Successful private-sector development calls for a business environment that is conducive to commerce, and that environment should be provided by the government. Thus, although economic liberalisation implies a reduced role for government, that role is nonetheless still a critical one and the government needs to be strong and effective. On the positive side, many interviewees had noted that the country's business environment was favourable, due to the many opportunities available, the availability of subsidised loans and the high degree of liquidity in the market. Some interviewees mentioned that the government had worked hard both to keep inflation low and to promote bilateral trade agreements.

Despite some limited praise for the government, the interviewees were very critical of the business environment, which, they implied, did not meet the needs of the private sector. They were particularly critical of the education system. When describing this the words used included 'disaster' and 'a major handicap'. Almost all the interviewees mentioned that there were serious failings in the system and that it was backward and outdated. They mentioned that some students were even unable to read, write or communicate on leaving school and some unable to spell in Arabic. In addition, very few were computer-literate. Training in the most basic skills was not provided, and most respondents asserted that the education system failed to meet the needs of the business sector. Many felt that the universities placed too little stress on technical and vocational courses and insufficient emphasis on research and development. The system, they suggested, was too focused on religion and neglected skills that the private sector needed.

All but one of the interviewees said that the legal system was a hindrance to the private sector. It was suggested that it lacked the tools necessary for the private sector to function effectively in terms of both property protection and the rapid settlement of disputes. The interview results suggested that these requirements were not being met by the current Saudi legal system, based on

132   *Monica Malik*

shariah or Islamic law, although several secular codes for commercial activity have been introduced, such as distributorship agreements, company laws and government contracts. These are subject to 'regulations' and 'implementing rules' issued by the Council of Ministers and various government ministries. Turck[5] further mentioned that apart from shariah courts, commercial disputes might be handled by special committees such as the Board of Grievances, the Saudi Arabian Monetary Agency's Committee for Banking Disputes or the Commission for Labour Disputes.

Many interviewees felt that much was lacking in the commercial codes and that a number of these were out of date. Many felt that a more comprehensive set of civil and commercial laws or regulations was needed to protect the interests of a company either leasing or lending. It was said that if the buyer reneged it was difficult to retrieve the money or the product in question. One interviewee mentioned that if security was provided this would give a boost to the economy as a whole as people would then be able to purchase homes, cars, furniture and kitchen equipment more readily. In discussions on this subject the selling of cars was repeatedly used as an example. Smaller businesses and less well-established companies within the private sector complained about the lack of commercial loans from banks despite, their good profits. This was due to the fact there was no regulation in force governing the recovery of money nor any dealing with such issues as bankruptcy; though it was noted that this situation was improving thanks to the setting up of the SAMA Committee for Banking Disputes. Another example given was the complex situation regarding mortgages: the process involves the borrower giving the title deed to the bank, which then passes the deed to a third party who holds the deed in their name on the bank's behalf.

Another area where the laws have to be improved and updated was that regarding the labour laws, which date from 1969 and cover labour relations and workers' and employers' rights. According to the interviewees, these make it difficult to terminate the contracts of Saudi Arabian employees, especially at managerial level. Not only does the process take a long time, but also disputes often end up at the Board of Labour, with considerable sums awarded as compensation. Difficulties also arise when it comes to firing non-Saudis. The labour laws seem to be extremely restrictive for management.

The interviewees also identified problems linked to dispute resolution. These included legal procedures that take a long time to process. One interviewee remarked that he had been fighting a case through the courts for the past fifteen years, with the system hoping he would just give up. A further point repeated by the interviewees was that the Board of Grievances took a long time. Business International[6] 'noted that this was because of the courts' emphasis on reconciliation.

Respondents also criticised the lack of legal transparency. They suggested this was a result of the fact that the laws were not codified. Due to this lack of transparency it was difficult to judge the outcome of a case, therefore, contracts with foreign partners were occasionally written under English law. One interviewee raised the point that he had very little trust in the court's

The role of the private sector   133

judgement since it could be influenced – especially in dealings connected with the royal family. He gave the example of one partner in a firm wanting to sell their share of the company and the other partner being obliged to buy at a price they considered very inflated. There was often poor enforcement once court decisions had been made.

Views of the government's role in business

Crony capitalism was seen as prevalent. As has been mentioned, personal contact is important for doing business, and the royal family has been influential in the success of certain private-sector families. Many interviewees felt that crony capitalism was one of the main challenges facing the private sector, as the royal family competed in every sector though not as equals. In addition, royalty and patronage detract from the viability of private-sector development and the culture required for sustainable development. The following section outlines some of the points mentioned by the interviewees indicating the presence of crony capitalism within Saudi Arabia.

Government tenders tend to be linked to favours and to whom you know, and the winning of government contracts is dependent on these. Some interviewees mentioned that although small contracts were distributed by open tender, large and valuable contracts were agreed behind closed doors. Princes and other prominent individuals were the main beneficiaries of the development programmes, and the most colourful examples of instant riches in Saudi Arabia suggest the importance of personal contact with the royal family. Yet the size and breadth of the new middle and upper class bespeak a much broader involvement on the part of the bureaucracy.

Subsidies go to those who are well connected rather than to the poor. It was remarked that previously there had been basic subsidies for the latter, such as on tea and sugar. All the interviewees felt that initially subsidies had been introduced to redistribute wealth but that these original aims were not being fulfilled. This was especially the case with agriculture, where subsidies had been intended to help redistribute money to poor Bedouin areas, encourage traditional farmers and increase the living standards of those in financial need. However, most had gone to wealthy, well-connected individuals with large estates.

Members of the royal family acted as intermediaries between the private sector and the decision-makers. Two different ways in which the Princes were involved were highlighted during the interviews. First, if a member of the royal family or the government asked you to do something, then you were obliged to do it, being then able to ask them for a favour in return. Second, when trying to win or develop a project you had to bring in a Prince for 'pulling power'. Then, when the private sector partner had done all the work, the Prince received a share of the profits. One interviewees said that he saw these payments to Princes as an extra tax necessary for business.

The royal family owns large sections of the economy, and one respondent said that the princes obtained money easily through land, being entitled to areas of a

134 *Monica Malik*

certain size. They went to the King and asked for a particular area, then either claimed the land or sold it to a third party. Alternatively, they took land that no one owned and cleared it, went to the government and make it legal, after which they sold it. The corruption occurs when the government bought back the land or they sold it to a third party and then claimed it back; or when it emerges that the land already belonged to someone else. The interviewee noted that while this was rare some high-profile cases nonetheless existed. Legislation was geared to personal interest. The interviewee said it was often designed to increase the importance of a ministry and could at the same time benefit an individual working within the private sector.

Shortcomings of the financial system

One of the three main elements required for private-sector development, according to the World Bank, is a financial system that mobilises and allocates financial resources efficiently. A large majority of the interviewees indicated that the financial system was insufficiently developed to meet private-sector needs. The main areas raised were the problems linked with the stock market, and a minority talked about the need for increased loans for commercial purposes. Both these areas were identified in the fourth and fifth development plans as areas requiring improvement.

The lack of commercial loans by the private banks to small businesses has already been mentioned. Some interviewees felt this ways due to the fact that banks mostly lent to a few large corporate clients and to the government – which is very profitable – and that as a result did not feel the need to expand their client base. Others noted that bank loans were predominantly short-term and that more sources of long-term financing were called for. In addition, it was noted that the difficulty in obtaining finance was most acute for small and medium-sized companies (which are needed for a healthy economy) as these are not able to apply for government agency loans such as those issued by the Saudi Industrial Development Fund.

The area most discussed was that relating to the problems of the stock market. Some interviewees suggested that this played a very limited role in the economy. One problem raised by the interviewees was that few companies were listed on the stock market. This did not provide many options for those wanting to invest in the country, especially in small and medium-sized businesses. This question was linked with the issue of the regulations for going public.

It was alleged that companies were controlled by a very small number of investors. Many of the interviewees said that it was the old, traditional families and money that owned the majority of company shares listed on the stock market. When a company is first floated it is greatly oversubscribed so does not encourage new investors or tap into new sources of capital. The stock market was not viewed as being run professionally. The interviewees suggested different ways in which it could be manipulated, and also said that board members made use of their privileged knowledge for their own personal gain as well as

The role of the private sector   135

providing their friends with inside information. The trading process was seen as time-consuming and inefficient. Regulation of the stock market had to be tightened as in the present situation it was people with power who made the substantial gains.

Generally the respondents complained that there were poor investment opportunities in Saudi Arabia compared with internationally. Overall they felt there was much to be improved in areas relating to the stock market, especially its regulation. It was not viewed as an important means for the private sector to raise capital or involve the public in the ownership of companies.

The inadequacy of the infrastructure

Despite government efforts to develop the infrastructure, the interviewees felt it was not at the level the private sector required. Indeed, they all expressed a great deal of frustration when discussing the matter. Many noted that while the infrastructure was being built there had been a failure to oversee its construction adequately, which had led to its becoming a huge burden on the economy. The interviewees also commented that continual government spending was needed both for its maintenance and its ability to keep pace with the demands of the economy. This had not happened, due to budgetary problems.

Industrial cites were the area of most concern. The interviewees remarked on a shortage of land, water and electricity. They mentioned having obtained their own electricity generators, something that more and more plants were doing. In addition, it was pointed out that there was a lack of the facilities necessary to deal with sewage and waste, which is often removed by trucks.

Telecommunications were also seen as a problem. One interviewee mentioned that in some of his plants there was only one telephone line, although many interviewees stated that improvements had been made in the quantity of lines provided and that they expected this to continue. One said it was difficult for one of his offices to contact another during the day, which resulted in difficulties with IT flows and networking. In addition, interviewees complained about the fact that the Internet had come so late to the kingdom, although it was possible to connect through Bahrain, which was expensive. They noted that mobile phones had also been introduced last into Saudi Arabia and that the more remote areas were not covered by the network. They added that despite cuts in tariffs, mobile phones there were still the most expensive in the GCC.

Excessive bureaucracy and regulation

Even though the government wants to play a smaller role in the economy, it is nonetheless important for that role to be both efficient and effective. A high level of bureaucracy and poor regulations can have a negative effect on the economy; these things can deter investment in a country as well as proving very time-consuming and costly for the private sector. In addition an oversized bureaucracy or civil service can place a financial burden on the government and taxpayers.

136 *Monica Malik*

The majority of interviewees felt that a great deal of time, money and efficiency were being wasted on bureaucratic matters or complicated and inappropriate regulations. Some interviewees added that one of the causes of the large size of the bureaucracy was the government's policy of hiring workers for social reasons. This had created a considerable amount of paperwork, and the level of corruption had risen as a result, partly reflecting the need for bribes due to the fact that salaries had not increased.

The interviewees noted that it took between three and six months merely to establish a company. The procedures are seen as being very tedious, as the private sector has to deal with a number of ministries – such as the Ministry of Commerce and the Ministry of Industry – each of which requires separate paperwork. Interviewees compared this with the UAE, where a company can be set up over the telephone. One of the main reasons for investing overseas was the high level of bureaucracy and red tape in Saudi Arabia.

Applying for licences was another example of a lengthy process that could take up to six months with no guarantee that the licence will eventually be given. Interviewees said that often licences were not granted as there were already many companies in the area. They added that it was not up to the licence office to make decisions on these criteria, and that if a company was unable to compete it would go out of business. Interviewees also mentioned that they were required to complete a large number of forms and demonstrate numerous capabilities when applying for SIDF loans, but that these could not be put to use when applying for bank loans. Thus much time was wasted on paperwork, and the situation needed to be standardised.

Regarding exporting and importing, interviewees complained about the high level of bureaucracy involved in trying to obtain export licences, which went against government rhetoric on the private sector increasing exports. Interviewees mentioned a new law stipulating that consignments of imported products had to be cleared at source, which was very time-consuming. Previously the product had just required to be inspected, and if it was cleared there had been a free flow.

Interviewees also complained that a new telephone line could take between two to three years to be installed once the initial application had been made. Whether the privatisation of telecommunications will improve this situation remains to be seen.

A further problem area linked with the bureaucracy is the fact that it is not service-oriented and lacks the flexibility to understand the needs of the private sector. Respondents asserted that ministries were always putting up hurdles and blocking the private sector. When discussing bureaucracy many interviewees also mentioned the difficulties surrounding regulation. One of the reasons for the private sector's taking a lead in the economy is to reduce the distortion of investment and resources due to government involvement.

The areas where the interviewees felt there were problems with the regulations included labour laws that were insufficiently flexible. There was also concern about regulations preventing mergers. Some interviewees remarked

The role of the private sector   137

that their main company was too small within the global context and that they wanted to merge and create alliances, but that government regulation was preventing them from doing so. Two interviewees felt that government regulation did not encourage companies to go public, with one asserting that due to a lack of transparency concerning the rules the process could take years.

There were complaints about the poor regulation and supervision of the insurance industry, for which Saudi Arabia possesses no legal framework. The ad hoc committees formed by the chambers of commerce and the Ministry of Commerce handled disputes between the insurance companies and their policyholders. The Saudi court system does not legitimise insurance activities and, accordingly, does not handle insurance conflicts. With no legal framework in place the protection of policyholders' rights is probably worse there than in other GCC countries.

The interviews were conducted before the new foreign investment laws had been introduced, but interestingly interviewees saw a need for more favourable regulations in order to attract foreign direct investment. To support this view one gave the example of an industrial project in another Arab country where the feasibility and marketing studies had already been completed and institutions were in place to encourage and attract foreign investment. Interviewees highlighted the problems of obtaining visas – especially for women, even if they happened to be the team leaders for a particular project – and compared this with the UAE, where one could get a visa at the airport. They also referred to the problems faced by joint venture partners who need a letter from their sponsor in order to obtain or disconnect a telephone line or to travel.

Most respondents considered there was inadequate regulation for the protection of intellectual property rights. Interviewees expanded on this by saying that Saudi Arabia was one of the worst offenders in this area and had done little to improve the enforcement, especially when compared to the UAE.

Interviewees complained about the poor monitoring and enforcement of the regulation of the stock market, which allowed the market to be manipulated. There was also a lack of vital, up-to-date economic information. Such knowledge was seen as crucial to the private sector for the making of business and investment decisions. Areas highlighted included macroeconomic indicators and information about the market, companies and financing.

Conclusion

The survey revealed a large number of challenges facing both the private sector and the government. Respondents believed the private sector had to improve its core capabilities and managerial competence, especially in the light of Saudi Arabia joining the WTO. It was clear, however, that many doubted the government's view regarding private-sector-led development. The sector needs to gain experience and overall is still dependent on government spending, which indicated the lack of diversification within the economy. The lack of development of private-sector capabilities was partly a result of the profitable

138 *Monica Malik*

market conditions due to the high levels of liquidity and government policies to protect the private sector. The interviewees suggested that despite the need for the private sector to mature there existed a greater role for it in the economy and that in many areas it could prove more effective than the state.

The respondents suggested that the government had to strengthen its institutions and restructure key areas such as the law and education. This was important not only for attracting greater private investment but also for the improved efficiency of the private sector. Moreover, the poor business environment affects the efficiency of the private sector as well as the foreign investments entering Saudi Arabia. There was also some feeling that, in addition to the environment created by the government, the official policy of replacing foreign workers with Saudis could reduce the private sector's ability to be competitive and efficient. All the interviewees believed that the policy of giving preference to the recruitment of Saudis affected private sector performance negatively as it resulted in increased costs and reduced productivity. Despite this some asserted that the substitution of Saudi workers for expatriates was important for the country's future sustainable development, while the remainder felt that it went against the ideal of private-sector development.

10 The electricity industry

Ahmed Al-Rajhi

Introduction

Saudi Arabia is considered a developing country, and for this reason the achievement of both economic and social development remains a national strategic objective. The country's investments have depended largely on the availability of government revenues generated from oil exports. The declining oil revenues and budgetary constraints have limited the ability of the public sector to provide sufficient funding for competing obligations. Arguably, the objective of economic diversification could be attained more successfully with a greater contribution from the private sector. Hence the current challenging task for the country is to allocate its resources efficiently between its different priorities. The clarification of the boundaries separating the private and public sectors would enhance efficiency in the economy through increased specialisation.

Privatisation has been a government objective since the mid 1980s, with the main candidates being the telecommunication sector, the national airline and the electricity industry. What differentiates the electricity industry different from the others is the fact that it has been in the private domain since its inception and the government's involvement has been viewed as a transitional process relating to specific objectives. One objective has been the modernisation of that industry through the creation of a new infrastructure. This was followed by the aim of restructuring the industry to prepare it for privatisation and exposure to market forces. Ideally, it was hoped that such an approach would lead to an increase in productive efficiency, through a lowering of costs, and in allocative efficiency, by making prices reflect these costs. In addition, this industry has the ability to provide highly valued products and value-added services that could increase its contribution to the economy.

This chapter introduces the reader to the economic and institutional changes that the electricity industry – worldwide – is undergoing. It also sheds light on the actual experiences of reform of some developed and developing countries and the challenges affecting the introduction of competitive markets to this important industry. The restructuring process of Saudi Arabia's electricity industry is under way, but some aspects of the reform remain at the formational stage. Hence the issues raised in the chapter – and the international experiences

140   *Ahmed Al-Rajhi*

discussed – are extremely relevant and should serve as a useful lesson for the country's electricity industry.

Restructuring of the electricity industry

The traditional literature on electricity economics focuses on the issue of regulation, while the more recent writing explores the widely debated alternatives for restructuring the industry and how competitive forces are introduced. Although different countries may have the same objectives – namely the establishment of efficient markets and competition – Hadjilambrinos[1] emphasises that political and institutional traditions influence the restructuring direction that each country takes. Some governments may view privatisation not as a part of a broad reform programme with competition as the main objective, but as a way of improving the government's fiscal position. Newbery[2] points out that the term 'restructuring' and 'privatisation' are not synonymous, as restructuring does not necessarily imply a change of ownership and privatisation does not necessarily imply a change of structure. Yet, he believes that in the case of the electricity industry, restructuring usually comprises the elements of restructuring, privatisation and deregulation.

Most restructuring cases involve, simultaneously, both a horizontal and a vertical break-up of the electricity industry. Klein[3] describes horizontal restructuring as the situation where a number of companies are created within a single area of economic activity, such as power generation, while vertical restructuring involves the separation of the different stages of the electricity industry. The vertical separation normally includes regulation of the natural monopoly segments (i.e. transmission and distribution) and allows the introduction of competition to generation and supply. Arocena *et al.*[4] argue that some governments may chose to corporatise the industry instead of unbundling it, which would amount to the government's raising money through an implicit tax on future electricity consumption. Though this caution is well founded, a dilemma arises from the fact that when the electricity industry is losing money it is unlikely to be sold easily. Thus it is worth trying to expose the industry to the market forces at an early stage of the process.

Uncertainty in restructuring

Despite the changing organisation of the industry, coordination both within and among the generation, transmission, and distribution segments remains necessary. Thus the move towards deregulated markets has created its own sceptics. Joskow and Schmalensee[5] have expressed some doubts that the introduction of competition into electricity markets could accommodate, without a loss of any economic efficiency, the organised cooperation required for least-cost planning and operation. These are reasonable doubts, but it is essential to consider the fact that the introduction of competition is based on the assumption that the long-term benefits, such as an increase in efficiency, will be much

The electricity industry 141

greater than short-term efficiency losses that might result form a reform of the industry.

Banks[6] believes that the unbundling of the electricity industry might only have created uncertainty without being able to introduce successful financial instruments to minimise the risks. Thus he thought it unwise for countries with successful electricity industries to rush into this process with no guarantees that it would be correctly applied. This argument might be accepted if the industry was performing well; however, many countries have been obliged to reform their industries precisely because of a failure to achieve the desired outcome. The policy dilemma, then, is to consider the expected benefits resulting from restructuring as opposed to the problems and costs associated with such a complicated process. The question of how this trade-off should be resolved is thus becoming one of the most interesting issues in electricity economics.

Competition in production and monopoly in delivery

Competition in generation

Although the notions of natural monopoly have influenced public policies and academic discussions for many years, they have become less relevant to certain activities of the modern electricity industries. Arocena *et al.*[7] argue that both static and dynamic (e.g. 'learning by doing') economies of scale do not exist in the generation segment. In addition, many empirical studies, such as Bernstein,[8] have examined the investment costs of power projects in the 400–600 MW range and reached the same conclusion. More recent studies, such as those conducted by Doyle and Maher[9] and Bayless[10] reveal that the new technology of Combined Cycle Gas Turbines (CCGT) has made it possible for efficient production in generation to be reached on a much smaller scale than ever before. According to Berrie[11] the prospects for Independent Power Producers (IPP) are greatly improved as these new technologies point downwards in scale, price and optimum size, away from 2000 MW and towards 200–500 MW power generators. This trend has obviously made market competition more possible, especially with the faster installation of these smaller generators.

There are continuous challenges to the claims about which segments of the industry remain natural monopolies. The potential for competition has been expanded and the extent of regulation limited. Trebing[12] indicated that the industry changes have made it possible to introduce competition into generation, while the natural monopolies of transmission and distribution have to remain under regulation. These changes in power generation have led Hyman and West[13] to emphasise that even if the industry is dominated by vertically integrated utilities, competition remains feasible. These utilities are able to choose between using their own generation or buying it from other utilities or private power producers. Regional utilities or independent producers are able to sell in the wholesale market, and customers able to choose either self-generation or purchase from the local utility or even from external sources.

142 *Ahmed Al-Rajhi*

New role of distribution and transmission

Armstrong *et al.*[14] point out that the distinction between these two activities is that the transmission network is high-voltage and national in scope, whereas the distribution network is low-voltage and local. When the electricity industry consists of vertically integrated utilities this distinction is less critical, but the breaking-up of that industry has highlighted certain significant practical and regulatory issues such as open access for competitors and customers. Sansom[15] argues that it is not economically or technically necessary for transmission and distribution to be operated by a single company in an unbundled structure. The option of regional separation is essential for yardstick competition, especially given the very limited economies of scope between distribution activities in different regions. A further advantage of this separation is the fact that retail-supply competition between regional companies become possible.

The move towards deregulation has enhanced the strategic role of the transmission network not only in terms of direct benefits from power exchange but also in facilitating broad competition. Bernstein *et al.*[16] examined the impact of transmission on competition in generation within the context of a model of two geographically separated markets, each dominated by a single supplier. The main finding of this investigation was that the availability of increased transmission capacity enhanced the potential for entry, in the form of electricity imports. Furthermore, even though there was no entry the mere presence of this threat discouraged monopolistic behaviour within each market. These findings reflect the role of transmission networks in creating competition between different sources of generation as well as providing the consumers with choices. However, the realisation of this advantage depends on the structural and regulatory approaches chosen to deal with this monopolistic segment. Tenenbaum and Henderson[17] emphasise that market power in the electricity industry is influenced by the ownership or control of the transmission network. The authors give the example of a combined generation and transmission utility being able to make use of its control over the transmission grid to block its competitors from reaching its consumers.

Functional transformation of the electricity industry

In the 1980s, Fred Schweppe and other colleagues at Massachusetts Institute of Technology anticipated a considerable transformation in the electricity industry. They envisioned the ideal of an unbundled marketplace for electricity to consist of the following three segments: (a) a regulated transmission and distribution company which functioned as an intermediary; (b) a number of private generating companies which sold electricity to the transmission and distribution company; (c) electricity consumers who bought electricity from the transmission and distribution company. Although Joskow and Schmalensee[18] expected the electricity industry to be restructured along lines similar to those outlined above, they did not agree that the transmission and distribution segments should

The electricity industry 143

necessarily be integrated into one company. However, both visions conform to what it is called a single-buyer structure, which is nowadays considered a transitional stage. Hence, these early works did not anticipate the vast transformation currently in progress in the electricity industry.

Restructuring models

Tenenbaum et al.,[19] and Hunt and Shuttleworth[20] are well-known authors who provided a comprehensive analysis of the ways to restructure an electricity industry. Tenenbaum et al.[21] presented four restructuring models, each of which differed in the extent to which it introduced privatisation, as in the following:

> *Model 1*: This model consists of one or more vertically integrated, privately owned companies with each one in a franchised market. In this model, privatisation is introduced without competition.

> *Model 2*: This model maintains the traditional structure of Model 1 but allows competition in generation, with continued regulation of transmission and distribution segments.

> *Model 3*: This model expands on Model 2 by emphasising the role of the transmission segment that must transmit electricity in a non-discriminatory way. In this model, the transmission owners are obliged to provide access to competitors and to other wholesale buyers and sellers.

> *Model 4*: This model assumes that the whole industry is privatised and vertically separated. In this model, the independent transmission company owns the network and controls the dispatching of generators. Regional distribution companies are obliged to provide access to competitors and to their own consumers.

Hunt and Shuttleworth[22] identified four similar restructuring models. These models are differentiated not on the basis of ownership but rather in terms of the degree of competition and choice each provides to the participants. The first is described as a monopoly model, the second as a single purchasing-agency (i.e. monopsony) model, the third as a wholesale competition model and the fourth as a retail-competition model. Figure 10.1 illustrates the general outlines of these four models.

The figure shows that these models are not based on ownership; for instance, the first can be a government-owned or private monopoly, but it clearly does not provide competition between generators or choice of supply for consumers. The second is the single-buyer model that introduces competition into the field of generation, and is considered transitional in nature. However, some authors such as Lovei[23] caution that this brings with it certain problems, especially in developing countries, such as inviting corruption, weakening payment

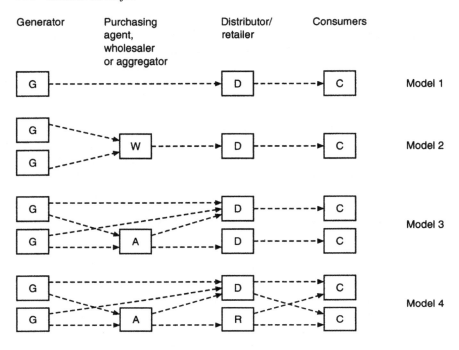

Figure 10.1 Restructuring models for an electricity industry

Source: Hunt, S. and Shuttleworth, G. (1996), Competition and Choice in Electricity, p. 24.

discipline and increasing government liabilities. The third model maintains competition in generation and introduces a choice of supply for distribution companies and large consumers. The fourth extends retail choice to small consumers, who might otherwise become captive to the distribution companies and hence end up subsidising large consumers. Thus the fourth model is considered the most efficient given that it has the most competitive market structure. However, applying these models to the real world revels that there is no single conform to the structure of a particular country, and that the distinction between them is really not always straightforward. Nevertheless the important point is that, regardless of which model is adopted, the technological changes and the dynamic nature of the industry reform has introduced many options.

Trading mechanisms in electricity markets

The cornerstone in terms of promoting competition in generation and within the wholesale electricity market is the structure of that market itself. Newbery[24] points out that this market should consist of both a spot (physical) market and a one for risk-sharing created through trading in financial instruments. The electricity spot market is normally described as a price-based pool where by

The electricity industry   145

physical transactions are carried out through the power pool that relies on the central dispatching of the generators based on the ranking of their operating costs (i.e. the merit order). Thus the market price – or system marginal price – is determined by the marginal operating cost of the most expensive generator at a specific hour. Ideally, the dispatcher is in effect matching the bids submitted by the two sides of the market, which are generators (i.e. supply), and distribution companies and large consumers (i.e. demand). The alternative for the pool mechanism is the bilateral contracts where the generators and distribution companies sign physical contracts outside the market but have to be scheduled through the independent system operator.

Mork[25] emphasises that the decision to choose between a pool or bilateral contract should be based on such factors as price volatility and security of supply on the one hand and price transparency and market liquidity on the other. The emphasis is on the claim that the price transparency associated with pool-based markets can lead to increased competition and efficiency. Murray[26] also favours this approach over bilateral contracts, which, while they benefit the involved parties individually, produce suboptimal outcomes and incur higher costs overall. However, the price transparency of the pool requires information availability, which, due to the repetitive nature of the electricity market, can create an incentive for collusion among generators.

Hunt and Shuttleworth[27] and Green[28] provide a very useful comparison of the two ways in which the electricity wholesale market can be structured. While acknowledging the disadvantages of the pool system, especially in terms of price volatility, the authors point out that bilateral contracts include the self-dispatching of generators which results in inefficiency in production. Furthermore, the presence of large transactions requiring to be managed by the system operator can give rise to disputes and even litigation. Also, the authors point out that bilateral trading creates a balancing market that is necessary to clear the mismatch between supply and demand. Thus bilateral contracts eventually result in the establishment of a spot market. It is, therefore, important that the design of the market has to consider from the start the long-term merits of a spot market for electricity.

These arguments for or against the two schemes focus on the functioning of the market overlooking the equally important factor of generation mix. Sioshansi and Morgan[29] believe that while a spot market would be more suited to a system where generation was mostly thermal, a contract market would be more appropriate for a one in which the bulk of its generation was hydro-based. This argument is well supported by the case of the Brazilian electricity system, thus indicating a considerable degree of complexity associated with hydroelectricity. Estache and Rodriquez-Paradina[30] studied this case and showed that the pool mechanism faced challenges in the hydro system. First, it is difficult to ensure open entry for new generation, especially when existing generators own the water rights. Second, the optimal dispatch depends not only on the demand and the availability of generators but also on water storage. Third, the hydroelectric generation involves very high sunk costs which are

146 Ahmed Al-Rajhi

difficult to recover when marginal prices remain very low over a long period. These findings show that the choice between a spot or bilateral market is more relevant to a thermal system than to a hydro system and, more broadly, that what may prove workable solutions for one system may not necessarily be suitable for another.

Financial contracts in the electricity market

The new electricity industry has introduced new entities and an innovative trading climate. With the creation of electricity markets new players such as marketers, brokers and retailers have become visible participants. Thus it is not surprising that the development of the electricity market is also enhanced by the role of financial contracts. Hunt and Shuttleworth[31] emphasise that some type of mechanism such as contract markets is needed for the transition from one model to another. For example, the move from a vertically monopolistic structure to a single-buyer structure requires purchasing contracts such as Power Purchase Agreements. Graves *et al.*[32] look at the growing importance of contracts in the electricity industry from a different angle. They point out that electricity can be stored 'synthetically' through forward contracts, where buying power at a given time and selling it at another is the financial equivalent of the storing and reselling of power.

Moreover, the restructuring of the electricity industry introduces considerable elements of risk and uncertainty. Berrie[33] believes that the new structure for electricity markets requires the various parties involved to enter into financial contracts and agree in advance on the assumptions regarding the probable patterns of prices in the months or years to come. Consequently, the participants in electricity markets need to undertake high-risk financial hedging transactions to protect their contract positions. The volatile prices associated with electricity markets make it necessary for generators and distribution companies to employ various kinds of financial instruments. These instruments provide hedging against future purchase prices, especially for those distribution companies obliged to supply their customers at fixed retail prices.

International experiences of reforming the electricity industry

It is reasonable to assume that different countries normally pursue different reform objectives which reflect the variations in their electricity industries' structure. However, as the following review of some cases from developed and developing economies indicates, countries sharing the same geographical region and even the same economic structure are able to adopt different approaches and paces for their reform programmes. This could be indicative of several factors, including the orientation in policy toward privatisation, the historical development of the industry in each country, and the extent to which each country has progressed in resolving the debate on whether electricity is a commercial commodity or a social service.

Developed countries

The advantage developed countries have over developing ones is that the former have more advanced financial and regulatory systems which make the introduction of the ownership and regulatory reforms to the electricity industry much simpler. However, as the experiences of countries such as the United Kingdom and the United States have shown, the introduction of competitive markets to this critical industry is easier said than done. The electricity industry of England and Wales went through major reform, including the transfer of ownership from the public to the private sector. In 1990, the Electricity Pool of England and Wales was introduced, but its success was less than expected. Green[34] attributes this mostly to the fact that the structure of the wholesale market was inconsistent with the way a competitive market was supposed to be. The continuous high concentration in generation led to the market being manipulated by large generators, and the demand side was completely ignored. Despite falling electricity prices since 1990, these factors – as well as political pressure from the coal industry and major electricity consumers – have caused the abolition of the pool in 2001 and led to its replacement by bilateral contracts.

According to Kahn and Stoft,[35] the reform experience of the United States differs from those of the United Kingdom and many other countries – with the exception of Spain and Alberta in Canada – in that the industry moved to wholesale competition from a structure dominated by private, vertically integrated utilities. The presence of private ownership and institutional fragmentation complicated the restructuring process and increased the transaction costs (e.g. stranded costs) of introducing competition. Although the regional wholesale markets in the United States have performed well, the Californian power crisis of 2001 caused second thoughts both in the state and beyond. Yet it is important to realise that the crisis was caused not by the introduction of market forces per se but rather, as is widely believed, by the flawed design of the market in this state. Kee[36] and, Silsbee and Jurewitz,[37] among others, studied this market and summarised its problems as follows: (a) the shortage of new generation and transmission capacity due to the price cap imposed on retail prices and too many site requirements; (b) the inability of the distribution companies to use financial contracts to hedge against risk caused by the volatility of wholesale prices; (c) a demand side which is unresponsive to market prices because these prices are not observed by final consumers.

New Zealand is one of the countries that has had a relatively successful experience of industry reform despite the considerable amount of public ownership. The drive towards electricity privatisation was not completely implemented due to a change of government, but the commercialisation of state-owned companies was a major feature. Gunn and Sharp[38] draw attention to another important characteristic of this industry, where the non-intervention style of regulation has emphasised open access to distribution networks that has made retail competition possible. The European electricity market is a complex

148 *Ahmed Al-Rajhi*

one as it involves different countries with different industry structures. While the French system remains closed to outside competition as it is dominated by Électricité de France, the more open countries such as Germany and Spain, have a high concentration in generation. Arocena *et al.*,[39] for example, shows that the two largest companies control about 83 per cent of the generation in the Spanish market. Thus it is not surprising that cross-border trade in power is one of the contentious issues facing the European Union. Scandinavia, on the other hand, was successful in introducing what Hjalmarsson[40] calls *club regulation* whereby voluntary cooperation exists between vertically integrated national utilities. This arrangement was very useful for the establishment of the currently existing competitive market, known as Nord Pool.

Developing countries

Ironically, Chile – a developing country – is considered a world pioneer in the restructuring of an electricity industry. The reform process of its electricity industry began in 1978, but the unbundling of that industry and the introduction of a wholesale spot market took its clearest shape after 1982. The lesson to be learnt from the Chilean experience is that political will and strong conviction are essential to the implementation of such an ambitious reform, in view of the fact that the country had an underdeveloped financial system and a very limited experience of regulation. The same approach spilled into other neighbouring countries in South America in the early 1990s, but to varying degrees. Hammons *et al.*[41] show that both the gas-based Argentinean system and the mostly hydro-based Bolivian one include wholesale markets. On the other hand, the hydro-based Brazilian system remains in the process of formation, but currently most of the system is still state-owned with the exception of private distribution companies.

The Asian countries' interest in reforming their power industries was driven – especially prior to the Asian crises – by the high-demand growth for electricity. Caruso and Chen[42] studied these countries and found that they had also differed in their chosen path of reform. Vietnam and China transformed their power ministries into corporate structures, while Indonesia and Thailand created commercial subsidiaries for their power authorities. Pakistan divested itself of its state ownership in generation by selling to private domestic as well as to international investors. Malaysia can be considered the most advanced, as it went ahead with privatising its national electricity authority by floating its shares on the financial market. The trend of reforming electricity industries has also reached sub-Saharan countries. Turkson and Redlinger[43] argue that for these countries the motive is mainly to satisfy the structural adjustment programmes recommended by the IMF and the World Bank. Interestingly enough, these nations differ in the approach they have selected to reform their electricity industries. While Zimbabwe has chosen a slow approach through corporatisation, Ghana and Kenya have opted for privatisation and wholesale competition.

The Middle East has proved slower than other regions in catching up with the liberalisation wave of the industry, partly because there remains some of the confidence of past decades in the public sector's ability to provide electricity, a provision widely believed to be a social service. The Arabian Gulf states had, until recently, less urgency to liberalise their economies, including the electricity industry. However, the opening up of the Egyptian electricity industry for private power producers and the adoption of a single-buyer model by Abu Dhabi, Oman and Saudi Arabia show that this region is no longer an exception.

The Saudi Arabian electricity industry: regulatory and organisational development

The electricity industry in Saudi Arabia has passed through distinct stages of development in the last seventy years. The following is a review of these stages, based primarily on the regulatory and organisational transformation of the industry over the decades.

First stage

Saudi Arabia's electricity industry began as a private enterprise. The 1930s witnessed the introduction of electricity by some entrepreneur's needing this service for their businesses. They were also able to sell excess capacity to neighbouring houses and streets for lighting. In 1949 some Saudi citizens and businessmen cooperated in establishing the first private electricity company in Dammam. Other cities and towns followed suit until the early 1970s, when the country had over a hundred small commercial companies and cooperative projects.

During the period 1961–1974 the Ministry of Commerce supervised the electricity industry, which may reflect how this resource was viewed as a commercial commodity as opposed to merely a social service. The industry was not subsidised and was dominated by profit-making private companies. Yet, the monopolistic power of these companies resulted in prices that were very high and varied both across regions and even cities within the same region. This variation in prices may have been caused by the companies' inability to reduce their average costs by exploiting their economies of scale. In addition to limited markets (the small size of the population in their franchised areas), these companies had no access to transmission lines, which resulted in their losing the opportunity to export their excess output to other markets.

Second stage

The creation in 1975 of the new Ministry of Industry and Electricity (MIE) meant that the supervision of electricity was shifted to the same ministry responsible for the pursuing the strategic objective of industrialisation. This development may have influenced government policy towards the electricity

150 *Ahmed Al-Rajhi*

industry and the expected role of the private sector within it. Since the country claims to adhere to the philosophy of a free-market economy, this objective does not in itself justify direct government involvement in the electricity industry. Thus, it seems that practical considerations as opposed to ideological dogma may lead to government intervention in this area.

The discussion of this issue may be illuminated by the views of Ghazi Algosaibi, the first official to head the Ministry of Industry and Electricity. Algosaibi[44] indicated that he had discovered to his disappointment shortly after taking office how the electricity companies lacked any constructive response to the challenges facing their industry. It is possible, however, that this attitude on the part of the companies was based on rational justifications. The introduction of a nationwide price regulation during the period 1971–1975 may have adversely affected the profitability of these companies. This period witnessed a reduction in electricity prices of as much as 50 per cent compared with previous years, which may well have contributed to underinvestment in the industry. In addition, the required capital costs were immense, which made the private sector unable to invest in them, at least in an expeditious manner. Even if the private companies had been able to raise sufficient funds from the domestic and international markets, they would have lacked the incentive to undertake unprofitable projects.

It seems that the rush towards economic development and industrialisation made the public officials impatient with these companies, who needed to consider what all the sudden changes would mean to them. The technocrats' patience may have been somewhat limited, especially as at that time they had substantial public funding at their disposal. Yet such a pragmatic approach may have been based on two important justifications. First, the aim of nationwide electrification and of providing Saudi citizens with electricity at low and affordable prices and second, the intention to attain the capacity required to meet the growing demand of energy-intensive industrialisation without delay. Thus these factors enhanced the perception that the electricity industry was unable to meet these new, high expectations by relying on the private sector alone.

Third stage

This stage, which lasted from 1976 to 1999, was the one that saw the largest expansion in the industry's capacity, made possible with the aid of government funding. Between 1976 and 1982 the government gradually subsumed individual operators under four vertically integrated companies, one in each area of the country. This led to the formation of the Saudi Consolidated Electric Companies (SCECOs) in the eastern, central, southern and western regions. Also the Electricity Corporation (EC) was created in 1976 as a public enterprise with two objectives. The first was to have the responsibility of financing and supervising the operation and expansion projects of the scattered companies in the northern region. The second was to represent the government's ownership share in the electricity companies, including SCECOs. This extensive ownership allowed the

The electricity industry 151

government to control day-to-day operations and decisions within the industry, and Table 10.1 shows that by the end of 1998 it was the major shareholder in these joint-stock companies, with about 84 per cent of total paid-up capital.

Fourth stage

This industry was singled out under the Sixth Development Plan (1995–2000) as the main candidate for full privatisation in the medium and long term. The Plan emphasises profit-making as the ultimate objective of this restructuring process. The government commitment to privatising the electricity industry has been presented within the context of providing the private investors in the industry with the opportunity to make profits on their investments. This notion is reiterated in the Seventh Development Plan (2000–2004), which places great emphasis on market-based pricing for such services. This official attitude is expected to contribute positively toward creating the conditions needed for the industry to raise finances based on its creditworthiness.

The restructuring plans announced in 1998 aim at preparing the industry for full privatisation when its institutions are developed. As a first step, in 2000 the regional SCECOs and the northern companies were merged into one holding company, the Saudi Electricity Company (SEC). The plan's immediate objective was to make the existing industry structure commercially viable and more attractive to private investors. The balance of ownership between the government and the private sector within the company reflects that which existed in the former companies prior to the merger, but this is expected to alter when further shares are offered for privatisation. The objective at this stage is to end direct government intervention in the industry's day-to-day affairs and make it operate on a commercial basis.

The setting up of this company is to be followed by that of a regulatory office, the Electric Services Regulatory Authority (ESRA), to be responsible for overseeing the industry's transformation into an unbundled structure. This reform is being carried out, not on a region-by-region basis but rather on an activity-by-activity one. The restructuring plan intends to make the industry ultimately a self-financing private enterprise, with the introduction of a market mechanism into its various segments. The plan's broad outline envisages the new structure to include:

Table 10.1 Government's shares in electricity companies (in million SR)

	Central	Western	Eastern	Southern	Northern	Total
Paid-up capital	8,000	7,350	4,151	3,564	37	23,102
Government share	5,742	6,281	3,764	3,513	21	19,322
Per cent	72	85	*91	99	57	84

Source: Council of Saudi Chamber of Commerce (1999).

Note: * Includes ARAMCO share of 41 per cent.

- An opening-up of the generation segment to competing private companies;
- a privately-owned transmission company;
- regional private distribution and supply companies;
- the industry's transformation from a single-buyer structure to a pool structure where electricity is traded in the wholesale market; and
- the establishment of an 'independent' regulatory body.

The implementation of this plan would result in important tasks for the regulator, which will be responsible for dealing with a number of issues after this decentralisation. Healthy competition in generation calls for the provision of well-thought-out rules and a regulatory system that is both fair and transparent. Thus the reform has to be made credible in practice by tackling directly some of the economic and regulatory issues likely to arise under the new structure. Reform of the industry should not result in a replacing of the public monopoly with a private one. This will be especially true during the time when SEC is the sole supplier of electricity. This situation requires detailed supervision on the part of the regulator to prevent any exploitation of its monopolistic powers. In addition, having a nationwide distribution company would have the effect of masking regional inefficiencies, which makes it essential to speed up the establishment of regional distribution companies. This step would make the job of the regulator much easier by facilitating yardstick competition. The unbundling of the industry will mean that the transmission grid plays a strategic role in linking consumption centres with generation sources. The benefits from competition in generation will not materialise unless this natural monopoly segment of the industry is well regulated. This becomes necessary at an early stage of the process in order to reduce potential disputes among the different participants, such as generators and distribution companies (or, indeed, major customers).

The gradualist approach taken by the reform plan could allow the necessary time for the institutional and legal reforms to take place. The advantage of having the Saudi Arabian state as the major shareholder from the beginning of the process is that reforming the existing structure becomes very flexible. The role for the government at such a stage has precedents in the experiences of other countries. For example, Yajima[45] contrasts the reform experience of the United States with those of countries such as Chile, where full-reform models have been easily realised with government engagement. This view indicates that the existence of large private interests in the industry prior to restructuring would complicate the process itself.

Salient features of the Saudi Arabian electricity industry

Operational features

The operational and financial issues are closely interlinked, and the following sections review the operational ones first. This is necessary in order to give the proper background for an understanding of the financial issues facing this industry.

Demand growth

In addition to industrialisation, urbanisation has been a major factor in the growth in electricity consumption in Saudi Arabia during the past three decades. The growth in demand between 1970 and 1990 reflects the time when the country was becoming more urbanised and was going through economic and social changes. The 1990s were a difficult time for the industry as it tried to keep up with the growth in electricity consumption, which proved faster than that in generation capacity. Although the country's infrastructure was then mostly completed and the economy beginning to slow down, the high population growth and diversification of the economy were the main driving forces behind the increase in demand. Figure 10.2, below, illustrates the growth in electricity consumption and generation over the last thirty years.

The annual growth in generated electricity, in MWh, since 1975 has been 13.8 per cent, insufficient to keep up with the 14.8 per cent growth in consumption. In 1999 about 106 million MWh were sold, while the industry itself was incapable of generating more than 94 million MWh. The by-product electricity generated by the desalination plants – owned by the Slain Water Conversion Corporation (SWCC) – covered the deficit of 18 per cent. This indicates the importance of SWCC plants for the electricity industry: their output has been crucial in closing this deficit since 1984. Furthermore, the very low costs of power they generated are likely to put additional pressure on the electricity industry by increasing generation competition.

Figure 10.2 shows the total energy losses, which represents the difference between total generation and total electricity sales. These losses declined in percentage terms from 13.4 in 1980 to a mere 7.9 in 1999. This percentage is very low, even in comparison with the electricity systems of many developed countries, which show an average loss of 9 per cent. This increase in efficiency in

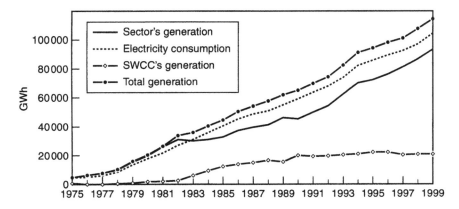

Figure 10.2 Development of electricity generation and consumption
Source: MIE Annual Report (1999).

transporting electricity is due to the establishment of modern transmission and distribution networks made possible with the help of public funding. However, as the industry moves into the private domain cost considerations rather than system reliability will become a determining factor for future investments. Hence economic regulation will be necessary to guarantee network expansion and prevent the occurrence bottlenecks likely to hinder the functioning of the market.

The factors behind the growth in electricity demand during the past thirty years may have become less vigorous, but they remain substantial. Thus, electricity demand is expected to grow at an annual rate of about 5 per cent, requiring the generation capacity to increase to 60,000 MW by the year 2020. In addition to this expansion the capacities for transmission and distribution will have to be proportionally available. Although these numbers – presented in the Long-Term Plan – have been considered an overestimate this Plan was nonetheless useful in drawing attention to future challenges. Figure 10.3 shows the estimated investment requirements up to the year 2020.

Demand characteristics

Storing electricity on a large scale is not economically feasible, which makes electricity a demand-driven industry. This would impose additional costs, as the generation and transmission capacities must be designed to meet the estimated demand at the peak hour. In the case of Saudi Arabia, the peak time for the country occurs during a number of days in the summer as the consumption – especially by residential customers – is closely influenced by the use of air-conditioning. The fluctuation of the electricity demand during the year, and even during the same day, has a considerable and direct effect on the system's capital

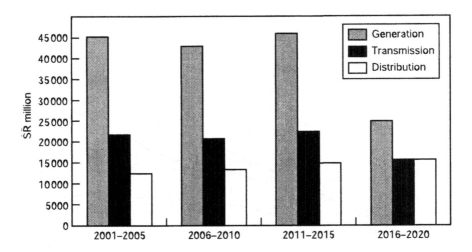

Figure 10.3 Investment requirements until 2020
Source: Long Term Electrification Plan, Electricity Corporation (1996).

costs. This would indicate a continuous need for installing additional generation units with high operation costs to meet the demand at its peak hour. Hence the shrinking of the large gap between off-peak and peak demand reduces the capital and operation costs significantly. This could be achieved through the implementation of efficient pricing which reflects the actual cost of production and utilising suitable demand-side management programmes (DSM). In addition, it is more economic to share generation reserves among the different interconnected regions. Table 10.2 reveals this potential by presenting the ratio of monthly peaks to the year peak for each of the five regions.

Although the peak load in Saudi Arabia usually occurs during the summer, there is a variation in terms of the peak times for the five regions. This would indicate the opportunity for cost savings as generation capacity in one region can function as a reserve for other regions. Table 10.2 demonstrates that the peaks for all regions do not occur in the same month and that for regions with the same peak month, the day of the month and even the time of day are different. These observations show the potential for utilising these regional differences and the urgent need to speed up the completion of the national transmission network. Thus this network and the expected interconnection with the other GCC countries are likely to produce financial benefits, including a reduction in capacity costs and higher system reliability, by meeting any unexpected increase in demand.

Types of consumption

The electricity industry provided its services to about three and a half million subscribers by the end of 1999, over 95 per cent of whom were in the areas

Table 10.2 The ratios of monthly peaks to the year peak for 1998

Months	Northern	Western	Southern	Central	Eastern	Country
Jan	0.86	0.55	0.81	0.59	0.66	0.65
Feb	0.74	0.56	0.85	0.52	0.62	0.62
Mar	0.67	0.69	0.93	0.52	0.61	0.66
Apr	0.61	0.88	0.97	0.73	0.76	0.84
May	0.78	0.9	0.95	0.85	0.85	0.89
Jun	0.93	0.92	1.00	1.00	0.96	0.96
Jul	0.91	0.91	0.94	0.87	0.92	0.93
Aug	1.00	0.96	0.96	0.93	1.00	0.99
Sep	0.99	1.00	0.95	0.94	0.98	1.00
Oct	0.81	0.96	0.96	0.86	0.9	0.94
Nov	0.53	0.76	0.87	0.51	0.7	0.7
Dec	0.64	0.66	0.76	0.5	0.63	0.64
Date	Aug-15	Sep-05	Jun-14	Jun-09	Aug-22	Sep-05
Time	n.a	4:00 pm	8:00 pm	3:00 pm	2:00 pm	4:00 pm

Source: Calculated from the MIE Report (1998).

156 *Ahmed Al-Rajhi*

supplied by the four SCECO companies. The following table shows the consumption types for the five regions of Saudi Arabia.

The type of consumers the company is serving affects its financial position through the impact on its revenues and its costs. Table 10.3 shows that, for the industry as a whole, more than 48 per cent of the consumption is by residential consumers and 24 per cent by industrial consumers, followed by the government at around 15 per cent. The situation varies between regions where SCECO-Eastern had the advantage of having 57 per cent of its electricity sold to large industrial consumers, which include ARAMCO, as well as SABIC with its large petrochemical companies. On the other hand, SCECO-Southern sold over 74 per cent of its electricity to residential consumers, but the disadvantage for this company is that it operates in the region with the lowest per capita income in the country. As the industry currently has only one nationwide distribution company, these variations not only conceal inefficiency differences but also could lead to cross-subsidisation between different types of consumers and different regions.

Fuel location

The location of any industry is determined by a combination of factors, but the most important among them is the proximity to consumption location (markets) and the availability of production inputs such as raw material including fuel. This is also true in the case of the Saudi Arabian electricity industry, where the fuel factor has a major influence on the location of generation. About 35 per cent of the industry's generation capacity is located in the eastern region, which contains the majority of the country's oil and gas fields as well as its petrochemical industries. Figure 10.4 shows the power generation usage of the different types of fuels by electricity companies situated in different regions of the country.

The availability of gas fields in the eastern region enables SCECO-Eastern to have 98 per cent of the fuel used in its plants coming from natural gas. Despite this company's high usage of gas, the industry as whole is still dominated by

Table 10.3 Electricity sold by type of consumption, %

Type	Eastern	Central	Southern	Western	Northern	Total
Residential	24.17	56.82	74.34	63.8	66.54	48.26
Commercial	5.74	9.12	7.67	12.36	10.62	8.7
Industrial	56.66	6.59	1.3	6.12	1.15	24.2
Agricultural	0.67	4.97	0.61	0.18	5.75	1.8
Government	11.94	19.05	13.03	14.48	13.23	14.6
Hospitals	0.54	2.2	2.12	1.15	1.64	1.25
Charties	0.28	1.25	0.92	1.91	1.6	1.6
Total	100	100	100	100	100	100

Source: Ministry of Industry and Electricity (1999).

The electricity industry 157

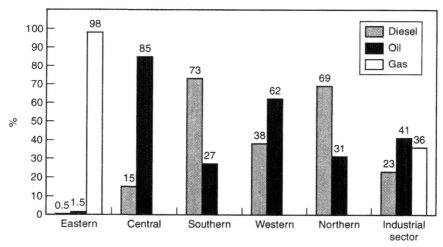

Figure 10.4 Relative usage of fuel types by each region
Source: Ministry of Industry and Electricity (1999)

crude oil and diesel. Most of the fuel usage in the central and western regions is of crude oil, while the bulk of the fuel usage in the southern and northern companies is of diesel. The difference in fuel usage could be explained in part by the transportation costs of these different types of fuel and the lack of a nationwide natural gas network. However, as the industry switches to natural gas in power generation and the national gas network is completed, the cost advantage of transmitting electricity relative to transporting gas may encourage more electricity producers to locate in the eastern region.

Financial features

Tariff structure

The prices for electricity consumption are set officially and uniform across the country. Although they distinguish between consumers based on their type and the level of their monthly consumption, the time of use is completely ignored. Table 10.4 shows the tariff structure for residential customers (commercial and government offices are also charged under the same structure) since 1995, which also includes the revised tariffs in 2000 as part of the restructuring plan.

The tariffs as presented in Table 10.4 could be described as inverted block tariffs. Under such tariffs the consumer is charged one price for consumption up to a certain number of kilowatt-hours per month and then charged a higher one for any additional consumption. These tariffs clearly exempt from the increase in tariffs groups of customers with any consumption below 5,000 kWh. These groups account for 75 per cent of total residential consumption or 93 per cent of consumers. This exemption reflects the attempt to protect lower and middle-

158 Ahmed Al-Rajhi

Table 10.4 Tariff structure for residential monthly consumption

Consumption Blocks, kWh	1995-Apr-00 Halalah	Apr-00 Halalah	Increase %	Oct-00 Halalah	Decrease %
1–500	5	5	0	5	0
501–1000	5	5	0	5	0
1001–2000	5	5	0	5	0
2001–3000	*10	10	0	10	0
3001–4000	*10	10	0	10	0
4001–5000	*13	13	0	12	7.7
5001–6000	*13	18	38.5	12	33
6001–7000	*20	23	15	15	35
7001–8000	*20	28	40	20	29
8001–9000	*20	32	60	22	31
9001–10000	*20	36	80	24	33
10001+	*20	38	90	26	32

Source: Ministry of Industry and Electricity (1999).

Note: * Includes the additional 5 Halalahs that go to the 'Halalah Fund'. 1SR = 100 Halalah.

income families. However, it remains to be seen whether revenues generated from the increase in prices for the highest 25 per cent of consumption will be sufficient. This depends on the price-sensitivity of the demand by high consumption groups as well as the efficiency in payment collection.

The table shows that the revised tariffs in April 2000 and October 2000 have nine and eight sets of prices respectively, in contrast to the previous structure with only four sets. Train[46] demonstrated that increasing the number of blocks led to welfare gains as prices reflected costs more and diminished the chance of creating what are known as 'collection points'. The collection points exist when the different consumers with different levels of consumption are paying the same price. So the existence of such points depends mainly on the size of each block, which means that the revised structure reduces these collection points for consumption levels above 5,000 kWh. Since the transaction costs associated with having a larger number of blocks are expected to be very small, it is economically justifiable to have a greater number of blocks even for consumption below 5,001 kWh.

It is worth noting that the table shows that the electricity prices were revised twice within six months in 2000. The first revision was in April as part of the new reform plan of the electricity industry, which aimed at improving the creditworthiness of SEC. The second revision came in October of the same year, as response to the complaints raised by consumers, many of whom were large commercial consumers. It seems that the timing of the April revision was inappropriate as it became effective during the summer and consumers were ill-prepared to adjust their consumption patterns to the price increase. This unexpected change may have pleased many consumers, but it increased uncertainty for potential private investors in electricity.[47] The uncertainty could

The electricity industry 159

have been minimised if the industry's regulator had been established at that time, which would have given the concerned investors some insight into the economic basis for the price reduction.

Although it is reasonable to expect that low production costs combined with competition will result in low electricity prices for consumers, it is informative to view current prices within their historical perspective. Figure 10.5 shows that the current tariff structure sets prices at a low level, both in nominal and real terms. This is especially true in comparison with the price level prior to 1971, when the industry was not subsidised and was operated by profit-making private companies.

It might be expected that the electricity price would be low in Saudi Arabia due to lower fuel costs, but setting prices below production costs has increased unnecessary electricity consumption and reduced the companies' ability to have an adequate internal stream of revenues. Figure 10.5 demonstrates the changes in electricity prices for industrial and non-industrial (including residential) consumers over the past three decades. It is worth pointing out that industrial prices are expected to be lower than those for non-industrial consumers. The reason is that the costs for the system to supply one kilowatt to large consumers are much lower than that for supplying the same amount to residential consumers, due to the difference in their voltages.

The reduction in prices since 1974 has been complemented by government subsidies to cover the difference between the costs and revenues of the companies. The shareholders of these companies continue to receive from the government a guaranteed annual dividend of 7 per cent for each share despite the fact that the companies incur losses. This policy is intended to keep private investors interested in the industry and hence provide indirect subsidies to the companies. The direct subsidies were also intended to help the companies offset increases in fuel costs. However, the decline in oil and fuel prices during the 1980s was not reflected in a reduction in subsidies. This may indicate a continuation of the public policy of supporting this industry during the period of

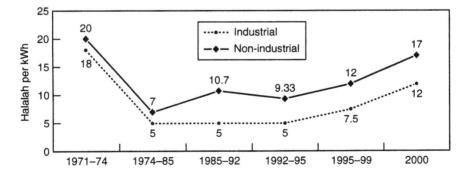

Figure 10.5 Development of electricity prices (1971–2000)
Source: Electricity Corporation (1996) and Ministry of Industry and Electricity (2000).

160 *Ahmed Al-Rajhi*

economic transformation. Nevertheless it is reasonable to assume that this well-intentioned policy has made electricity producers and consumers more dependent on these subsidies, which might result in inefficient decisions.

Financial losses

The lack of interest on the part of private investors in the electricity industry had been directly linked to its weak financial performance, due mainly to uneconomic prices. This performance had a negative impact on the ability of the electricity companies to expand their operations and on their ability to borrow. Table 10.5 shows the financial position of SCECOs for the last five years prior to their merger in SEC in 2000.

Table 10.5 shows that the four companies collectively had about 3.7 billion riyals in net losses at the end of 1999, which caused their accumulated debt since 1995 to reach 15.8 billion riyals. Some financial and organisational factors may have contributed to this negative outcome, but the most frequently cited factor is the tariff structure itself. Table 10.6 shows that a limited adjustment to the tariff structure could help significantly with the reduction, if not elimination, of these losses.

Table 10.6 also reveals that the average revenue per kWh for the SCECO companies is in line with the industry average of 7.1 halalahs. This can be explained by the fact that all these companies were selling their energy under the same tariff structure. The situation is very different on the cost side, which

Table 10.5 Financial losses of SCECOs (in billion SR)

Exhibit	1995	1996	1997	1998	1999	Total
Total Revenues	6.5	6.7	7.2	7.3	7.9	35.6
Total Expenses	9.5	9.7	10.1	10.6	11.6	51.5
Net Results	−2.96	−3.02	−2.89	−3.24	−3.69	−15.8
%	−31.3	−31	−28.7	−30.7	−31.8	−30.7

Source: SCECOs annual reports (1995–1999).

Table 10.6 Revenue, cost and loss per kWh sold by SCECOs in 1998 (in Halalahs)

SCECO Companies	Revenue	Cost	Loss
Central	7.88	11.5	−3.62
Eastern	7.2	8.8	−1.6
Southern	6.3	20.8	−14.5
Western	7.17	11.9	−4.73
Average	7.1	13.3	−6.2
Average (Excluding Southern)	7.42	10.73	−3.32

Source: Companies' Annual Reports (1998).

The electricity industry   161

reflects the variation in the cost structures of these companies. The lowest average cost is for SCECO-Eastern which benefits from its location in a fuel-abundant region, as well as having the advantage that most of its output is sold to bulk industrial consumers. On the other hand, SCECO-Southern has very large residential consumers and is located in a region with very difficult geographical conditions, which places limits on its ability to generate enough revenues and/or cut costs. In general, an improvement in the industry's financial performance would result if the proposed reform and new tariffs were combined with reductions in generation costs, which account for about 60 per cent of the industry's costs.

Financing sources

Government support to the electricity industry in the past came through direct funding from the Electricity Corporation (EC) and interest-free loans provided by the Saudi Industry Development Fund (SIDF). This support, in addition to subsidies, has enabled the industry to meet its obligations but has also made the electric companies lack the incentives to be profitable. Azzam pointed out that the 'Halalah Fund', introduced in 1995, was very useful in attracting contractors to finance fund-backed projects.[48] The commercial banks' involvement clearly increased during the 1990s, which indicates the potential for further debt financing from domestic and international banks when the right schemes are used.

The innovative methods such as Build-Own-Operate (BOO), Build-Operate-Transfer (BOT) and Build-Own-Operate-Transfer (BOOT) are new concepts for the country. The first indication of interest in this method was in 1997, when SCECO-Western invited bids to build the Shoaiba power plant. According to Khoshaim,[49] two international groups were commissioned to study the feasibility of the BOOT scheme. By 1998 it became apparent that the scheme would not materialise given the existing tariff structure and the restrictive foreign investment laws, which needed to be liberalised to minimise the project risk. Nevertheless, this case should not be used to make a sweeping judgement on the potential of these schemes. The timing coincided with the merger of the SCECOs, as this long-term contract was expected to be arranged by the new company. Furthermore since then the government had approved many measures to improve the investment climate, likely to prove helpful for such risky projects. These changes mean that various forms of equity and debt-financing will remain relevant for the future. Internal cash flows also may benefit from revising the tariffs, but they will remain insufficient. Sufficient cash flows do not exclude the need for funding diversification, which is necessary for reducing the financing costs.

Policy issues and recommendations

The literature regarding the economic and institutional transformation of the electricity industry in the last two decades, and international experiences of

162 *Ahmed Al-Rajhi*

restructuring provide ample lessons for the Saudi Arabian electricity industry. Hence, there follows a list of useful policy issues and recommendations that have arisen from this chapter.

1) The consistency and continuity of the industry reforms are necessary ingredients of a suitable climate for private investors, as well as for the long-term success of the reform itself. More importantly, the industry restructuring does not take place in isolation from other reforms taking place in the Saudi Arabian economy. Thus establishing a successful competitive market for electricity is very much dependent on the presence of a developed financial market and regulatory system.

2) The international experiences of introducing market forces to the electricity industry indicate that this process is very difficult, but the setbacks are not sufficient reasons to halt it. The temptation for developing countries, including Saudi Arabia, is that the less risky single-buyer structure, which is designed to be temporary and transitional, may become permanent. Consequently, the industry may face similar problems to those that the reform is actually intended to correct, such as inefficient pricing and investment decisions that lack transparency.

3) Although there is no shortage of domestic private wealth, foreign investment would bring to the Saudi electricity industry not only finance but also know-how, managerial skills and expertise. This investment initially comes in the form of international private placements (IPP) and variants of BOOT power projects, which have the advantage of raising cheaper sources of finance than those arranged by the government or even local commercial banks. However, these schemes are associated with high prices, due mainly to their sensitivity to the foreign exchange risk and to the uncertainty about rules for setting electricity tariffs.

4) Privatisation with no credible competition may lead to higher electricity prices, which not only hinder the objective of industrialisation but also have a negative distributional effect. Hence, the reform of the industry should result in lower, but cost-based, prices through competition and choice in as many parts of the industry as possible. Saudi Arabia is in a fortunate position in that its thermal system could reduce the complexity associated with the electricity spot market. The current switch to natural gas as fuel could help the move to a competitive market for power generation. This replacement not only reduces production costs considerably but also increases pressure on competing generators to be more efficient as their production costs become very similar.

5) Restructuring of the electricity industry requires effective regulation, as there are strong incentives for rent-seeking behaviour and monopolistic power within this industry. Also, the opportunity that will be given to large consumers to choose their suppliers should be extended as soon as possible to small consumers, who as captive consumers may end up subsidising those large ones. As the move towards competition may take longer than initially

The electricity industry 163

anticipated, the immediate task of regulation should be dealing with the monoposony (i.e. a single-buyer company) facing generators and the distribution monopoly facing consumers.

6) An important lesson that Saudi Arabia can learn from international experiences is that not only should the market rules be predictable and transparent, but more importantly they should be announced in advance of the electricity market becoming operational. This is necessary to limit the potential sources of dispute, as changing the rules in the middle of the process would create objections and could even impede the creation of the market itself.

7) Having a single nationwide distribution company makes it socially unacceptable to have residential electricity consumers paying regionally differentiated prices. As the restructuring plan envisages that the industry will include regional private distribution companies, spatial differences can feed into retail prices. However, ignoring these differences would lead to overconsumption in some remote regions and underconsumption in others. Similarly, electricity consumption should be in line with production costs, which vary throughout the hours of the day and throughout the year. Consequently, neglecting consumers' responses to real-time prices, or at least time-of-use prices, would create an incomplete electricity market as well as resulting in inefficient decisions.

8) The electricity industry is a capital-intensive enterprise requiring highly skilled labour. Hence, while privatisation may improve labour productivity it may also have a negative impact on the employment of Saudi Arabian nationals. This would create a potential for a conflict between the objectives of Saudi-isation and privatisation. An incremental approach to the hiring and firing of employees – especially during the initial years of the process – and well-designed training programmes, would minimise this impact.

9) Saudi Arabia can benefit from the GCC interconnection on three fronts. First, additional sources of cheap generation could put pressure on the Saudi electricity industry to improve its performance. Second, the large market size for electricity would justify the transaction costs caused by the introduction of a wholesale spot market. Third, trading in an electricity spot market requires the use of a variety of financial instruments. Thus the establishment of a pool for GCC power would open the way for the participants in the Saudi electricity industry to have access to the more liberal financial markets, such as that of Bahrain.

Conclusion

The last twenty years have witnessed a clear turning point in the history of the electricity industry, due mainly to tremendous technical and economic changes taking place in power generation. Interestingly, these changes have coincided with a worldwide shift away from the direct involvement of the public sector in this industry and with the increasing popularity of economic policies involving privatisation and liberalisation. However, the reform of the industry and the introduction of competition remain challenging tasks and involve overcoming many complexities and problems. The Saudi Arabian electricity industry can learn from the experiences of other countries, which shows that its restructuring can be carried out neither in haste nor in isolation from economic and social factors. Thus the adoption of a gradualist approach is a wise policy to follow, but it is equally important that prudence should not slip into excessive caution; otherwise the status quo will prevail and the long-term objectives of the reform may not materialise.

Notes

2 Which development paradigm?

1 Beblawi, H. and Luciani, G. (eds) (1987) *The Rentier State*, London: Croom Helm.
2 Presley, J. (1984) *A Guide to the Saudi Arabian Economy*, pp. 49–85, London: Macmillan.
3 Turner, L. and Bedore, J. M. (1979) *Middle East Industrialisation: A Study of Saudi and Iranian Downstream Investments*, pp. 104–105, London: Saxon House.
4 Al-Farsy, F. (1982) *Saudi Arabia: A Case Study in Development*, pp. 194–196, London, KPI.
5 Rostow, W. W. (1960) *The Stages of Economic Growth: A Non-Communist Manifesto*, Cambridge University Press.
6 Todaro, M. (1994) *Economic Development*, fifth edition, p. 661, Longmans; Thirwall, A.P. (1994) *Growth and Development*, fifth edition, pp. 348–349, Macmillan.
7 El Mallakh, R. (1982) *Saudi Arabia: Rush to Development*, p. 37, London: Croom Helm.
8 Johany, A. D., Berne, M. and Mixon, J. W. (1986) *The Saudi Arabian Economy*, p. 111, London: Croom Helm.
9 Moliver, D. M. and Abbondante, P. J. (1980) *The Economy of Saudi Arabia*, p. 54, New York: Praeger.
10 Porter, M. E. (1990) *The Competitive Advantage of Nations*, p. 72, New York: Free Press.
11 Niblock, T. 'Social structure and the development of the Saudi Arabian political system', in Niblock, T. (ed.), (1982) *State, Society and Economy in Saudi Arabia*, pp. 75–77, London: Croom Helm
12 Al-Awaji, I. M. (1971) *Bureaucracy and Society in Saudi Arabia*, Ph.D. dissertation, University of Virginia. Cited in Garawi, A. and Schmidt, M. E. 'The Saudi Managerial Environment', in Wright, J. W. (ed.) (1996) *Business and Economic Development in Saudi Arabia*, p. 88, London: Macmillan.
13 Al-Shalan, F. A. (1991) *Participation in Managerial Decision Making in the Saudi Arabian Public Sector*, Ph.D. dissertation, University of Pittsburgh, p. 245. Cited in Wright, J. W., op. cit., p. 89.
14 Al-Malik, S. M. (1989) *Strategic Decision Makers: A Study of Business and Government Top Executives in Saudi Arabia*, Ph.D. dissertation, Georgia State University, p. 427. Cited in Wright, J. W., op. cit., p. 89.
15 *Sura 2:275* and elsewhere.
16 Esposito, J. L. (1998) *Islam: the Straight Path*, third edition, p. 192, Oxford University Press.
17 Kuznets, S. (1955) 'Economic growth and income inequality', *American Economic Review*, (March), pp. 1–28; Kuznets, S. (1963) 'Quantitative aspects of the economic growth of nations', *Economic Development and Cultural Change*, (March), pp. 1–80.

166 *Notes*

18 United Nations Development Programme, *Human Development Report*, Oxford University Press 1999, p. 146.
19 www.the-saudi.net/saudi-arabia/taxation.htm
20 *Sura* 9:60
21 *Sura* 4:29
22 an-Nabhani, T. (2000) *The Economic System in Islam*, p. 106, London: Al-Khilafah Publications.
23 El-Ghonemy, M. R. (1998) *Affluence and Poverty in the Middle East*, pp. 143–144, London: Routledge.
24 Al-Shoshan, A. (1991) *Saudi Arabia: the Country Nutrition Profile*, Paper presented at the FAO/WHO International Conference on Nutrition, Rome, 1991, pp. 11–12.
25 World Bank Atlas Development Indicators, Washington, 2000, pp. 24–25.
26 Cinar, E. M. 'Earnings profiles of women workers and education in the Middle East', in Shahin, W. and Dibeh, G. (2000) *Earnings Inequalities, Unemployment and Poverty in the Middle East and North Africa*, pp. 88–91, Wesport: Greenwood Press.
27 Richards, A. and Waterbury, J. (1990) *A Political Economy of the Middle East: State, Class and Economic Development*, Boulder, Colorado: Westview. See especially Chapter 8, 'Contradictions of state-led growth', pp. 219–237.
28 Tripp, C. 'States, elites and the management of change', in Hakimian, H. and Moshaver, Z. (2001) *The State and Global Change: the Political Economy of Transition in the Middle East and North Africa*, pp. 211–231, London: Curzon.
29 Hopwood, D. 'The ideological basis: Ibn Abd Al-Wahhab's Muslim revivalism', in Niblock, T. (ed.), (1982) *State, Society and Economy in Saudi Arabia*, London: Croom Helm. op. cit., pp. 23–35.
30 Islahi, A. A. (1988) *Economic Concepts of Ibn Taimiyah*, p. 173, Leicester: Islamic Foundation.
31 Sluglett, P. and Farouk-Sluglett, M. 'The precarious monarchy: Britain, Abd Al-Aziz Ibn Saud and the establishment of the kingdom of Hijaz, Najd and its dependencies, 1925–1932', in Niblock, T. (ed.), (1982) *State, Society and Economy in Saudi Arabia*, pp. 36–39, London: Croom Helm.
32 Al-Hegelan A. and Palmer, M. (1985) 'Bureaucracy and development in Saudi Arabia', *Middle East Journal*, vol. 39, no. 1, 1985, pp. 48–68. Reprinted in Niblock T. and Wilson, R. (1999) *The Political Economy of the Middle East*, volume 5, pp. 1–22, Cheltenham: Edward Elgar.
33 www.saudinf.com/main/e111.htm

3 Government economic policy

1 Saudi Arabian Monetary Agency, *Thirty-Seventh Annual Report*, Riyadh, 2001, pp. 363–364.
2 Ibid. p. 365. Author's calculations.
3 Stern, N (1989) 'The economics of development', *Economic Journal*, (September), p. 616; reprinted in Gerald M. Meier (1995), *Leading Issues in Economic Development*, p. 556 Oxford University Press, sixth edition.
4 Kumar Bagchi (1989) 'Development planning', in Eatwell, J. Milgate, M. and Newman, P. (eds), *The New Palgrave: Economic Development*, pp. 98–99, London, Macmillan.
5 Hershlag, Z.Y. (1988) *The Contemporary Turkish Economy*, pp. 4–10 London: Routledge. 1988, pp. 4–10.
6 Lange, O. (1960) *Essays on Economic Planning*, pp. 11–20, London: Asia Publishing House, reprinted in Bernstein, H. (ed.), (1973) *Underdevelopment and Development*, pp. 207–215. Harmondsworth: Penguin.
7 Amin, S. (1990) *Maldevelopment: Anatomy of a Global Failure*, p. 184, London: Zed Books.

Notes 167

8 Todaro, M. *Economic Development*, pp. 622–623, London: Addison Wesley Longman.
9 El Mallakh, R. (1982) *Saudi Arabia: Rush to Development*, p. 141, London: Croom Helm.
10 Ibid. pp. 142–143.
11 Central Planning Organisation, *Report of the Central Planning Organisation*, Jeddah, 1974, p. 17.
12 Al-Farsy, F. (1986) *Saudi Arabia: A Case Study in Development*, p. 148, London: KPI.
13 Ibid. p. 149.
14 El Mallakh, R. (1982) *Saudi Arabia: Rush to Development*, pp. 178–180, London: Croom Helm.
15 Al-Farsy, F. (1986) *Saudi Arabia: A Case Study in Development*, p. 106, London: KPI.
16 Ibid. pp. 80–81.
17 SAMA, *Annual Report*, Riyadh, 1978, p. 9.
18 Al-Farsy, F. (1986) *Saudi Arabia: A Case Study in Development*, pp. 158–173, London: KPI.
19 El Mallakh, R. (1982) *Saudi Arabia: Rush to Development*, pp. 250–251, London: Croom Helm.
20 SAMA, *Annual Report*, Riyadh, 2001, pp. 43–44.
21 Ibid. pp. 45–46.
22 Saudi British Bank, *Saudi Economic Bulletin*, vol. 5, no. 19, p. 7.
23 *Statement of the Ministry of Planning on the Seventh Development Plan*, Riyadh, 2000, p. 6.
24 SAMA, *Annual Report*, Riyadh, 2001, op. cit., p. 139.
25 'Saudi Arabia's Seventh Five Year Plan', *Middle East Economic Survey*, vol. 43, no. 41, 9 October 2000, pp. D1–D5.
26 Vineeta Shetty, 'Telecoms: winds of change', *Middle Eastern Economic Digest Special Report on Saudi Arabia*, 15 September 2000, pp. 30–32.
27 Rudnick, D. 'Telecommunications: a market ripe for development', *The Times Special Report on Saudi Arabia*, 28 November 2000, p. 8.
28 Reuters, Riyadh, 4 July 2001.
29 *Gulf News*, Dubai, 14 November 2001.
30 Vineeta Shetty, 'Telecoms: winds of change', *Middle Eastern Economic Digest Special Report on Saudi Arabia*, 15 September 2000, pp. 30–32.
31 'Demand growth drives expansion', *Middle Eastern Economic Digest Special Report on Saudi Arabia*, 15 September 2000, op. cit., pp. 35–36.
32 Economist Intelligence Unit Country Report, *Saudi Arabia*, August 2000, p. 22.
33 Saudi British Bank, *Saudi Economic Bulletin*, vol. 5, no. 19, p. 6.
34 *Statement of the Ministry of Planning on the Seventh Development Plan*, Riyadh, 2000, op. cit., pp. 18–19.
35 SAMA, *Annual Report*, Riyadh, 2001, op. cit, p. 146.
36 *Middle East Economic Digest, Database*, 2001.
37 SAMA, *Annual Report*, Riyadh, 2001, op. cit, pp. 87–88.
38 Borland, B., 'The Saudi economy in 2002', *Saudi Economic Survey*, vol. 36, no. 1756, 20 February 2002, p. 75.
39 Ministry of Finance Statement, Riyadh, 8 December 200
40 Khan, Z. and Abu-Dahesh, A. (2001) 'Saudi budget', *Riyadh Bank Quarterly Economic Review*, fourth quarter p. 4.
41 *Middle East Economic Digest, Database*, 2001 op. cit.
42 SAMA, *Annual Report*, Riyadh, 2001, op. cit, p. 300.
43 Kawach, N. (2002) 'Saudi budget deficit soars past $200 billion', *Gulf News*, 1 January.
44 www.muslimtrade.net/tradeguide/saudia
45 'GCC brings forward customs unity schedule', *Middle East Economic Digest*, 4 January 2002, p. 2.

168 Notes

46 'GCC summit', *Oxford Analytica Daily Brief*, 14 January 2002, p. 15.
47 Wilson, R. *Islamic Finance*, Financial Times Financial Publishing, London, pp. 95–97.
48 'Taxation in Saudi Arabia', Whinney Murray and Co., Riyadh, January 2001, p. 2.
49 Borland, B. (2001) 'Outward flows, inward investment needs in the GCC', *Arab Banker*, vol. 16, no. 2, pp. 49–51.
50 SAMA, *Annual Report*, Riyadh, 2001, op. cit, p. 300.
51 'New privatisation structure elicits positive reaction', *Middle Eastern Economic Digest*, 16 February 2002, p. 19.
52 Ministry of Industry and Electricity, *Guide to the Licensing of Foreign Investment in the Kingdom of Saudi Arabia*, Riyadh, 2000, p. 13.
53 Saudi Arabian General Investment Authority, *The New Foreign Investment Laws of the Kingdom*, Riyadh, 2000, p. 2.
54 McDowall, A. (2002) 'Two cheers for Saudi Arabia', *Middle Eastern Economic Digest*, 23 February, pp. 4–5.
55 SAMA, *Annual Report*, Riyadh, 2001, op. cit, pp. 52–53.
56 McDowall, A. (2002) 'Two cheers for Saudi Arabia', op. cit, *Middle Eastern Economic Digest*, 23 February, pp. 4–5.
57 Ministry of Industry and Electricity, *Guide to the Licensing of Foreign Investment in the Kingdom of Saudi Arabia*, Riyadh, 2000, p. 25.
58 McDowall, A. (2002) 'Two cheers for Saudi Arabia', op. cit, *Middle Eastern Economic Digest*, 23 February, p. 5.
59 Butter, D. (2001) 'Special Report Saudi Arabia: Strength in adversity', *Middle Eastern Economic Digest*, 30 November, pp. 28–29
60 'Green light for foreign investors', *Middle Eastern Economic Digest*, 18 January 2002, p. 21.

4 Oil, gas and petrochemicals

1 Gelb, A. and associates, *Oil Windfalls: Blessing or Curse?* Oxford University Press for the World Bank, New York, 1988.
2 Anon., *Chevron and Saudi Arabia*, Chevron Publication, Riyadh, 1999, p. 2.
3 Moliver, D.M. and Abbondante, P.J. (1980) *The Economy of Saudi Arabia*, p. 17, New York: Praeger.
4 Danielsen, A.L. (1982) *The Evolution of OPEC*, p. 144, New York: Harcourt Brace.
5 Ibid. p. 140.
6 Roncaglia, A. (1985) *The International Oil Market*, p. 47, London: Macmillan.
7 Robinson, J. (1988) *Yamani: the Inside Story*, London: Simon and Schuster.
8 Johany, A.D. (1980) *The Myth of the OPEC Cartel: the Role of Saudi Arabia*, Chichester UK: Wiley.
9 Based on data in *OPEC Annual Statistical Bulletin*, Vienna, 2002, p. 114.
10 Ibid. p.9.
11 *BP Statistical Review of World Energy*, London, 2001, p. 12.
12 Data from Ministry of Petroleum and Minerals cited in Saudi Arabian Monetary Agency *Thirty Seventh Annual Report*, Riyadh, 2001, p. 414.
13 Data from Saudi American Bank, *Facts and Figures, 1998–2002*, Riyadh, 2002.
14 www.saudiaramco.com
15 Data from Ministry of Petroleum and Minerals cited in Saudi Arabian Monetary Agency *Thirty-Seventh Annual Report*, Riyadh, 2001, p. 415.
16 CWC Group, (2002) 'Breaking the deadlock', *Saudi Review: Economic and Political Analysis*, Issue 18, pp. 20–21.
17 'ARAMCO mulls gas supply options', *Middle East Economic Digest*, 13 September 2002.
18 'Fresh offer for gas initiative', *Middle Eastern Economic Digest*, 4 October 2002.

Notes 169

19 'Saudi Arabia offers further gas concessions', *Petroleum Argus*, 7 October 2002.
20 Turner, L. and Bedore, J.M. (1979) *Middle East Industrialisation: A Study of Saudi and Iranian Downstream Investments*, pp. 8 and 18, London: Saxon House Publishing for the Royal Institute of International Affairs.
21 SABIC, *Potential Realised*, Riyadh, 2001, p. 1.
22 www.sabic.com/en/products/metals.htm
23 www.sabic.com/en/products/polymers.htm
24 www.sabic.com/en/press/press_master.asp
25 'Saudi petrochemicals sector reaches level of saturation', *Alexander's Gas and Oil Connections*, vol. 6, Issue 19, 2001.
26 'Company News: Middle East', *Alexander's Gas and Oil Connections*, vol. 4, Issue 13, 1999.

5 Banking and financial markets

1 Patrick, H.T., (1996) 'Financial development and economic growth in underdeveloped countries', *Economic Development and Cultural Change*, vol. 14, no. 2, pp. 174–177. Reprinted in Meier, G.M. (1995) *Leading Issues in Economic Development*, pp. 202–204, Oxford University Press.
2 Cameron, R., (1963) 'The bank as entrepreneur', *Explorations in Entrepreneurial History*, pp. 50–55, series 2, vol. 1.
3 Wilson, R. (1983) *Banking and Finance in the Arab Middle East*, p. 19 London: Macmillan.
4 Ibid. pp. 7–13.
5 Johany, A.D. Berne, M.J. and Wilson Mixon, J. (1986) Jr., *The Saudi Arabian Economy*, pp. 150–152, London: Croom Helm.
6 Abdeen, A.M. and Shook, D.N., (1984) *The Saudi Financial System*, p. 60, Chichester and New York: Wiley.
7 Wilson, R. (1982) 'The evolution of the Saudi banking system and its relationship with Bahrain', in Niblock, T. (ed.), (1982) *State, Society and Economy in Saudi Arabia*, p. 280, London: Croom Helm.
8 History of Al-Bank Al-Saudi Al-Fransi, www.alfansi.com/English/Cocd/History.htm
9 Young, A. (1983) *Saudi Arabia: the Making of a Financial Giant*, p. 26, New York University Press.
10 Ibid. pp. 29–30.
11 Ibid. pp. 61–64.
12 Ibid. p. 145.
13 Presley, J. and Wilson, R. (1991) *Banking in the Arab Gulf*, pp. 18–19 London: Macmillan.
14 Wilson, R. *Banking and Finance in the Arab Middle East*, op. cit., p. 88.
15 Banking Control Law, Royal Decree No. M/5, 22/2/1386 AH, articles 9 and 10.
16 Ibid., article 6.
17 Abdeen, A.M. and Shook, D.N. (1984) *The Saudi Financial System in the Context of Western and Islamic Finance*, p. 134, Chichester: Wiley.
18 Saudi Arabian Monetary Agency, *Annual Report, 1398*, Riyadh, 1978, p. 34.
19 Wilson, R. (1998) *Banking and Finance in the Middle East*, Financial Times Publications, p. 19.
20 Moliver, D.M. (1998) and Abbondante, P.J. (1980) *The Economy of Saudi Arabia*, p. 93, New York: Praeger.
21 Wilson, R. *Banking and Finance in the Middle East*, op. cit., pp. 234–235.
22 Ibid. p. 238.
23 Al-Rajhi Banking and Investment Corporation, *Annual Report*, 1999, p. 12.
24 Wilson, R. 'Three decades of modern Islamic banking', *Arab Banker*, vol. 16, no. 2, 2001, p. 39.

170 *Notes*

25 In 2001 Al-Baraka's international banking operations were merged with those of the International Investor of Kuwait, an Islamic investment company. The new company will manage assets worth 3 billion dollars, with Al-Baraka having a 35 per cent stake. See *New Horizon*, Institute of Islamic Banking and Insurance, London, no. 119, July 2001, p. 24.
26 IDB Annual Report 2000, www.islamic-banking.int
27 Al-Rajhi Banking and Investment Corporation, *Annual Report, 1999*, p. 17.
28 Saudi Arabian Monetary Agency, *Thirty Seventh Annual Report, 2001*, p. 75.
29 Saudi Arabian Monetary Agency, *Quarterly Statistical Bulletin*, third quarter 2001, pp. 25.
30 Saudi Arabian Monetary Agency, *Thirty Seventh Annual Report, 2001*, op. cit., p. 75.
31 Saudi Arabian Monetary Agency, *Quarterly Statistical Bulletin*, op. cit., third quarter 2001, pp. 80–81.
32 National Commercial Bank, *Market Review and Outlook*, 2 November 2001, p. 6.
33 Saudi Arabian Monetary Agency, *Quarterly Statistical Bulletin*, op. cit., third quarter 2001, p. 33.
34 Saudi Arabian Monetary Agency, *Monthly Statistical Bulletin*, September 2001, p. 23.
35 Affara, F.M.S. (1995) *The Role of Financial Intermediaries in Saudi Arabia with Particular Reference to the National Commercial Bank*, Ph.D. thesis, University of Durham.
36 Wilson, R. (1998) *Banking and Finance in the Middle East*, pp. 239–240, Financial Times Publications.
37 Dowling, K. (2000) 'The ties that bind: Barclays, a bin Laden relative, Carlyle and the BCCI boys', *Online Journal*, 3 November.
38 Sage, M. 'Bin Laden's brother-in-law an Irish citizen', PA News, 4 October 2001.
39 www.ireland.com/special/tribunals/flood/
40 www.ncb.com.sa/utils/NCBoverview.asp
41 National Commercial Bank, *Press Release*, 10 November 2001. www.alahli.com/utils/Pr3.asp
42 Saudi Arabian Monetary Agency, *Monthly Statistical Bulletin*, September 2001, op. cit. p. 10.
43 Saudi Arabian Monetary Agency, *Thirty Seventh Annual Report, 2001*, op. cit., p. 307.
44 Al-Shaikh, S. (1999) 'Structure of Gulf banking and the effect of globalisation and financial liberalisation', p. *NCB Economist*, volume 9, number 2, March/April.
45 Saudi American Bank, *Annual Report 2000*, pp. 12–15.
46 Sabri, S. (2001) *The House of Saud in Commerce: A Study of Royal Entrepreneurship in Saudi Arabia*, pp. 140, 174, 220 and 267, New Dehli: I.S. Publications.
47 The Saudi Investment Bank, *Annual Report 2000*, p. 3.
48 Ibid. pp. 6–7.
49 Saudi Arabian Monetary Agency, *Thirty-Seventh Annual Report, 2001*, op. cit., p. 107–110.
50 The market capitalisation has remained stable in relation to GDP since the early 1990s. See Azzam, H. 'Gulf capital markets: development prospects and constraints', in *Development of Financial Markets in the Arab Countries, Iran and Turkey*, Economic Research Forum for the Arab Countries, Iran and Turkey, Cairo, 1995, pp. 185–186.
51 Seznec, J.-F. (1987) *The Financial Markets of the Arabian Gulf*, pp. 51–67, London: Croom Helm.
52 Wright, J.W. and Albatel, A.H. 'Private sector finance: problems faced by the fourth and fifth development plans', in Wright, J.W. (ed.) (1996) *Business and Economic Development in Saudi Arabia*, p. 60 London: Macmillan.
53 Borland, B. (2001) 'Outward flows, inward investment needs in the GCC', *Arab Banker*, vol. 16, no. 2, pp. 49–51.

Notes 171

54 Darwiche, F. *The Gulf Stock Exchange Crisis: the Rise and Fall of the Souq Al-Manakh*, pp. 86–139, London: Croom Helm, London.
55 Abdul-Hadi, A.S.F. (1988) *Stock Markets of the Arab World*, pp. 49–51, London: Routledge.
56 Al-Shaikh, S.A. (2000) 'The mutual funds market in Saudi Arabia', *NCB Economist*, vol. 10, no. 2, p. 7.
57 *An Introduction to Short-Term Savings through Mutual Funds*, National Commercial Bank, Jeddah, 1999, p. 3.
58 Al-Ahli Long-Term Mutual Funds, *Achieve Your Long-term Investment Goals,* National Commercial Bank, Jeddah, 2000, p. 10.
59 Al-Shaikh, S.A. (2002) 'The mutual funds market in Saudi Arabia', *NCB Market Review and Outlook*, 1 February, p. 4.
60 www.failaka.com/Funds.html See list in *New Horizon*, Institute of Islamic Banking and Insurance, London, October 2001, no. 113, pp. 10–11.
61 Wilson, R. 'Islamic mutual funds unveiled', *New Horizon*, Institute of Islamic Banking and Insurance, London, no. 115, December 2001-January 2002, pp. 8–9.
62 Al-Shaikh, S. 'The mutual funds market in Saudi Arabia', *NCB Economist*, vol. 10, no. 2, March/April 2000, op. cit., pp. 5–12.
63 www.ncb.com.sa/islamic_banking/
64 Al-Shaikh, S. 'The mutual funds market in Saudi Arabia', *NCB Market Review and Outlook*, 1 February 2002, op. cit., pp. 4–6.
65 www.ncb.com.sa/funds_prices
66 www.ncb.com.sa/islamic_banking/short_term_funds.asp
67 www.ncb.com.sa/funds_prices
68 Al-Shaikh, S. 'The mutual funds market in Saudi Arabia', *NCB Economist*, vol. 11, no. 1, First quarter 2001, p. 7.
69 'Saudi Arabia focus', *Arab Banker*, vol. 14, no. 2, 2000, pp. 20–31.
70 Allen, R. 'Envy of the neighbours: Saudi banking', *Financial Times Survey of Middle Eastern Banking*, April 9 2001, op. cit., p. 4.
71 Allen, R., 'Saudi Banking: envy of the neighbours', *Financial Times Survey of Middle Eastern Banking*, 9 April 2001, p. 5.
72 Al-Shaikh, S. 'The evolving role of financial institutions in the new decade', *NCB Economist*, volume 11, number 1, First quarter 2001, p. 13.
73 Saudi Arabian Monetary Agency, *Thirty Seventh Annual Report, 2001*, op. cit., p. 214
74 Sharaf Sabri, *The House of Saud in Commerce: A Study of Royal Entrepreneurship in Saudi Arabia*, I.S. Publications, New Delhi, 2001, p. 250.

6 International trade and GCC economic relations

1 WTO, *World Trade in 2000: Overview*, www.wto.org
2 WTO, *World Merchandise Exports by Region and Selected Economy, 1980, 1985, 1990, 1995 and 1999–2001*, www.wto.org
3 WTO, *World Merchandise Imports by Region and Selected Economy, 1980, 1985, 1990, 1995 and 1999–2001*, www.wto.org
4 Wilson, R. (1995) *Economic Development in the Middle East*, p. 147, London: Routledge.
5 Salvatore, D. (2001) *International Economics*, seventh edition, pp. 29–51, New York: Wiley.
6 Vernon, R. (1996) 'International investment and international trade in the product life cycle', *Quarterly Journal of Economics*, (May) pp. 190–207.
7 Daniels, J.D. and Radebaugh, L.H. (1998) *Interenational Business: Environments and Operations*, Addison Wesley, eighth edition, pp. 212–213.
8 Brander, J.A. and Spencer, B. (1985) 'Export subsidies and international market share rivalry', *Journal of International Economics* (February) pp. 83–100.

172 Notes

9 Porter, M. (1990) *The Competitive Advantage of Nations*, p. 72, New York: Free Press.
10 'Jeddah aims to make its mark', *Middle East Economic Digest*, 17 May 2002.
11 'Ports: the keys to the Kingdom', *Middle East Economic Digest*, 30 November 2001.
12 SAMA, *Thirty-Seventh Annual Report*, 2001, p. 372.
13 *The Kingdom's First Bonded and Re-export Zone*, Saudi Trade and Export Development Company, Jeddah, 2001.
14 *Damman Bonded and Re-Export Zone*, Saudi Trade and Export Development Company, Damman, 2001.
15 Trade Partners UK: www.tradepartners.gov.uk/saudi_arabia/doingbusiness
16 *Clothing, footwear and fashion market in Saudi Arabia:* www.tradepartners.gov.uk/clothing/saudi_arabia/profile/overview.shtml
17 Al-Shaikh, S.A. (1999) 'Changing pattern of Saudi foreign trade: implications for industrial structure', *NCB Economist*, Jeddah, vol. 9, no. 4, July–August, pp. 1–8.
18 SAMA, *Thirty-Seventh Annual Report* 2001, p. 372.
19 WTO, *Leading exporters and importers in world trade in commercial services, 2000*, www.wto.org
20 Borland, B. (2001) 'Outward flows, inward investment needs in the GCC', *Arab Banker*, vol. 16, no. 2, (Autumn) p. 50.
21 SAMA, Thirty Seventh Annual Report 2001, p. 426.
22 'Korean exporters face hard times', *Middle East Economic Digest*, 24 May 2002.
23 'Trade: taking a tumble', *Middle East Economic Digest*, 29 March 2002.
24 'BAE: Al-Yamamah weathers the changes', *Middle East Economic Digest*, 17 May 2002.
25 Azzam, H. (2001) 'Inter-Arab cooperation vital to boost economic growth', *Arab News*, Jeddah, 1 May.
26 'Riyadh – Capital's top trade partner', *Gulf News*, Dubai, 21 July 2002.
27 'Riyadh Cables in joint venture with UAE firm', *Gulf News*, Dubai, 24 March 2002.
28 'Saudi date producers join forces to enter global market', *Arab News*, Jeddah, 3 May 2001.
29 *Oxford Analytica Daily Brief*, 14 January 2002, section 5.
30 Bashir, A.W. and Hassan, J. (2001) 'Consumers to gain substantially from tariff cuts, economists say', *Arab News*, Jeddah, 31 May.
31 Bashir, A.W. and Hassan, J. (2001) 'Kingdom cuts import duties to 5 per cent', *Arab News*, Jeddah, 28 May.
32 'GCC customs chiefs to hold key talks next month', *Arab News*, Jeddah, 4 May 2002.
33 'Kingdom to implement GCC plans', *Arab News*, Jeddah, 2 July 2002.
34 'GCC states to scrap list of businesses', *Arab News*, Jeddah, 9 May 2001.
35 'Prince Sultan lauds GCC summit', *Arab News*, Jeddah, 2 January 2002.
36 Wilson, R. (2002) *The Gulf-EU Trade Relationship: Challenges and Opportunities*, Emirates Centre for Strategic Studies and Research, Lecture Series no. 37, 2002, pp. 1–35.
37 Al-Nayyif, B. (2002) 'Faqeeh blames lack of clear WTO rules for delay in entry', *Arab News*, Jeddah, 19 April.
38 Al-Amoudi, M.O. (2001) 'Saudi agenda and WTO', *Arab News*, Jeddah, 13 June.
39 www.wto.org/wto/english/thewto_e/acc_e/status_e.htm
40 Banoon, J. (2001) 'Kingdom's accession to WTO still some way off says Faqeeh', *Arab News*, Jeddah, 2 October.
41 'Kingdom can't open market to banned goods', *Arab News*, Jeddah, 22 April 2001.
42 'Saudi Arabia bans companies over Israel imports', *Saudi Times* (citing Associated Press) 5 August 2002.
43 Binzagr, W. (2001) 'WTO: the good and the bad', *Arab News*, Jeddah, 25 June.
44 'Saudi's plan tribunals to settle trade disputes', *Gulf News*, Dubai, 20 January 2002.
45 Hanware, K. and Bashir, A.W. 'Saudi products will compete well in global markets', *Arab News*, Jeddah, 2 May.

Notes 173

7 Employment issues

1 www.devdata.worldbank.org
2 *The Little Data Book*, World Bank, 2001, p. 185.
3 *Saudi Economic Survey*, 12 April 2000, p. 12.
4 Ba-Isa, M. (2001) 'Kingdom demographic map undergoes dramatic change', *Arab News*, Jeddah, 27 April.
5 Wilson, R. (1995) *Economic Development in the Middle East*, pp. 50–54, London: Routledge.
6 SAMA, *Thirty Seventh Annual Report* 2001, p. 247.
7 Source: Ministry of Planning, *Seventh Development Plan 2000–2004*, p. 47.
8 Borland, B. 'The Saudi Economy in 2002', *Saudi Economic Survey*, 20 February 2002, pp. 65–66.
9 'Government tries to unite conflicting unemployment estimates', *Middle East Economic Digest*, London, 11 October 2002.
10 Staff writer, 'Efforts under way to eradicate unemployment', *Arab News*, Jeddah, 4 October 2002.
11 Tash, A.Q. (2002) 'Dealing with unemployment', *Arab News*, Jeddah, 23 June.
12 Borland, B. (2002) 'The Saudi economy in 2002', *Saudi Economic Survey*, vol. 36, no. 1756, 20 February, pp. 65–66.
13 Khan, G.A. (2001) 'Unemployment rate alarming: study', *Arab News*, Jeddah, 4 January.
14 Hassan, J. *Arab News*, Jeddah, 14 October 2002.
15 Yamani, M. (2000) *Changed Identities: the Challenge of the New Generation in Saudi Arabia*, pp. 76–78, London: Royal Institute of International Affairs.
16 Weiss-Armush, A.M. (1993) 'Women in Saudi society', in Al-Sweel, A. and Wright, J.W. (eds.), *Saudi Arabia: Tradition and Transition'*, Michigan: Westland, Hayden– McNeil, p. 103.
17 Al-Awadh, K. (2002) 'Saudi staff challenge BAE Systems move', *Arab News*, Jeddah, 6 July.
18 Al-Awadh, K. (2002) 'BAE plans to cut jobs', *Arab News*, Jeddah, 15 August.
19 Ministry of Planning, *Seventh Development Plan 2000–2004*, pp. 209–211.
20 Wahba, J. 'Returns to education and regional earnings differentials in Egypt' in Salehi-Ishfahani, D. (ed.), (2001) *Labour and Human Capital in the Middle East: Studies in Market and Household Behaviour*, pp. 369–391, Reading: Ithaca Press.
21 Borland, B. (2002) 'Saudi Arabia's employment profile', *Saudi American Bank Newsletter*, 8 October, p. 4.
22 The Saudi Arabian Information Resource: www.saudinf.com/main/y0721.htm
23 The World Bank, *Little Data Book*, Washington, 2001, p. 185.
24 Ibid.
25 United Nations, *Statistical Abstract of the ESCWA Region*, twentieth issue, New York, 2000.
26 Presley, J. (2000) 'The Seventh Development Plan', *Saudi Economic Bulletin*, Saudi British Bank, Riyadh, fourth quarter, issue 19, p. 6.
27 Yamini, M. (2000) *Changes Identities: the Challenge of the New Generation in Saudi Arabia*, op. cit, p. 64, London: Royal Institute of International Affairs.
28 Ibid. p. 101.
29 Al-Yamani, I. (2002) 'Career woman carries the day', *Arab News*, Jeddah, 20 June.
30 Al-Zobidy, O. (2001) 'Shoura opens debate on high marriage costs', *Arab News*, Jeddah, 31 December.
31 Anonymous staff writer, 'Manpower council to address female unemployment', *Arab News*, Jeddah, 10 May 2002.
32 Al-Maeena, T.A. (2002) 'It's always their fault!' *Arab News*, Jeddah, 12 May.
33 Yamani, M. (2000) *Changed Identities: the Challenge of the New Generation in Saudi Arabia*, op. cit, pp. 141–145, London: Royal Institute for International Affairs, London.

174 *Notes*

34 Al-Orabi, H.M. (1999) 'Attitudes of Saudi women towards participating in the labour force', *Humanomics*, vol. 15, no. 4, pp. 123–140.
35 Gamburd, M.R. (2000) *The Kitchen Spoon's Handle: Transnationalism and Sri Lanka's Migrant Housemaids*, Cornell University Press.
36 Abdullah S. Al-Shetaiwi, 'Factors Affecting the Under-utilisation of Qualified Saudi Women in the Saudi Private Sector', Ph.D. thesis, Loughborough University Business School, 2002.
37 Ibid, p. 167 and p. 172.
38 Ibid. p. 177.
39 Ibid. p. 190.

8 Employment conditions in SABIC

1 The full results of the survey are set out in Abdullah Hamad Al-Salamah, *Employee Perceptions in Multinational Companies, A Case Study of the Saudi Arabian Basic Industries Corporation*, Ph.D thesis, University of Durham, April 1994.
2 Hambleton, H.G. (1982) 'The Saudi Arabian Petrochemical Industry: its Rationale and Effectiveness', in Niblock, T. *State, Society and Economy in Saudi Arabia*, p. 236, London: Croom Helm.
3 El Mallakh, R. (1982) *Saudi Arabia: Rush to Development*, p. 414, London: Croom Helm.
4 For an account of the initial investments see Presley, J.R. (1984) *A Guide to the Saudi Arabia Economy*, London: Macmillan.
5 Hambleton, H.G. op. cit., p. 238.
6 Johany, A.D., Berne, M. and Mixon, W. (1986) *The Saudi Arabian Economy*, p. 128, London: Croom Helm.
7 Al-Salamah, A.H., op. cit., p. 48.
8 SABIC Annual Report, 1990.
9 Yilmaz, F.M. (2000) 'New Saudi law permits 100 per cent ownership', *IslamiQ.com*, 30 March, Allen, R. and Corzine, R. 'Saudi Arabia: New council to push for energy reform', *Financial Times*, London, 11 February 2000.
10 The dependence on Arab manpower was much less by the late 1980s in Saudi Arabia than that noted in earlier studies. See Naiem A. Sherbiny and Ismail Serageldin, 'Expatriate labour and economic growth: Saudi demand for Egyptian labour', in Kerr, M.H. and El Sayed Yassin (1982) *Rich and Poor Countries in the Middle East: Egypt and the New Arab Social Order*, pp. 225–257, Boulder Colorado: Westview Press. This was to some extent due to concerns over its social consequences. See Ibrahim, S.E. (1982) *The New Arab Social Order: A Study of the Social Impact of Oil Wealth* pp. 95–122, Boulder, Colorado: Westview Press.
11 Evidence from developed countries suggests that married men with children advanced faster in their careers. See Tharenou, P. 'Is there a link between family structures and women's and men's managerial career advancement?' *Journal of Organizational Behaviour*, vol. 20, no. 6, pp. 837–863.
12 There is an extensive literature on training issues, much of which has relevance to SABIC. For an introduction see Chapman, P.G. (1993) *The Economics of Training*, London: Harvester Wheatsheaf. Zinderman, A. (1978) *Manpower Training: Theory and Policy*, London: Macmillan.
13 For a discussion of training issues specific to developing countries see: Bas, D. (1988) 'Cost-effectiveness of training in developing countries', *International Labour Review*, vol. 127, no. 3, pp. 355–369; Roberts, L. 'Manpower consulting and training in developing countries', *Training and Development Journal*, vol. 37, no. 10, 1983, pp. 48–52; Bennell, P. and Segerstrom, J. 'Vocational education and training in developing countries: has the World Bank got it right?' *International Journal of Education Development*, vol. 18, no. 4, pp. 271–287.

Notes   175

14 For an example of how another Saudi Arabian employer, Al-Bank Al-Saudi Al-Fransi, regards training, see: www.arab.net/sfbbank/general/employment.html
15 Arguably there are greater risks in working abroad which justify the higher salaries. Some of the standard arguments about risk versus pay may be applicable to expatriate executives. See Aggarwal, R.K. and Samwick, A.A. (1999) 'The other side of the trade-off: the impact of risk on executive compensation', *Journal of Political Economy*, vol. 107, no. 1, pp. 65–105.
16 For a survey of the literature on career advancement see Tharenou, P. (1997) 'Explanations of managerial career advancement', *Australian Psychologist*, vol. 32, no. 1, March, pp. 19–28.
17 Cultural context is important for labour relations and company employment practices. See Hyman, R. (1997) *Globalisation and Labour Relations*, London: Sage.
18 For a review of some of the issues see Bosch, G. (1999) 'Working time: tendencies and emerging issues', *International Labour Review*, vol. 138, no. 2, p. 131.
19 An earlier study of Saudi Arabian managers also revealed some dissatisfaction over working hours. See Ali, A. and Al-Shakhis, M. (1989) 'Managerial beliefs about work in two Arab states', *Organisation Studies*, vol. 10, no. 2, pp. 169–186.
20 There is scope for studies of the social impact of SABIC working hours. One model might be the work of Barton, J. Aldridge, J. and Smith, P. (1998) 'The emotional impact of shift work on the children of shift workers', *Scandinavian Journal of Work Environment and Health*, vol. 24, no. 3, pp. 146–150.
21 Abrahamsson, L. (2000) 'Production economics analysis of investment initiated to improve the working environment', *Applied Ergonomics*, vol. 31, no. 1, pp. 1–7.
22 Melchior, A. 'Globalisation and labour standards: a look at Asia', *Internasjonal Politikk*, vol. 57, no. 2, 1999, p. 295.
23 There have been numerous investigations into workers' attitudes towards safety in many countries. See, for example, Hayes, B.E. Perander, J. Smecko, T. and Trask, J. (1998) 'Measuring perceptions of workplace safety: development and validation of the work safety scale', *Journal of Safety Research*, vol. 29, no. 3, pp. 145–161.

9 The role of the private sector

1 Evans, P. (1995) *Embedded Autonomy: States and Industrial Transformation*, p. 11, New Jersey: Princeton University Press.
2 Cammack, P., (1991) 'States and markets in Latin America', in Moran, M. and Wright, M. (eds.) *The Market and the State: Studies in Interdependence*, New York: St Martin's Press.
3 Evans, P., op. cit., p. 59.
4 Roumasset, J.A., (1992) 'Introduction: the role of government in economic development' in Roumasset, J.A. and Barr, S. (eds), *The Economics of Cooperation: East Asian Development and the Case for Pro-Market Intervention*, p. 7, Boulder, Colorado: Westview.
5 Turck, N. (1998) 'Dispute resolution in Saudi Arabia', *International Lawyer*, vol. 22 (Summer) pp. 415–440.
6 Business International (1981) *Saudi Arabia – Issues for growth*: an inside view of an economic power in the making, London: Business International.

10 The electricity industry

1 Hadjilambrinos, C. (1999) 'Electricity restructuring: Lessons for the US from the British and Norwegian experience', *The Structure of the Energy Industries: The Only Constant is Change*, Twentieth Annual North American Conference of IAEE, Florida (29 August–1 September 1999), pp. 56–63.

176 *Notes*

2 Newbery, D. (1999) *Privatization, Restructuring, and Regulation of Network Utilities*: Massachusetts, MIT.
3 Klein, M. (1998) 'Network industries', in Helm, D. and Jenkinson, T. (eds.) *Competition in Regulated Industries*, Oxford: Oxford University Press.
4 Arocena, P., Kuhn, K. Regibeau, P. (1999) 'Regulatory reform in the Spanish electricity industry: A missed opportunity for competition', *Energy Policy*, vol. 27, no. 7, pp. 387–399.
5 Joskow, P. and Schmalensee, R. (1985) *Markets for Power: An Analysis of Electric Utility Deregulation*, Massachusetts: MIT Press.
6 Banks, F. (1999) *Energy Economics: a Modern Introduction*, Boston: Kluwer.
7 Arocena *et al.* (1999) op. cit.
8 Bernstein, S. (1988) 'Competition, marginal cost tariffs and spot pricing in the Chilean electric power sector', *Energy Policy*, vol. 16, no. 8 (August), pp. 369–377.
9 Doyle, C. and Maher, M. (1992) 'Common carriage and the pricing of electricity transmission', *Energy Journal*, vol. 13, no. 3, pp. 63–94.
10 Bayless, C. (1994) 'Less is more: Why gas turbines will transform electric utilities', *Public Utilities Fortnightly*, vol. 132, no. 22, pp. 21–25.
11 Berrie, T. (1992) *Electricity Economics and Planning*, London: Peter Peregrinus.
12 Trebing, H. (2000) 'Electricity: Changes and issues', *Review of Industrial Organization*, vol. 17, no. 1, pp. 61–74.
13 Hyman, L and West, H. (1989) 'Diversification, deregulation, and competition: Cost of capital implications for electric utilities', in Crew, M. (ed.) *Deregulation and Diversification of Utilities*, pp. 165–181, London: Kluwer.
14 Armstrong, M., Cowan, S. and Vickers, J. (1997) *Regulatory Reform: Economic Analysis and British Experience*, Massachusetts: MIT Press.
15 Sansom, R. (1995) *Privatising the UK Electricity Supply Industry*, SEEBOARD International, United Kingdom.
16 Bernstein, S., Bushnell, J. and Stoft, S. (1997) 'The competitive effects of transmission capacity in a deregulated electricity industry' *National Bureau of Economic Research Working Papers*, no. 6293, Massachusetts.
17 Tenenbaum, B. and Henderson, S. (1991) 'Market-based pricing of wholesale electric services', *The Electricity Journal*, vol. 4, no. 10 (December), pp. 30–45.
18 Joskow and Schmalensee, op. cit.
19 Tenenbaum, B. Lock, R. and Barker, J. (1992) 'Electricity privatization: Structural, competitive and regulatory options', *Energy Policy*, vol. 20, no. 12, pp. 1134–1160.
20 Hunt and Shuttleworth (1996) *Competition and Choice in Electricity*, Chichester, UK: Wiley.
21 Tenenbaum *et al.* (1992), op. cit.
22 Hunt and Shuttleworth (1996), op. cit.
23 Lovei, L. (2000) 'The single-buyer Model: A dangerous path toward competitive electricity markets', World Bank: *Public Policy for the Private Sector*, note no. 225.
24 Newbery, D. (1999), op. cit.
25 Mork, E. (2001) 'Emergence of financial markets for electricity: A european perspective', *Energy Policy*, vol. 29, no. 1, pp. 7–15.
26 Murray, B. (1998) *Electricity Markets: Investments, Performance and Analysis*, Chichester, UK: John Wiley & Sons, Chichester.
27 Hunt and Shuttleworth (1996), op. cit.
28 Green, R. (1999) 'Draining the pool: The reform of electricity trading in England and Wales', *Energy Policy*, vol. 27, no. 9, pp. 515–525.
29 Sioshansi, F. and Morgan, C. (1999) 'Where function follows form: International comparisons of restructured electricity markets', *The Electricity Journal*, vol. 12, no. 3, pp. 20–30.

Notes 177

30 Estache, A. and Rodriquez-Paradina, M. (1997) 'The real possibility of competitive generation markets in hydro systems – The case of Brazil', World Bank: *Public Policy for the Private Sector*, note no. 106.
31 Hunt and Shuttleworth (1996), op. cit.
32 Graves, F. Read, G. Hanser, P. and Earle, R. (2000) 'One-part markets for electric power: ensuring the benefits of competition' in Ilic, M.; Galiana, F. and Fink, L. (eds.) *Power Systems Restructuring: Engineering and Economics*, pp. 243–280, Boston: Kluwer.
33 Berrie, T. (1992), op. cit.
34 Green, R. (1999), op. cit.
35 Kahn, E. and Stoft, S. (1995) 'Organization of bulk power markets: A concept paper', *Lawrence Berkeley National Laboratory, LBL-37508*, University of California, www.stoft.com.
36 Kee, E. (2001) 'Vesting contracts: A tool for electricity market transition', *The Electricity Journal*, vol. 14, no. 7, pp. 11–22.
37 Silsbee, C. and Jurewitz, J. (2001) 'Wholesale generator incentives to exercise market power in the California electricity market', *The Electricity Journal*, vol. 14, no. 7, pp. 51–56.
38 Gunn, C. and Sharp, B. (1999) 'Electricity distribution as an unsustainable natural monopoly: A potential outcome of New Zealand's regulatory regime', *Energy Economics*, vol. 21, pp. 385–401.
39 Arocena *et al* (1999) op. cit.
40 Hjalmarsson, L. (1996) 'From club-regulation to market competition in the Scandinavian electricity supply', in Gilbert, R. and Kahn, E. (eds.) *International Comparisons of Electricity Regulation*, New York: Cambridge University Press, pp. 126–178.
41 Hammons, T., Franco, N., Sbertoli, L., Khelil, C. Rudnick, H., Clerici, A. and Longhi, A. (1997) 'Energy market integration in South America', *IEEE Power Engineering Review* (August), pp. 6–14.
42 Caruso, G. and Chen, X. (1997) 'Experiences of electricity-sector restructuring in Asia', *Journal of Energy and Development*, vol. 22, no. 3, pp. 1–16.
43 Turkson, J. and Redlinger, R. (2000) 'Cross-country comparison', in Turkson, J. (ed.) *Power Sector Reform in SubSaharan Africa*, pp. 186–203, London: Macmillan.
44 Algosaibi, G. (1999) *Yes, (Saudi) Minister!: A Life in Administration*, London: London Centre of Arab Studies.
45 Yajima, M. (1997) *Deregulatory Reforms of the Electricity Supply Industry*, London: Quorum.
46 Train, K. (1994) *Optimal Regulation: The Economic Theory of Natural Monopoly*, Massachusetts: MIT Press.
47 Azzam, H. (1996) 'The Saudi electricity industry', *The NCB Economist*, no. 4 (July/ August), pp. 1–12.
48 Ibid.
49 Khoshaim, B. (1997) 'How the Shoaiba deal can establish BOO techniques in Saudi Arabia', *Arab Banker*, vol. 4, no. 4, pp. 18–20.

Bibliography

Books, monographs and chapters in edited volumes

Abdeen, Adnan M. and Shook, Dale N. (1984) *The Saudi Financial System*, Chichester and New York: Wiley.

Abdul-Hadi, Ayman Shafiq Fayyad (1988) *Stock Markets of the Arab World, London:* Routledge.

Abdulrahman Garawi and Schmidt, Mary E. (1996) 'The Saudi managerial environment', in Wright, J.R. Jr. (ed.), *Business and Economic Development in Saudi Arabia*, pp. 87–104, London: Macmillan.

Al-Farsy, Fouad (1982) *Saudi Arabia: A Case Study in Development*, London: KPI.

Algosaibi, G. (1999) *Yes, (Saudi) Minister!: A Life in Administration*, London: London Centre of Arab Studies.

Al-Shoshan, A. (1991) *Saudi Arabia: the Country Nutrition Profile*, Paper presented at the FAO/WHO International Conference on Nutrition, Rome.

Amin, Samir (1990) *Maldevelopment: Anatomy of a Global Failure*, London: Zed Books.

an-Nabhani, Taqiuddin (2000) *The Economic System in Islam*, London: Al-Khilafah.

Armstrong, M., Cowan, S. and Vickers J. (1997) *Regulatory Reform: Economic Analysis and British Experience*, Cambridge, Mass.: MIT Press.

Azzam, Henry (1995) 'Gulf capital markets: development prospects and constraints', in Heba Handoussa (ed) *Development of Financial Markets in the Arab Countries, Iran and Turkey*, Cairo: Economic Research Forum for the Arab Countries, Iran and Turkey.

Bagchi, Amiya Kumar, 'Development planning' in Eatwell, J., Milgate, M. and Newman, P. (eds) (1989) *The New Palgrave: Economic Development*, pp. 98–99, London: Macmillan.

Banks, F. (1999) *Energy Economics: a Modern Introduction*, Boston: Kluwer.

Beblawi, Hazem and Luciani, Giacomo (eds) (1987) *The Rentier State*, London: Croom Helm.

Berrie, T. (1992) *Electricity Economics and Planning*, London: Peter Peregrinus.

Borenstein, S., Bushnell, J. and Stoft, S. (1997) 'The competitive effects of transmission capacity in a deregulated electricity industry', *National Bureau of Economic Research Working Papers*, no. 6293, Massachusetts.

Cammack, P. (1991) 'States and Markets in Latin America', in Moran, M. and Wright, M. (eds) *The Market and the State: Studies in Interdependence*, New York: St Martin's Press.

Chapman, Paul G. (1993) *The Economics of Training*, London: Harvester Wheatsheaf.

Bibliography 179

Cinar, E. Mine (2000) 'Earnings profiles of women workers and education in the Middle East', in Shahin, W. and Dibeh, G. (eds) *Earnings Inequalities, Unemployment and Poverty in the Middle East and North Africa*, Westport, Conn.: Greenwood.

Daniels, John D. and Radebaugh, Lee H. (1998) *International Business: Environments and Operations*, eighth edition, Reading, Mass. and Harlow: Addison-Wesley.

Danielsen, Albert L. (1982) *The Evolution of OPEC*, New York: Harcourt Brace Jovanovich.

Darwiche, Fida (1986), *The Gulf Stock Exchange Crisis: the Rise and Fall of the Souq Al-Manakh*, London: Croom Helm.

El-Ghonemy, M. Riad (1998) *Affluence and Poverty in the Middle East*, London: Routledge.

El Mallakh, Ragaei (1982) *Saudi Arabia: Rush to Development*, London: Croom Helm.

Esposito, John L. (1998) *Islam: the Straight Path*, third edition, Oxford: Oxford University Press.

Estache, A. and Rodriquez-Paradina, M. (1997) 'The real possibility of competitive generation markets in hydro systems – The case of Brazil', *Public Policy for the Private Sector*, note no. 106, World Bank.

Evans, P. (1995) *Embedded Autonomy: States and Industrial Transformation*, New Jersey: Princeton University Press.

Gamburd, Michele Ruth (2000), *The Kitchen Spoon's Handle: Transnationalism and Sri Lanka's Migrant Housemaids*, Ithaca, NY: Cornell University Press.

Gelb, Alan and associates (1988) *Oil Windfalls: Blessing or Curse?* New York: Oxford University Press for the World Bank.

Graves, F; Read, G; Hanser, P. and Earle, R. (2000) 'One-part markets for electric power: Ensuring the benefits of competition' in Ilic, M., Galiana, F. and Fink, L. (eds) *Power Systems Restructuring: Engineering and Economics*, pp. 243–280, Boston: Kluwer.

Hadjilambrinos, C. (1999) 'Electricity restructuring: Lessons for the US from the British and Norwegian experience', *The Structure of the Energy Industries: The Only Constant is Change*, Twentieth Annual North American Conference of IAEE, Florida (29 Aug–1 Sept. 1999), pp. 56–63.

Hambleton, H.G. (1982) 'The Saudi Arabian Petrochemical Industry: its Rationale and Effectiveness', in Niblock, T., *State, Society and Economy in Saudi Arabia*, pp. 233–277, London: Croom Helm.

Hershlag, Z.Y. (1988) *The Contemporary Turkish Economy*, London: Routledge.

Hjalmarsson, L. (1996) 'From club-regulation to market competition in the Scandinavian electricity supply', in Gilbert, R. and Kahn, E. (eds) *International Comparisons of Electricity Regulation*, pp. 126–178, New York: Cambridge University Press.

Hopwood, Derek (1982) 'The ideological basis: Ibn Abd Al-Wahhab's Muslim revivalism' in Niblock, T. (ed.), *State, Society and Economy in Saudi Arabia*, pp. 23–35, London: Croom Helm.

Hunt, S. and Shuttleworth, G. (1996) *Competition and Choice in Electricity*, Chichester: Wiley.

Hyman, Richard (1997) *Globalisation and Labour Relations*, London: Sage.

Hyman, L. and West, H. (1989) 'Diversification, deregulation, and competition: Cost of capital implications for electric utilities', in Crew, M. (ed.) *Deregulation and Diversification of Utilities*, pp. 165–181, London: Kluwer.

Joskow, P. and Schmalensee, R. (1985) *Markets for Power: An Analysis of Electric Utility Deregulation*, Cambridge, Mass.: MIT Press.

Kahn, E. and Stoft, S. (1995) 'Organization of bulk power markets: A concept paper', *Lawrence Berkeley National Laboratory, LBL-37508*, University of California, 1995.

180 *Bibliography*

Ibrahim, Saad Eddin (1982) *The New Arab Social Order: A Study of the Social Impact of Oil Wealth*, Boulder, Colo.: Westview Press.

Islahi, Abdul Azin (1988) *Economic Concepts of Ibn Taimiyah*, p. 173, Leicester: Islamic Foundation.

Johany, Ali D. (1980) *The Myth of the OPEC Cartel: the Role of Saudi Arabia*, Chichester: Wiley.

Johany, Ali D., Berne, Michel and Mixon Jr, J. Wilson. (1986) *The Saudi Arabian Economy*, London: Croom Helm.

Klein, M. (1998) 'Network Industries' in Helm, D. and Jenkinson, T. (eds) *Competition in Regulated Industries*, Oxford: Oxford University Press.

Lange, O. (1960) *Essays on Economic Planning*, pp. 11–20, London: Asia Publishing House; reprinted in Henry Bernstein (ed.) (1973) *Underdevelopment and Development*, pp. 207–215, Harmondsworth: Penguin.

Lovei, L. (2000) 'The single-buyer model: A dangerous path toward competitive electricity markets', *Public Policy for the Private Sector*, note no. 225, World Bank.

Moliver, Donald M. and Abbondante, Paul J. (1980) *The Economy of Saudi Arabia*, New York: Praeger.

Murray, B. (1998) *Electricity Markets: Investments, Performance and Analysis*, Chichester: Wiley.

Newbery, D. (1999) *Privatization, Restructuring, and Regulation of Network Utilities*, Cambridge, Mass.: MIT.

Niblock, Tim (1982) 'Social structure and the development of the Saudi Arabian political system' in Niblock,T. (ed.) *State, Society and Economy in Saudi Arabia*, London: Croom Helm.

Porter, Michael E. (1990) *The Competitive Advantage of Nations*, New York: Free Press.

Presley, John R. (1984) *A Guide to the Saudi Arabia Economy*, London: Macmillan.

Presley, John and Wilson, Rodney (1991) *Banking in the Arab Gulf*, London: Macmillan.

Richards, Alan and Waterbury, John (1990) *A Political Economy of the Middle East: State, Class and Economic Development*, Boulder, Colo.: Westview.

Robinson, Jeffrey (1988) *Yamani: the Inside Story*, London: Simon and Schuster.

Roncaglia, Alessandro (1985) *The International Oil Market*, London: Macmillan.

Rostow, Walt W. (1960) *The Stages of Economic Growth: A Non-Communist Manifesto*, Cambridge: Cambridge University Press.

Roumasset, J.A. (1992) 'Introduction: the role of government in economic development' in J.A. Roumasset, J.A. and Barr, S. (eds), *The Economics of Cooperation: East Asian Development and the Case for Pro-Market Intervention*, Boulder, Colo.: Westview.

Sabri, Sharaf (2001) *The House of Saud in Commerce:* A Study of Royal Entrepreneurship in Saudi Arabia, New Dehli: I.S. Publications.

Salvatore, D. (2001) *International Economics* seventh edition, New York: Wiley.

Sansom, R. (1995) *Privatising the UK Electricity Supply Industry*, SEEBOARD International, UK.

Seznec, J-F. (1987) *The Financial Markets of the Arabian Gulf*, London: Croom Helm.

Sherbiny, N.A. and Serageldin, I. (1982) 'Expatriate labour and economic growth: Saudi demand for Egyptian labour' in Kerr, M.H. and Yassin, E.S., *Rich and Poor Countries in the Middle East: Egypt and the New Arab Social Order*, Boulder, Colo.: Westview.

Sluglett, P. and Farouk-Sluglett, M. Marion (1982) 'The precarious monarchy: Britain, Abd Al-Aziz Ibn Saud and the establishment of the kingdom of Hijaz, Najd and its dependencies, 1925–1932', in Niblock, T. (ed.) *State, Society and Economy in Saudi Arabia*, pp. 36–39, London: Croom Helm.

Bibliography 181

Thirwall, A.P. (1994) *Growth and Development*, fifth edition, London: Macmillan.

Todaro, M. (1994) *Economic Development*, fifth edition, London: Longmans.

Train, K. (1994) *Optimal Regulation: The Economic Theory of Natural Monopoly*, Cambrdige, Mass.: MIT Press.

Turkson, J. and Redlinger, R. (2000) 'Cross-country comparison' in Turkson, J. (ed.) *Power Sector Reform in Sub-Saharan Africa*, pp. 186–203, London: Macmillan.

Turner, L. and Bedore, J.M. (1979) *Middle East Industrialisation: A Study of Saudi and Iranian Downstream Investments*, London: Saxon House.

Tripp, C. (2001) 'States, elites and the 'management of change' in Hassan Hakimian, H. and Ziba Moshaver, Z. (ed.) *The State and Global Change: the Political Economy of Transition in the Middle East and North Africa*, pp. 211–231, London: Curzon.

Wahba, J. (2001) 'Returns to education and regional earnings differentials in Egypt' in Salehi-Ishfahani, D. (ed.) *Labour and Human Capital in the Middle East: Studies in Market and Household Behaviour*, pp. 369–391, Reading, Mass.: Ithaca.

Weiss-Armush, A.M. (1993) 'Women in Saudi society' in Abdulaziz Al-Sweel and J.W. Wright (eds) *Saudi Arabia: Tradition and Transition'*, pp. 101–117, Westland, Mo.: Hayden-McNeil.

Wilson, R. (1982) 'The evolution of the Saudi banking system and its relationship with Bahrain', in Tim Niblock, (ed.) *State, Society and Economy in Saudi Arabia*, pp. 278–300, London: Croom Helm.

Wilson, R. (1983) *Banking and Finance in the Arab Middle East*, London: Macmillan.

Wilson, R. (1998) *Banking and Finance in the Middle East*, London: Financial Times Publications.

Wilson, R. (1995) *Economic Development in the Middle East*, London: Routledge.

Wilson, R. (1997) *Islamic Finance*, London: Financial Times Financial Publications.

Wilson, R. (2002) *The Gulf–EU Trade Relationship: Challenges and Opportunities*, Lecture Series no. 37, Abu Dhabi: Emirates Centre for Strategic Studies and Research.

Wright, J.W. and Albatel, A.H. (1996) 'Private sector finance: problems faced by the fourth and fifth development plans' in Wright, J.W. (ed.) *Business and Economic Development in Saudi Arabia*, pp. 53–70, London: Macmillan.

Yajima, M. (1997) *Deregulatory Reforms of the Electricity Supply Industry*, London: Quorum Books.

Yamani, M. (2000) *Changed Identities: the Challenge of the New Generation in Saudi Arabia*, London: Royal Institute of International Affairs.

Young, A. (1983) *Saudi Arabia: the Making of a Financial Giant*, New York: New York University Press.

Zinderman, A. (1978) *Manpower Training: Theory and Policy*, London: Macmillan.

Articles

Abrahamsson, L. (2000) 'Production economics analysis of investment initiated to improve the working environment', *Applied Ergonomics*, vol. 31, no. 1, pp. 1–7.

Aggarwal, R.K. and Samwick, A.A. (1999) 'The other side of the trade-off: the impact of risk on executive compensation', *Journal of Political Economy*, vol. 107, no. 1, pp. 65–105.

Al-Hegelan, A. and Palmer, M. (1985) 'Bureaucracy and development in Saudi Arabia', *Middle East Journal*, vol. 39, no. 1, pp. 48–68. Reprinted in Niblock, T. and Wilson, R. (1999) *The Political Economy of the Middle East*, vol. 5, pp. 1–22, Cheltenham: Edward Elgar.

182 Bibliography

Al-Orabi, H.M. (1999) 'Attitudes of Saudi women towards participating in the labour force', *Humanomics*, vol. 15, no. 4, 1999, pp. 123–140.

Ali, A. and Al-Shakhis, M. (1989) Mohammed, 'Managerial beliefs about work in two Arab states', *Organisation Studies*, vol. 10, no. 2, 1989, pp. 169–186.

Arocena, P., Kuhn, K. and Regibeau, P. (1999) 'Regulatory reform in the Spanish electricity industry: a missed opportunity for competition', *Energy Policy*, vol. 27, no. 7, pp. 387–399.

Barton, J., Aldridge, J. and Smith, P. (1998) 'The emotional impact of shift work on the children of shift workers', *Scandinavian Journal of Work Environment and Health*, vol. 24, no. 3, pp. 146–150.

Bas, D. (1988) 'Cost-effectiveness of training in developing countries', *International Labour Review*, vol. 127, no. 3, pp. 355–369.

Bayless, C. (1994) 'Less is more: why gas turbines will transform electric utilities', *Public Utilities Fortnightly*, vol. 132, no. 22, pp. 21–25.

Bennell, P. and Segerstrom, J. (1999) 'Vocational education and training in developing countries: has the World Bank got it right?' *International Journal of Education Development*, vol. 18, no. 4, pp. 271–287.

Bernstein, S. (1988) 'Competition, marginal cost tariffs and spot pricing in the Chilean electric power sector', *Energy Policy*, vol. 16, no. 8, pp. 369–377.

Bosch, G. (1999) 'Working time: tendencies and emerging issues', *International Labour Review*, vol. 138, no. 2, p. 131.

Brander, J.A. and Spencer, B. (1985) 'Export subsidies and international market share rivalry', *Journal of International Economics* (February), pp. 83–100.

Caruso, G. and Chen, X. (1997) 'Experiences of electricity-sector restructuring in Asia', *Journal of Energy and Development*, vol. 22, no. 3, pp. 1–16.

Doyle, C. and Maher, M. (1992) 'Common Carriage and the Pricing of Electricity Transmission', *Energy Journal*, vol. 13, no. 3, pp. 63–94.

Green, R. (1999) 'Draining the Pool: the Reform of Electricity Trading in England and Wales', *Energy Policy*, vol. 27, no. 9, pp. 515–525.

Gunn, C. and Sharp, B. (1999) 'Electricity distribution as an unsustainable natural monopoly: a potential outcome of New Zealand's regulatory regime', *Energy Economics*, vol. 21, pp. 385–401.

Hammons, T., Franco, N., Sbertoli, L., Khelil, C. Rudnick, H., Clerici, A. and Longhi, A. (1997) 'Energy market integration in South America', *IEEE Power Engineering Review* (August), pp. 6–14.

Hayes, B.E., Perander, J., Smecko, T. and Trask, J. (1998) 'Measuring perceptions of workplace safety: development and validation of the work safety scale', *Journal of Safety Research*, vol. 29, no. 3, pp. 145–161.

Kee, E. (2001) 'Vesting contracts: A tool for electricity market transition', *The Electricity Journal*, vol. 14, no. 7, pp. 11–22.

Kuznets, S. (1955) 'Economic growth and income inequality', *American Economic Review* (March), pp. 1–28.

Kuznets, S. (1963) 'Quantitative aspects of the economic growth of nations', *Economic Development and Cultural Change* (March), pp. 1–80.

Melchior, A. (1999) 'Globalisation and labour standards: a look at Asia', *Internasjonal Politikk*, vol. 57, no. 2, pp. 290–299.

Mork, E. (2001) 'Emergence of financial markets for electricity: a European perspective', *Energy Policy*, vol. 29, no. 1, pp. 7–15.

Bibliography 183

Roberts, L. (1983) 'Manpower consulting and training in developing countries', *Training and Development Journal*, vol. 37, no. 10, pp. 48–52.

Silsbee, C. and Jurewitz, J. (2001) 'Wholesale generator incentives to exercise market power in the California electricity market', *The Electricity Journal*, vol. 14, no. 7, pp. 51–56.

Sioshansi, F. and Morgan, C. (1999) 'Where function follows form: International comparisons of restructured electricity markets', *The Electricity Journal*, vol. 12, no. 3, pp. 20–30.

Stern, N. (1989) 'The economics of development', *Economic Journal* (September), pp. 599–616; reprinted in Meier, G.M. (1995) *Leading Issues in Economic Development*, sixth edition, p. 556, Oxford: Oxford University Press.

Tenenbaum, B. and Henderson, S. (1991) 'Market-based pricing of wholesale electric services', *The Electricity Journal*, vol. 4, no. 10 (December), pp. 30–45.

Tenenbaum, B; Lock, R. and Barker, J. (1992) 'Electricity privatization: Structural, competitive and regulatory options', *Energy Policy*, vol. 20, no. 12, pp. 1134–1160.

Tharenou, P. (1997) 'Explanations of managerial career advancement', *Australian Psychologist*, vol. 32, no. 1 (March), pp. 19–28.

Tharenou, P. 'Is there a link between family structures and women's and men's managerial career advancement?' *Journal of Organizational Behaviour*, vol. 20, no. 6, pp. 837–863.

Trebing, H. (2000) 'Electricity: Changes and Issues', *Review of Industrial Organization*, vol. 17, no. 1, pp. 61–74.

Vernon, R. (1966) 'International investment and international trade in the product life cycle', *Quarterly Journal of Economics* (May), pp. 190–207.

Theses

Affara, F.M.S. (1995) 'The role of financial intermediaries in Saudi Arabia with particular reference to the National Commercial Bank', Ph.D. thesis, University of Durham.

Al-Awaji, I.M. (1971) 'Bureaucracy and society in Saudi Arabia', Ph.D. thesis, University of Virginia.

Al-Malik, S.M., (1989) 'Strategic decision makers: A study of business and government top executives in Saudi Arabia', Ph.D. thesis, Georgia State University.

Al-Salamah, A.H. (1994) 'Employee perceptions in multinational companies, A case study of the Saudi Arabian Basic Industries Corporation', Ph.D. thesis, University of Durham.

Al-Shalan, F.A. (1991) 'Participation in managerial decision making in the Saudi Arabian public sector', Ph.D. thesis, University of Pittsburgh.

Al-Shetaiwi, A.S. (2002) 'Factors affecting the under-utilisation of qualified Saudi women in the Saudi private sector', Ph.D. thesis, Loughborough University Business School.

Official and company reports and international agency publications

Banking Control Law, Royal Decree no. M/5, 22/2/1386 AH.

Central Planning Organisation (1974) *Report of the Central Planning Organisation*, Jeddah.

Electricity Corporation (1996) *Electricity Corporation in Service of Economic Development*.

184 *Bibliography*

Electricity Corporation (1996) *Long Term Electrification Plan.*

Ministry of Industry and Electricity (1999) *Electricity Industry Development During One Hundred Years* (in Arabic).

Ministry of Industry and Electricity (2000) *Guide to the Licensing of Foreign Investment in the Kingdom of Saudi Arabia*, Riyadh.

Ministry of Industry and Electricity, *Electricity Growth and Development in Saudi Arabia* (several issues).

Ministry of Planning, *General Objectives and Strategic Bases of the Sixth Development Plan 1995–2000.*

Ministry of Planning, *General Objectives and Strategic Bases of the Seventh Development Plan 2000–2005.*

Saudi Arabian General Investment Authority (2000) *The New Foreign Investment Laws of the Kingdom*, Riyadh.

Saudi Arabian Monetary Agency (2001) *Thirty Seventh Annual Report*, Riyadh.

Saudi Consolidated Electricity Companies SCECOs (1999) *Annual Report.*

Saudi Industrial Development Fund (1995) *Annual Report.*

Saudi Trade and Export Development Company (2001) *Damman Bonded and Re-Export Zone.*

Saudi Trade and Export Development Company (2001) *The Kingdom's First Bonded and Re-export Zone, Jeddah.*

Statement of the Ministry of Planning on the Seventh Development Plan (2000) Riyadh.

Trade Partners UK (2002) *Clothing, footwear and fashion market in Saudi Arabia*, London.

United Nations Development Programme (1999) *Human Development Report*, Oxford University Press.

Whinney Murray and Co., (2001) *Taxation in Saudi Arabia.*

World Bank Atlas Development Indicators (2000) Washington.

Periodicals

Al-Rajhi Banking and Investment Corporation Annual Reports
Arab Banker
BP Statistical Review of World Energy
CWC Group Saudi Review: Economic and Political Analysis
Economist Intelligence Unit Country Reports on Saudi Arabia
Financial Times Surveys of Middle Eastern Banking
Gulf News
Islamic Development Bank Annual Reports
Middle East Economic Survey
Middle Eastern Economic Digest
National Commercial Bank Economist
National Commercial Bank Market Review and Outlook
New Horizon Monthly Magazine of the Institute of Islamic Banking and Insurance London
OPEC Annual Statistical Bulletin
Oxford Analytica Daily Brief
Petroleum Argus
Riyadh Bank Quarterly Economic Review
Saudi American Bank Annual Reports
Saudi American Bank Newsletter

Bibliography 185

SABIC Annual Reports
Saudi Arabian Monetary Agency Annual Reports
Saudi Arabian Monetary Agency Quarterly Statistical Bulletins
Saudi Arabian Monetary Agency Monthly Statistical Bulletins
Saudi British Bank Saudi Economic Bulletin
Saudi Economic Survey
Saudi Investment Bank Annual Reports
WTO, Leading exporters and importers in world trade in commercial services, 2000
WTO, World Trade in 2000: Overview
WTO, World Merchandise Exports by Region and Selected Economy
WTO, World Merchandise Imports by Region and Selected Economy
United Nations, Statistical Abstract of the ESCWA Region, twentieth issue, New York, 2000

Index

Abdulaziz bin Hamad Algosaibi 66
Abdullah bin Faisal bin Turki, Crown
    Prince 3, 19, 48, 52, 66
    and economic policy 26, 33, 36–7
Abdullah Faisal bin Turki Al-Saud, Prince
    51
Abdullah Salim Bahamdan, Sheikh 64–5
Abu Dhabi 12, 42, 84, 88, 149
Aden 79
Africa 3, 58, 70, 79, 98, 148
Agip 42
Agricultural Bank 11
Al-Ahli European Trading Equity 71
Al-Ahli Global Trading Fund 72
Al-Ahli Saudi Equity Fund 71
Al-Ahli Saudi Riyal *Murabaha* Fund 72
Al-Ahli Saudi Riyal Trading Fund 71–2
Al-Ahli Saudi Trading Equity Fund 71–2
Al-Ahli Short Term Dollar Fund 70
Al-Ahli US Trading Equity 71
Al-Arabi Saudi Company Shares 72
Al-Awaji, Ibrahim M. 13
Al-Farsi, Fouad 23
Al-Fifi, Yahya 101
Al-Hegelan, Abdelrahman 19
Al-Jazira Bank 64, 66
Al-Jubail Fertiliser Company 113
Al-Khobar 59
Al-Malikh, S.M. 13
Al-Namiah, Ali 96
Al-Orabi, Hekmat 108
Al-Rajhi, Ahmed 5
Al-Rajhi Banking and Investment
    Corporation 14, 61–4, 66, 71
Al-Rajhi Local Share Fund 71
Al-Salamah, Abdullah 5
Al-Shalan, Fahad A. 13
Al-Shetaiwi, Abdullah 109
Al-Shuaibaa electricity project 61

Al-Yamanah defence contract 86
Al-Zamel group 55
Alaska 44
Alberta 147
Alexandria 57
Algeria 16, 42
Algosaibi, Ghazi 150
Ali, Anwar 22
American Express 67
Amin, Samir 22
Arab Fertiliser Company 69
Arab Free Trade Agreement (1998) 87
Arab League (1945) 41, 84–5, 87
Arab Monetary Fund 84
Arab National Bank 64, 66, 72
Arab Socialist Union 22
Arab–Israeli conflict (1973) 40
Arab–Israeli war (1967) 42
Arabian American Oil Company
    (ARAMCO) 3, 7, 13, 15, 77
    and economic policy 35–7
    and electricity 151, 156
    and employment 112, 120
    and oil industry 40–4, 50–2
Arabian Oil 40
Arabian peninsula 16–17, 56–7, 88, 91
Arabic 108, 131
Argentina 148
Armstrong, M. 142
Arocena, P. 140–1, 148
Asia 56, 79, 81, 85, 148
    East Asia 9, 89, 127
    South Asia 84, 90, 95, 103–4, 113
    Southeast Asia 89
    Western Asia 9
Asian Islamic funds 71
Asir Province 11, 94, 102
Association of South-East Asian Nations
    (ASEAN) 87

Index 187

Atatürk, Mustafa Kemal 22
al-Aziz al-Zamil, Abd 112
Azzam, Henry 161

BAE Systems 87, 100–1
Baghdad 41, 80
Bahrain 40, 68, 135, 163
  and economic policy 35–6
  and employment 95, 106
  and trade 85, 87–91
Bandar, Prince 66
Bank of Credit and Commerce
  International 64
Bank Misr of Egypt 57
Bank Saudi-ization Act (1976) 60
Banking Control Law (1966) 59
banking sector and financial markets
  56–74
  banking history 57–9
  commercial banking 59–60
  competition 62–5
  corporate finance and investment 65–7
  Islamic finance 60–2
Banks, F. 141
Banque de l'Indochine 58, 60
Bayless, C. 141
Bechtel Corporation 112
Bedouin 15, 106, 129, 133
Berrie, T. 141, 146
Berstein, S. 141–2
Bin Mahfouz family 57–8, 64–5
Bin Mahfouz, Salim 64
Booz Allen Hamilton 28
Brander, J.A. 78
Brazil 145
British Aerospace 100
British Bank of Iran and the Middle East
  59–60
British Petroleum (BP) 42, 50
Bu Hlaika, Ihsan 32
Build-Operate-Transfer (BOT) 161
Build-Own-Operate (BOO) 161
Build-Own-Operate-Transfer (BOOT)
  161–2
bureaucracy and regulation 135–7
Bush, George H. W. 52
business environment 131–3
Business International 132

Cairo 41
California 5, 58, 147
Calvinism 14
Cammack, P. 127
Canada 147

Capital Markets Authority 70
Capital Markets Law (2002) 69–70
capitalism 12–14
Caruso, G. 148
Central Department of Statistics 96–8, 105
Central Intelligence Agency (CIA) 40
Central Planning Organisation (CPO) 23–4
Chapra, Umer 60
Chase Manhattan International Finance 66
Chen, X. 148
Chevron 43
Chile 148, 152
China 47, 92, 148
Citibank 65
Clifford Chance 28
colleges 107
Combines Cycle Gas Turbines (CCGT)
  141
Commerce, Minister of 26, 34
commercial banking 59–60
Commission for Labour Disputes 132
Communications, Minister of 23
Communism 17, 21
Conoco 51
Council of Ministers 23, 27, 36, 89
Council of Saudi Chamber of Commerce
  151
'crony capitalism' 9, 56, 133
Cyprus 92

Da'awa 18
Dallah Al-Baraka Group 14, 61
Damman 40, 79–80, 87–8, 149
Dar al-Maal al-Islami 61
debt 31–2
Defence, Minister of 26
Delaby, Christian 58
Demand-Side Management (DSM) 155
development paradigms 6–19
  capitalism 12–14
  feudalism 10–12
  historical perspectives 7
  income distribution 15–17
  role of the state 17–19
  self-sustaining growth 8–10
development plans 38, 127–8
  First Development Plan (1970–1975) 23
  Second Development Plan (1975–1980)
    24–5
  Third Development Plan (1980–1985) 25
  Fourth Development Plan (1985–1990)
    25, 68
  Fifth Development Plan (1990–1995)
    25, 68

188 *Index*

Sixth Development Plan (1995–2000)
25, 29, 151
Seventh Development Plan (2000–2005)
6, 27–9, 99–107 *passim*, 151
Djibouti 58
Dow Chemicals 54
Doyle, C. 141
dualism, economic 37–8
Dubai 35, 79–80, 87, 89, 91
Durham, University of 4
Dutch East Indies 57

Eastern Petrochemical Company 113
Eastern Province 40, 78, 80, 112, 131
and development 5, 7, 11, 16
economic policy *see* government economic
policy
Ecuador 42
education and training 22, 106–8
Egypt 1–2, 41–2, 53, 149
and banking 56–8, 61, 68
and development 11, 14, 16
and economic policy 22, 31, 33
and employment 95, 103–4, 107, 113
and trade 75, 77, 85, 88, 90–1
El Mallakh, Ragaei 9
El-Ghonemy, Mohammed Riad 17
Electric Services Regulatory Authority
(ESRA) 151
Électricité de France 148
Electricity Corporation (EC) 150, 154,
159, 161
electricity industry 24, 139–64
competition and monopoly 141–2
functional transformation 142–6
international reform 146–9
policy issues 161–3
regulatory and organisational
development 149–52
restructuring 140–1
salient features 152–61
Electricity Pool of England and Wales 147
Electrification Plan, Long Term 154
Elf 42
Emirates Holdings 88
employment conditions in SABIC 111–25
industrialisation and jobs 111–13
management and labour relations 120–2
promotion 119–20
respondents' profile 113–15
salaries 118–19
survey 113
time management 122–5
training 115–18

employment issues 94–110
demographic transition 95–7
education and training 106–8
employment structure 101–3
expatriate labour 103–6
labour market trends 99–101
unemployment 97–9
women and 108–10
Enron 52
Ericsson of Sweden 28
Eritrea 79
Esso 40
Estache, A. 145
Ethiopia 79
Eurofighter aircraft 87
Europe 30, 43, 71, 113, 123, 147
European Union (EU) 34, 47, 100, 48
and trade 85–7, 89, 91–2
Evans, Peter 126–7
Exxon 40, 42–3
ExxonMobil 3, 50–3

Fahd bin Salman, Prince 66
Fahd, Crown Prince 112
Fahd, King 26, 31, 43–4, 48, 57–8
Faisal Islamic Banks 61
Faisal, King 64
Faqih, Osama 34
Far East 30, 112
feudalism 10–12
Finance, Minister of 23, 43, 58
Finance and National Economy, Minister
of 26
financial markets *see* banking sector and
financial markets
financial system 134–5
Fiqh Academy 18
First Gulf War 81
First National City Bank 60
Five Year Plans *see* development plans
Flood Enquiry 64
Ford Foundation 23
Foreign Affairs, Minister of 51–3
France 42, 51, 57–9, 85–6, 148
funding and investment 33–7

gas *see* oil, gas and petrochemicals
Gellatly Hankey 57
General Agreement on Tariffs and Trade
(GATT) 91
General Investment Authority 27
General Organisation for Social Insurance
65
General Presidency for Female Education 61

Index 189

Geneva 34, 61
Germany 85–6, 116, 148
Getty Oil 40
Ghana 148
gharar (deception) 15
Ghawar 43, 50
girls' colleges 107
globalisation 2–3
al-Gosaibi, Dr Ghazi A. 112
government economic policy 20–38
  and business 133–4
  coordinated planning 28–9
  debt 31–2
  dualism 37–8
  fiscal choices 32–3
  funding and investment 33–7
  macroeconomic priorities 29–31
  management reorganisation 26–7
  planning 21–4, 21–5
  Seventh Five-Year Plan 27–8
Government Ministries *see* Ministries
Graves, F. 146
Green, R. 145, 147
Grievances, Board of 132
Gross Domestic Product (GDP) 1–3, 7,
  48–9, 67, 73
  and economic policy 20, 27, 31, 33,
  37–8
Gross National Product (GNP) 20, 106
Gulf Co-operation Council (GCC) 2–3, 7,
  16, 53–4, 75, 106–7
  and economic policy 32, 35
  and electricity 135, 137, 155, 163
  and trade 80, 84–5, 87, 92
  see also international trade and GCC
Gulf countries 4, 5, 17, 109, 112
  and trade 78–80, 87, 89
Gulf International Bank 69, 90
Gulf (oil company) 42
Gulf Stevedoring Company 79
Gulf War 31
Gunn, C. 147

HADEED steel company 37, 54
Hadjilambrinos, C. 140
halal 15
Halalah Fund 158, 161
Hammons, T. 148
Hanbali School of Islamic jurisprudence 14
haram 15, 59
al Hasa 11, 57, 78, 88, 94, 102
Haughey, Charles 64
Hawiyah 51
Hawk aircraft 87

Hejaz 4, 15, 17–18, 57, 76, 78
Henderson, S. 142
Hjalmarsson, L. 148
Hofuf 11, 78, 94
Holland 39, 59
Hong Kong 71
Houston, Texas 55
Human Resources Development Fund 27
Hunt, S. 143–6
Hussein, Saddam 45, 53
Hyman, L. 141

IBM 128
Ibn Saud, King Abdul Aziz 15, 17–18, 40,
  58–60, 78
ijara (leasing) 62
ijara wa-iqtina (hire purchase) 62
ijtihad 14
Iman University 107
income distribution 15–17
Income Tax, Department of *Zakat* and 16
India 85, 113
Indonesia 42, 75, 85, 87
Industrial Bank of Japan 66
Industry, Minister of 26
infrastructure 135
inheritance 16
initial public offerings (IPOs) 65–6, 73
International Finance Corporation 67, 127
International Monetary Fund (IMF) 30, 84,
  90, 148
international private placements (IPP) 162
international trade and GCC 75–93
  economic trade rationale 76–8
  GCC and regional trade 87–9
  GCC single market 89–91
  import and export trends 80–1
  regional implications 78–80
  surpluses and payments 82–4
  trading partners 85–7
  World Trade Organisation (WTO) 91–3
Internet 28, 67
Iran 14, 39–41, 44–5, 53
  and trade 79–80, 88
Iranian Council of Guardians 14
Iraq 11, 16, 22, 96
  and banking 56, 58
  and oil industry 40–2, 45, 53
  and trade 75, 80–1, 87
Ireland 64
Islam 13–14, 17, 64, 78
  finance 60–2
  law 14, 16, 56, 59–60, 132
  studies 107–8

190 *Index*

Islamic Affairs, Ministry of 18
Islamic Development Bank (IDB) 30,
    61–2, 84, 90
Islamic Revolution (1979) 14
Islamic University 107
Israel 1, 37, 86, 88, 92
istisna 62
Italy 42

Japan 30, 47, 66–7, 71, 85–6
    and employment 111, 113, 116
Java 57
Jebel Ali 35, 80, 87, 89
Jeddah 5, 7, 18, 108, 118
    and banking 57–9, 62
    and economic policy 30, 35–6
    and trade 76, 78–80, 84, 87, 89
Jeddah Islamic Port 79
Johany, Ali D. 45
Joint Defence Council 91
Jordan 16, 53, 68, 90, 92
    and employment 95, 103, 113
    and trade 90, 92
Joskow, P. 140, 142
JP Morgan 28, 66
Jubail 24, 26, 40, 50, 54
    and employment 112, 114, 118
Jurewitz, J. 147

Kaaba 18
Kahn, E. 147
Kaki Salih Company 57, 59
Kee, E. 147
Kenya 148
Khalid, Prince 64
Khoshaim, B. 161
King Abdul Aziz University 107
King Fahd University 107
King Faisal University 107
King Khalid University 107
King Saud University 107–8
Klein, M. 140
Koran 14, 16
Kruskal-Wallis technique 113
Kuala Lumpur 70
Kuwait 40–1, 45, 68–9, 106
    and trade 80, 85, 87–8, 90, 92
Kuznets, Simon 15

Labour, Board of 132
Labour Committee, Higher 101
Labour Committee of Saudi Workers 101

labour market *see* employment issues
Labour, Minister of 26
Labour and Social Affairs, Minister of 96
Lange, Oskar 22
Lebanon 58, 68, 103
legal system 131–3
Libya 42
Lovei, L. 143
Lucent Technology 28

Maher, M. 141
Malaysia 2, 35, 67, 75, 87, 148
Malaysian Securities Commission 70
Malik, Monica 4
management 26–7, 129–31
Manpower Council 98
Marathon 51
Marxism 10, 12, 22
Massachusetts Institute of Technology 142
Massawa 79
Mecca 18, 35, 57, 78, 108
Medina 35, 57, 78
Ministerial Oil Committee 111
Ministries:
    Agriculture 22
    Commerce 69, 70, 136, 136–7, 137, 149
    Commerce and Industry 24
    Communications 23
    Defence 101
    Education 22, 61
    Finance 19, 31
    Finance and National Economy 60
    Health 22
    Industry 136
    Industry and Electricity (MIE) 24, 34,
        36, 112, 149–59 *passim*
    Interior 35
    Islamic Affairs 18
    Oil 22
    Petroleum 54
    Petroleum and Mineral Resources 34
    Planning 10, 19, 24–6, 96–107 *passim*
    Posts, Telephones and Telegraphs 28
Mitsubishi 54
Mobil 40, 42–3, 54
Mohammed Bin Faisal, Prince 61
Morgan, C. 145
Moriarty Tribunal 64
Mork, E. 145
Morocco 33, 68, 85
Mossadegh, Muhammad 40
murabaha 72

Index 191

Murray, B. 145
Musa Kaki family 57, 64
Muscat summit 3, 32, 88–91
musharakah 59
Muslim countries 56, 62, 70
Muslim society 15, 18, 57, 78, 107

Naimi, Ali 51–2
Najd 17–18, 76, 78
Nasser, Gamal Abdel 41
National Commercial Bank 56–60, 63–6, 68, 70–2, 74
National Guard 13, 19, 26
National Methanol Company 113
National Plastics Company 113
Nazer, Hisham 44–5
Netherlands 85
Netherlands Trading Society 57–8
New Zealand 147
Newbery, D. 140, 144
Niblock, Tim 13
Nigeria 42, 44
Nord Pool 148
North American Free Trade Agreement (NAFTA) 87
North Sea 44, 85

Occidental 51
October War (1973) 42
oil, gas and petrochemicals 22, 39–55
  and economic development 48–50
  gas development 50–3
  oil industry development 40–1
  oil pricing 45–6
  oil production 43–5
  oil reserves 46–8
  petrochemicals 53–5
  Saudi Arabia and OPEC 41–3
Oil, Minister of 43, 44, 48, 51
Oman 51, 68, 87–8, 90, 149
Organisation of Arab Petroleum Exporting Countries (OAPEC) 42
Organisation of the Islamic Conference 17–18, 61, 85
Organisation of Petroleum Exporting States (OPEC) 39, 41–8, 50
Orix Leasing Group 67
Osama bin Laden 64
Ottoman Bank 57
Ottoman Empire 4, 15, 57, 78

Pakistan 85, 113, 148

Palestine 42, 103
Palmer, Monte 19
petrochemicals *see* oil, gas and petrochemicals
Petroleum, Minister of 26
Philby, John 40
Philippines 84, 95, 104
Phillips 50
Planning Board 23
Planning, Minister of 24, 26, 43–4, 48
Port Sudan 79
Porter, Michael 78
Power Purchase Agreements 146
PricewaterhouseCoopers 28
private sector 126–38
  bureaucracy and regulation 135–7
  business environment and legal system 131–3
  development initiative 127–8
  efficiency of 128–9
  financial system shortcomings 134–5
  infrastructure inadequacy 135
  management capability 129–31
  role of government 133–4
  and the state 126–7
Protestantism 14
Public Investment Fund 23

Qatar 12, 39, 42, 51, 106
  and trade 87–8, 90, 92
Qatif 11

Ramadan 16
Raymond, Lee 51–3
Real Estate Development Bank 63, 73
Red Sea 35, 51, 54, 57–8, 79, 112
Redlinger, R. 148
regulation 135–7, 149–52
Revolution, Islamic (1979) 14
riba 30, 57, 59, 61, 70–1
Ricardo, David 77
Riyadh 5, 7, 18, 49, 52
  and banking 67, 69
  and economic policy 22, 31, 36
  and employment 99, 101, 105, 118
  and trade 76, 78, 84, 87, 89, 90–1
Riyadh Bank 56, 59–60, 63–4, 66, 72, 74
Riyadh Cables 88
Riyadh Equity Fund 72
Rodriquez-Paradina, M. 145
Rostow, Walt W. 8
Rotterdam 85

192 *Index*

Roumasset, J. A. 127
Royal Commission for Jubail and Yanbu 112
Royal Dutch Shell 50
Royal Saudi Air Force 87

Saleh Kamel, Sheikh 61
Sansom, R. 142
Saud Al-Faisal, Prince 51–3
Saud, House of 2
Saud, King 64
Saudi American Bank 4, 33, 35, 60, 63–6
Saudi Arabia Basic Industries Corporation (SABIC) 40, 53–5, 68–9, 156
  and development 2, 5, 9, 12, 14
  and economic policy 23, 25–6, 34–5
  and trade 77–8, 84
  see also employment conditions in SABIC
Saudi Arabian Fertiliser Company (SAFCO) 54
Saudi Arabian General Investment Authority (SAGIA) 34–6, 51
Saudi Arabian Investment Bank 63–4, 66–7
Saudi Arabian Monetary Agency (SAMA) 44, 46–7, 96, 105
  and banking 58–61, 63–4, 68–70
  and economic policy 22, 26, 30–2
  and trade 80–4, 86, 88
Saudi British Bank 60, 64, 66
Saudi Consolidated Electric Companies (SCECOs) 150–1, 156, 160–1
Saudi Consulting House 34
Saudi Development and Re-Export Services Company 80
Saudi Dutch Bank 63–4
Saudi Electricity Company (SEC) 29, 151–2, 158, 160
Saudi French Bank 60, 64, 66
Saudi Holland Bank 64, 66
Saudi Industrial Development Fund (SIDF) 7, 12, 14, 36, 161
  and banking 68, 73
  and employment 102, 106
  and private sector 129, 134, 136
Saudi International Petrochemichals Company 55
Saudi Iron and Steel Company 37, 113
Saudi Maintenance Corporation 79
Saudi Orix Leasing Corporation 67
Saudi Petrochemical Company 113
Saudi Ports Authority 79

Saudi Real Estate Development Fund 17
Saudi Telecom 2
Saudi Telecommunications Company (STC) 28, 54
Saudi Trade and Export Development Company 79–80
Saudi-isation 60, 74, 94–5, 111, 125, 163
Saudia (airline) 33
Scandinavia 148
Schmalensee, R. 140, 142
Schweppe, Fred 142
Second World War 41
Shah of Iran 14
shariah law 14, 56, 70, 132
Sharp, B. 147
Shayif, Abdulhadi A. 65
Shell 42, 51, 54
Shoaiba power plant 161
Shuttleworth, G. 143–6
Silsbee, C. 147
Singapore 35, 87
Sioshani, F. 145
Slain Water Conversion Corporation (SWCC) 153
Smith, Adam 76
Somalia 79
Souk al-Manakh 69
South America 148
South Korea 85–6, 111, 116
Soviet Union 22
Spain 147–8
Spencer, B. 78
Sri Lankan housemaids 108–9
Standard Oil of California (SOCAL) 40, 42–3
Stanford Research Group 24
Statistical Package for Social Sciences (SPSS) 113
stock exchanges 71
Stoft, S. 147
Sudan 2, 61, 98
Suez Canal 22, 79, 89
Suez-Mediterranean pipeline 85
Sulayman, Sheikh Abd Allah 58–9
Sultan, Prince 26
Supreme Council for Petroleum and Mineral Affairs 35
Supreme Economic Council 19, 26–7, 33, 70
Syria 11, 56, 58, 75, 77, 84
Syria, Ba'athist 22

Tadawul 69
Taimiyah, Ibn 17

Index 193

Taiwan 111, 116
Taiwan Fertiliser Company 54
technical colleges 107
Tehran 45
Tenenbaum, B. 142–3
Texaco 40, 42
Texas 52, 55
Tornado aircraft 36, 86–7, 100
Total 42
TotalFinaElf 51
trade 75–93
trade unions 101
Train, K. 158
training 106–8, 115–18, 131
Trebing, H. 141
Tripp, Charles 17–18
Tunisia 33, 68
Turkey 22, 32, 53, 75, 85
Turkson, J. 148
Twitchell, Karl 40
Typhoon aircraft 87

Umm Al-Qura University 107
Umm Qasr 80
Unified Economic Agreement (1981) 87
United Arab Emirates (UAE) 51, 95–6, 106, 136–7
  and trade 75, 82, 85, 87–9, 90
United Kingdom 30, 36, 42, 85–6, 101, 147
United Nations 81, 84
United Nations Team for Social and Economic Planning 23
United States of America 30–1, 60, 70, 147, 152
  and employment 100, 112–13, 116

and oil industry 40–3, 45–7, 50–2
and trade 83, 85–6, 91–2
United States of America Securities Exchange Commission 70
University of Durham 4

Venezuela 41, 45
Vernon, Raymond 77
Vietnam 148
vocational colleges 107

al-Wahhab, Ibn Abd 17
Wahhabi Muslim society 14–18, 57
West, H. 141
Western Region 61
women 107–10
World Assembly for Muslim Youth 18
World Bank 1, 23, 39, 67, 127, 134, 148
World Trade Organisation (WTO) 32, 34, 65–6, 112, 125
  and development 3, 6–7, 9
  and private sector 129–30, 137
  and trade 75–6, 82, 91–3

Yajima, M. 152
Yamani, Mai 108
Yamani, Sheikh 43–5, 49
Yanbu 40, 51, 54, 112
  and economic policy 24, 26, 37
Yemen 11, 22, 33, 57
  and employment 95, 98, 103
  and trade 84, 87, 91
Young, Arthur 58–9

Zakat 15–16, 32
Zimbabwe 148